ADVENTURES OF AN
ACCIDENTAL
SOCIOLOGIST

PETER L. BERGER

ADVENTURES OF AN
ACCIDENTAL
SOCIOLOGIST

HOW TO EXPLAIN THE WORLD
WITHOUT BECOMING A BORE

 Prometheus Books

59 John Glenn Drive
Amherst, New York 14228–2119

Published 2011 by Prometheus Books

Cover image © 2011 Media Bakery, Inc.
Cover design by Grace M. Conti-Zilsberger

Inquiries should be addressed to
Prometheus Books
59 John Glenn Drive
Amherst, New York 14228–2119
VOICE: 716–691–0133
FAX: 716–691–0137
WWW.PROMETHEUSBOOKS.COM

15 14 13 12 11   5 4 3 2 1

Library of Congress Cataloging-in-Publication Data

Berger, Peter L., 1929–
      Adventures of an accidental sociologist : how to explain the world without becoming a
bore / by Peter L. Berger.
            p. cm.
      ISBN 978–1–61614–389–3 (cloth : alk. paper)
      ISBN 978–1–61614–390–9 (e-book)
      1. Berger, Peter L., 1929– 2. Sociologists—United States—Biography. 3. Sociology.
I. Title.

HM479.B47A3 2011
301.092—dc22
[B]   2011004919

Printed in the United States of America on acid-free paper

CONTENTS

PREFATORY NOTE

In the summer of 2009 I was invited to give a public lecture at the Central European University in Budapest. When asked what they wanted me to lecture on, they said that this was completely up to me. I hate that. I'm not a missionary, and I don't have a sermon to be preached in Budapest. They then said that they found useful a format they called "ego-histoire." Did they mean autobiography? No, they meant an account of the lecturer's intellectual career—the issues he had dealt with, the people and adventures he had encountered on the way. I thought that would be fun. Not only did I have fun giving the lecture, but apparently the audience had fun listening to it. Back home, I went to work on a book. Here it is.

The same summer, just before traveling to Budapest, I had a conversation in Vienna with the daughter of a friend of mine. She had just started studying sociology at the university, and she was disappointed. She had read my old book *Invitation to Sociology* and had expected an exciting intellectual experience. Instead, she was very bored. I don't know what kind of sociology is being taught at the University of Vienna these days (when I am back in my hometown, I have more interesting things to do than inspect the state of Austrian sociology). But if the curriculum there is similar to what is mostly taught elsewhere in Europe or in America, I'm not surprised that this very bright young woman was bored.

There are very few jokes about sociology. One of those few is directly relevant here: A patient is told by his doctor that in all likelihood he has only a year to live. After absorbing this awful news, the patient asks what the doctor would recommend.

"Marry a sociologist and move to North Dakota."

"Will this cure me?"

"No, but the year will seem much longer."

In recent decades sociology has been suffering from two diseases—methodological fetishism, only studying phenomena that lend themselves to quantitative methods, and ideological propaganda, repeating the same old mantras (sometimes with an enriched vocabulary). Both diseases produce deepening boredom. There is nothing wrong with quantitative methods in themselves, and they can be useful, but because of the interests of those willing to fund the expensive budgets of survey research, the result is often increasingly sophisticated methods to explore increasingly trivial topics. As to the ideological mantras, they may have been exciting thirty years ago, but today they are prone to provoke yawns. Of course there are exceptions. Some sociologists produce interesting and important work. I think it is fair to say that they are a minority.

I told the young woman in Vienna that sociology need not be boring. If she continues in this field, it will be up to her to do things that are not boring. Especially after an academic has achieved a tenured position, she can do pretty much what she likes. There are lots of niches even in universities run by petty bureaucrats, the pay is usually adequate at that level, and (perhaps most important) there are all those long summers. There are also jobs for sociologists outside academia. Sociology, unlike most other social sciences (except anthropology), allows its practitioners to deal with a very broad array of topics. As I found it to be, it is well suited for someone who has an abiding fascination with the vast panorama of the human world, someone who has a passion for discovering what is really going on—someone who, if necessary, will look through keyholes and read other people's mail.

During my days as a graduate student, I once committed the latter offense. My then girlfriend shared an apartment with another young woman, a law student. This individual was rather sloppy and left her things lying around all over the apartment. One day, while I was sitting in the bathroom, I came across a letter of hers to her boyfriend. I read it with mounting fascination. It was about four pages long, in single-spaced typescript. Almost all of it was a psychological dissection of their past weekend together with each incident explained in basically Freudian terms what he said, what he *really* meant to say, how the weekend's events related to his underlying neuroses, how his mother entered the picture, what all this was doing to the letter writer, and so on and on. I stole the letter. I found it to be a priceless cultural document that had to be preserved for posterity (somewhere along the line, I'm sorry to say, it got lost).

A final acknowledgment: I want to express my appreciation to Laura Gross, my agent. She has been greatly supportive throughout, and she has been so with an unusual combination of intelligence and personal warmth.

1

BALZAC ON TWELFTH STREET

My intellectual career was launched by a mistake. I came to America with my parents, who settled in New York. I was barely eighteen years old, inspired by religious fervor (which, happily, I soon lost in that distinctive American immigrant experience that John Murray Cuddihy called "the ordeal of civility").[1] I wanted to become a Lutheran minister. Perhaps I already had doubts about this vocational intention. In any case, I got the idea of postponing the beginning of my theological education in order to learn more about the American society in which I was to work. I had only the vaguest notion about sociology, but it seemed to be the right discipline to find out about a society.

I had no money; neither did my parents. I had to work full-time to support myself and to come up with tuition. To my knowledge, the New School for Social Research was the only academic institution in the city where one could do all one's graduate work in the evening. Thus I enrolled there in a master's program in sociology. Of course I had no idea how marginal the New School was on the American social science scene.

There is rather cruel Jewish joke: A man goes into a kosher restaurant in New York. To his surprise he is served by a Chinese waiter, who speaks to him in elegant Lithuanian Yiddish. Upon leaving, he spots the owner of the restaurant.

"You have a Chinese waiter here?"

"Yes, he came here from Shanghai a year ago."

"But he speaks perfect Yiddish!"

"Psst!" says the owner. "He thinks he's learning English."

I thought I was learning American sociology.

I could only afford one course during my first semester—the first course I ever took in sociology. Taught by Albert Salomon, it was called "Balzac as a Sociologist." The idea was brilliant, and Salomon was a brilliant lecturer. It was also a very plausible pedagogical idea: Balzac had intended for his collection of novels, *The Human Comedy*, to provide a comprehensive picture of French society in the nineteenth century, from the aristocracy to the criminal underworld. And indeed the novels provide a detailed panorama of the many layers of this society. What Salomon did in his course was to use Balzac's opus to introduce students to the major categories of sociology—class, power, religion, social control, social mobility, marginality, crime. I must have read at least ten of Balzac's novels during the semester.

Salomon, who had no qualms about being an authoritarian professor, handed out assignments. Mine was to write a term paper on a novella by Balzac about a salesman, *Felix Gaudissart*, comparing it with Arthur Miller's play *Death of a Salesman*, which had just come out. My term paper (which I must still have somewhere) was hardly a masterpiece of sociological commentary, but I had fun with it. I compared Balzac's Gaudissart, a figure of early capitalist triumphalism, with Miller's Willy Loman, who (Salomon supposed) represented capitalism in a phase of decline.

At the end of the semester I had become quite familiar with nineteenth-century French society. I knew as little about twentieth-century American society as I had known before my Balzacian adventure. But I had acquired a sense of the excitement of a sociological perspective, which Salomon passionately expounded.

That perspective, which Salomon (rightly or wrongly) ascribed to Balzac, was an endless curiosity about every aspect of human behavior, especially those aspects that are normally hidden from view and denied in polite circles. It was a perspective that was inherently irreverent, debunking, subversive. I don't know whether Balzac was really how Salomon presented him: walking the streets of Paris, preferably at night, in quest of its secrets—trying to understand everything that went on in the city's salons, government offices, businesses, taverns, and brothels. But this was the image of the sociologist that was imprinted in my mind, and it has stayed that way ever since, even if its youthful exuberance has been moderated over the years.

The French government maintained a cultural center in a palatial building on upper Fifth Avenue; I think it is still there, presumably intended as an agent of the French *mission civilisatrice* in barbaric America. There happened to be a Balzac program there at the time, an exhibition and some lectures, none of which I recall. But there was also an attractive catalog with a reproduction of a caricature of Balzac. He is dressed in a sort of monk's cowl, topped by an oversized head with a leering look. I cut the picture out and had it framed. It still hangs in my study.

It reminds me of another insight I acquired from the beginning of my studies—that good sociology has a kinship with good novels, from which one can learn a lot about a society. In the course of my studies at the New School, I made the acquaintance of a professor of French literature who taught in the school's adult education division. He listened to me talking about my work, then said: "You belong with us. You are a *littérateur*." He meant it as a compliment. In later years I was occasionally regaled with this term as a pejorative epithet.

The New School was a peculiar place, and it had a peculiar history. It was founded in 1919 by a group of intellectuals who were disappointed by what they thought was the stuffy atmosphere of American academia. They wanted to create a "university for adults," and they did. It was essentially an adult education program, and it awarded no degrees. Admission was open to anyone, and one could take courses ranging from the most abstruse (say, Buddhist metaphysics) to the most practical (say, pottery). This program was almost instantly popular and thus became self-supporting. It continues to this day and has become a well-known New York institution. Other programs, including the graduate one that I attended, were added to the adult education operation and at least initially funded by it.

Among the founders of the institution were some prominent academics, including John Dewey. Thorstein Veblen, one of the classical American sociologists, taught there for a while. But the president from the beginning, still in office in the 1950s, was Alvin Johnson. An idiosyncratic, volatile, and highly entrepreneurial educator, he came from a Norwegian background in the upper Midwest, actually very similar to Veblen's. His daughter, Felicia Deyrup (a surprisingly quiet, definitely nonvolatile individual), taught economics.

In 1934 Johnson became concerned with the fate of German academics persecuted by the Nazis. With funding from various sources, he started something he called the European University in Exile, soon to be renamed the Graduate Faculty of Political and Social Science of the New School for Social Research—quite a mouthful, commonly abbreviated to "the Graduate Faculty." At first the original group of professors were all from Germany, some Jewish, some not. As the Nazi empire expanded, academics from other European countries joined the faculty—from Austria, Italy, Spain, and France. Some were quite famous, such as Leo Strauss, who moved on to the University of Chicago to found an influential school of political philosophy, and Claude Levi-Strauss, who returned to France after the war. The Graduate Faculty was accredited early on and started to award master's and doctoral degrees in a limited number of fields—philosophy, political science, sociology, and economics (later anthropology was added). The institution was indeed unique—a graduate school in the social sciences superimposed on an adult education program. There was no undergraduate program (again, one was added much later).

The Graduate Faculty and the adult education program had very little to do with each other. But the origins of the New School in the latter program had one distinctive consequence—*all classes were taught in the late afternoon or evening*, specifically in three two-hour slots beginning, respectively, at 4:00 p.m., 6:00 p.m., and 8:00 p.m. This fact, as mentioned above, was decisive for my decision to study at the New School. But it also determined the atmosphere of the place: nocturnal, somewhat mysterious, erotically charged—in my mind, Balzacian. Add to this the location of the New School in Greenwich Village, which enveloped the place in its bohemian atmosphere. Needless to say, for young people of my age, all this made for a heady experience.

In the 1950s, when I was a student there, the New School had only one building, at 66 West Twelfth Street, between Fifth and Sixth Avenues. Everything was crammed into that building—all classes, adult education as well as graduate; all offices; the library, such as it was; a cafeteria; and an auditorium. There were socialist-realist murals from the 1930s in various rooms, including a huge one by the Mexican revolutionary painter José Clemente Orozco, which featured heroic pictures of Lenin and Stalin. (In the 1950s, after a heated debate by the faculty, it was hidden behind a full-sized curtain, though anyone who wanted to see it could ask for the curtain to be lifted.) The "library" was essentially nonexistent; the few books it held were always out.

Our library was the New York Public Library further up on Fifth Avenue, where I spent many hours in the ornate general reading room and, later, in the reading room of the Oriental collection (which I needed for my dissertation research). The cafeteria was famous, justly so, as one of the best pickup places in the Village: how many fiery glances were exchanged over open copies of Kafka or Sartre!

As to the revolutionary murals (I have no idea how they got there), they were a sore point. The New School had a reputation as being left-wing and was sometimes confused with the Jefferson School of Social Science, which trained cadres for the Communist Party of the United

States. The faculty was eager to refute this reputation—hence the curtain. In fact, the core of the émigré faculty ranged from social democrats to center-right moderates; it was fiercely anticommunist in addition to its creedal antifascism. Indeed, the charter of the Graduate Faculty contained a clause, clearly directed against communists, that barred any professor whose teaching would be dictated by an outside organization. (In the 1960s this clause was invoked, unsuccessfully, by a militantly secularist faculty member who wanted to bar a Roman Catholic priest from being appointed to the Philosophy Department.)

The total number of graduate students was small, the number in sociology even smaller. We all knew each other. Most of us lived in or around the Village, typically as subtenants in rented rooms or attics. Thus we did not have long trips home after evening classes. Those of us who worked (most of us) could not take classes that began before 6:00 p.m. We emerged from the New School building after 8:00 or even 10:00 in the evening. And of course we were wide-awake. So we would sit together and argue, not often in each other's rooms (these were too uncomfortable). We favored two places, a dingy eatery called Alex's Borsht Bowl off Sixth Avenue and the Oviedo bar on Fourteenth Street. The latter place had an inscription over the urinal that read *"Muerte a Franco!"* ("Death to Franco!"). The owner claimed to be a veteran of the Republican forces during the Spanish Civil War. He once opined to me that, regardless of political views, every decent person was at heart an anarchist. Sleep was not a high priority.

A number of individuals came into our group, most of them for short periods of time. Most of them were bright. And of course there was a shifting contingent of Kafka-reading young women. My best friend during most of my time at the New School was Lenny Kornberg, who was a little older (he was a war veteran). He studied sociology at the New School, then moved on to get a degree in education. He had a room in a brownstone at 38 West Twelfth Street, on the same block as the New School. It was inhabited by an odd assortment of individuals—the superintendent was a Swiss woman who sent notes to the tenants in poetry, and a Chinese fellow meditated in a broom closet off the staircase. I sometimes stayed there myself. But the friendship that had the most important intellectual consequences for me was that with Thomas Luckmann. We met in a philosophy class, immediately hit it off, and spent much time together. My collaboration with Luckmann, which led to our coauthorship of an influential book, could of course not be foreseen at that time. It will have to be discussed later on in this book.

After my encounter with Balzac, I carried out my initial plan: I spent a little over a year getting a master's degree in sociology and went on to the Lutheran Theological Seminary in Philadelphia. I spent another year there, a happy one at that, but then decided that I would not pursue a ministerial vocation after all. (The reasons for this do not belong to this decidedly nontheological narrative. Suffice it to say that I did not feel that I could without reservations subscribe to the full text of the Unaltered Augsburg Confession—in retrospect a very quixotic decision, since there would be very few Lutheran clergy indeed if such a subscription were taken seriously as a condition for ordination.) By then I had become hooked on sociology as a discipline, or at any rate the view of sociology that the New School had conveyed to me. It thus seemed natural to return to the New School and to go on for a doctorate. And so an original mistake led to a lifelong professional career.

Just what was that view of sociology? And has it stood up over time?

My view of sociology, as it was shaped by my years of study at the New School (I began in 1949 and received the doctorate in 1954), can be traced to the influence of three teachers—Albert Salomon, Alfred Schutz, and Carl Mayer. All three belonged to the cadre of European refugee scholars, but they were very different both as personalities and in their intellectual profiles. I owe a debt of gratitude to each of them.

I have already described the impact of Salomon's course on Balzac. It was this vision of the endless effort to understand the inner workings of a society, and of the endless curiosity about the motives of individuals (including their passions and crimes), that hooked me on sociology. But that was not all that I learned from Salomon. He mainly lectured on two topics—the roots of sociology in the Enlightenment and the Durkheim school of French sociology. Salomon understood sociology as a child of the Enlightenment, especially the French Enlightenment, as being the relentless application of reason to achieve an understanding of the human world and, as a result, had adopted an essentially debunking spirit. I still think that Salomon was correct in his interpretation of what he called the "prehistory" of sociology. It was no accident that the very notion of sociology, and the word itself, was invented by Auguste Comte, a French philosopher.

Equally important was Salomon's interpretation of Emile Durkheim and the school of sociology he founded. Of all the classical sociologists, Durkheim was most obviously a child of the Enlightenment, as evidenced both in his political activity and in his understanding of the public role of sociology. He was very much engaged on the republican side in the Dreyfus affair. When, in the wake of that side's victory in the conflict, the separation of church and state was enacted in 1905, Durkheim served on the commission to create a republican catechism to replace Catholic instruction in the public schools. Salomon showed in class the textbook produced by this commission; it was entitled *Course of Study in Sociology and Morality*. A key concept of Durkheim's was "solidarity"; Salomon opined that, when one comes across that concept in Durkheim's writings, one can hear as an undertone the third principle of the French Revolution—"liberty, equality, *fraternity*."

I was not taken with this, as it were, Jacobin understanding of sociology; for one thing, I was early on much more impressed by Max Weber's more sober view of the discipline. But other Durkheimian themes permanently influenced my thinking: the objectivity of social phenomena, their hard reality (Durkheim: "Consider social facts to be *things*"); society requiring an overarching moral consensus in order to survive (Durkheim's "collective conscience"); modernity as a change in the character of institutional order (Durkheim: the shift from "mechanical" to "organic" solidarity), which now comes to be based on contractual relations; religion as a sacred symbolization of society; and "anomie" as the unbearable condition of being deprived of social ties. Durkheim's disciples then further developed this understanding of society with the concepts of "collective memory" (Maurice Halbwachs) and mental structure, or *mentalité* (Marcel Granet, Lucien Levy-Bruhl). As I absorbed this radically objectivist view of society, I was very much aware of its tension with the Weberian view of society as based on the subjective meanings of social actors. Much later, in the collaboration with Thomas Luckmann, we conceived of a way to integrate these two perspectives.

Salomon was a brilliant, passionate lecturer. He was also a quirky, irascible character. He did not suffer fools gladly, and he could cut down students sarcastically if their comments struck him as foolish. He did assemble around himself a small group of devoted followers. I was not one of them, though I greatly appreciated what he taught.

In terms of my later work as a sociologist, especially in sociological theory, it was the influence of Alfred Schutz that had the most lasting impact. It is somewhat ironic that, at the time, he impressed me less than either Albert Salomon or Carl Mayer. I was interested in his lectures, and I felt an affinity with him as a fellow Viennese (the other two were Germans). I could not, however, get too intrigued by the wider implications of phenomenology, which was Schutz's philosophical framework. The importance of the sociological implications did not become clear to me until considerably later, when Thomas Luckmann and I were working on our book *The Social Construction of Reality* about a decade after I finished my graduate studies. By contrast, Luckmann delved much more intensely into phenomenology; he became more explicitly a Schutzian and more competent in philosophy than I.

Thus it is somewhat difficult for me to disentangle what I learned from Schutz as a student from what I learned subsequently (mostly from reading his posthumously published works and from conversations with Luckmann). I heard Schutz lecture in two areas—the methodology of the social sciences and the sociology of knowledge. Ironically again, the second area occupied a much smaller place in Schutz's course offerings—as far as I can recall, a single course under that title, which was mainly an exposition of the history of that subdiscipline from its invention by Max Scheler and its introduction to the English-speaking world by Karl Mannheim. Part of this exposition was a trenchant critique of Marxist theories about the relation of ideas and social processes. It was in his methodological lectures that Schutz developed his own application of phenomenology to the understanding of society.

His most brilliant pedagogical tool for this was a seminar I took twice, rather ponderously entitled "Current Events and Situations of Everyday Life in the Light of Sociological Theory." Students were allowed to write papers on almost any topic; when they read the papers in class, Schutz would then comment in terms of his own theoretical approach. In one seminar I wrote a paper, called "The Case of Gustav," about different ways (Freudian, Marxist, theological) of understanding a young man's crisis of faith. (This exercise proved to be useful as I dealt with my own problems with faith, but Schutz was unaware of this.) I cannot recall what paper I wrote for the other seminar. My friend Lenny Kornberg wrote on the world of the blind.

I suppose that the central concept I learned from Schutz was that of "multiple realities," including the manner in which a sense of reality is kept going in the consciousness of individuals. The concept of course was elucidated in a phenomenological manner. Its maintenance in consciousness was elaborated by Schutz in an ingenious synthesis of phenomenology with a distinctively American tradition of social psychology derived from the work of George Herbert Mead.

Around the central concept Schutz constructed an array of, as it were, subsidiary concepts explaining how the different realities are organized in the subjective consciousness of individuals and how they are communicated intersubjectively: the primary reality of everyday life (the "paramount reality"); the various enclaves within that reality ("finite provinces of meaning"—such as dreams, aesthetic experiences, theoretical universes of discourse, and, last but not least, religious experiences, though Schutz was not much interested in those); the processes of transition from one reality to another (most wonderfully described in what I would consider Schutz's best piece of writing, the essay "Don Quixote and the Problem of Reality"); the individual's relations with those he interacts with face-to-face, with those who live at the same time but without such interaction, with those who preceded and those who will succeed him (respectively, "consociates," contemporaries, predecessors, and successors). All this added up to a detailed description of *The Meaningful Structure of the Social World*, which was the title of the only book Schutz published in his lifetime, in German and prior to his move to America.[2] After that move Schutz published a large number of articles in English, which were only collected after his death in three volumes of *Collected Papers*; they were published by a Dutch publisher at a prohibitive price, which made them quite inaccessible to American students.

It is remarkable that, nevertheless, Schutz has become quite well known in the social sciences in this country, partly through the efforts of New School students of his (in philosophy as well as sociology), but also through the efforts of others (such as Harold Garfinkle and other so-called ethnomethodologists). It is sad that Schutz died, in 1959 at the age of fifty-nine, before he achieved this influence. In a remarkable labor of love, Thomas Luckmann systematized the Schutzian approach in *The Structures of the Life-World* (with Luckmann as the coauthor with the long-deceased Schutz, this was probably a unique and certainly a profoundly moving case of collaboration between a predecessor and a successor).[3]

Schutz's own writings in the sociology of knowledge all dealt, in one way or another, with what he called "the social distribution of knowledge." This was elaborated in such cameo essays as the ones on "common-sense knowledge" (more or less synonymous with "the world-taken-for-granted"), "the well-informed citizen," the stranger, and the homecomer. Of course the ideas of these writings were communicated in class, but, except for scarce reprints, they were not accessible to his students. As already mentioned, his course on the sociology of knowledge dealt mainly with the presentation and critique of other people's works. But, as far as I can recall, Schutz during this course let fall, almost casually, one sentence that stuck in Luckmann's and my own mind. I'm not sure that I can reproduce it verbatim, but it went something like this: "If the sociology of knowledge is going to be true to its name, it will have to deal with everything that passes for knowledge in everyday life." At the time, this sentence impressed neither Luckmann nor me as a bolt from heaven. But that one sentence became, as it were, the basic marching order for our reformulation of the sociology of knowledge in the 1960s.

Schutz was a genial, sociable individual. His lifestyle was very much that of the Central European educated bourgeoisie from which he came. He was an amateur musician and held regular sessions of chamber music in his apartment. He loved the theater (which provided many of his examples), he was a good raconteur, and he smoked a lot. His life organization was somewhat peculiar: While he was a full member of the Graduate Faculty, he also owned an export-import business, apparently a reasonably successful one. According to gossip (I cannot verify this), he was paid a token one dollar per year as an annual salary from the New School, while he lived quite comfortably on his business income. He was in his business in the morning, he taught in the evening, and the afternoons he spent in the New York Public Library (like the rest of us).

If Salomon's lectures sometimes took on the passionate character of prophecy, Schutz's were low-keyed and informal, perhaps ultimately derived from the relaxed atmosphere of the coffeehouse. Schutz inspired several students to follow in his footsteps, but he did not crave disciples and he welcomed criticism. He was personally kind, but he had a sharp wit, which he did not use maliciously.

He came to my dissertation defense. He said almost nothing, except for one question on a minor detail in a footnote. After I passed, there was a little sherry party. He came over to me and said (in German): "Very well, Berger. You are now a doctor. Congratulations. But tell me: Do you really believe all the nonsense you wrote in this dissertation?" He smiled warmly as he said this. His intention was clear: He knew that there was no way of replying to his question without appearing to be foolish: "Yes, I believe the nonsense"? "I don't think I wrote any nonsense"? I said nothing, just laughed; he laughed too. He just wanted to make me a little uncomfortable and to stop me from having delusions of grandeur. In this he succeeded.

Carl Mayer was very different from the other two figures in the dominant trio of sociology teachers, both personally and professionally. He was a quiet, almost shy individual. So was his lecturing style. He was also remarkably thorough and lucid in his lectures. When he had finished discussing a topic, one obtained the impression that there was nothing more to be said about it.

He mostly lectured on two topics—the sociology of religion and the works of Max Weber. The two topics, of course, were related; both were crucially important for my formation as a sociologist. Since I was struggling with my own theological problems at the time, it was natural that I made the sociology of religion my primary area of specialization. And Mayer's teaching persuaded me that Weber's conception of sociological method made the most sense to me—a view that I have had no reason to change ever since.

A superb teacher, Mayer wrote very little: a single book, in German—his doctoral thesis on the concepts of church and sect—and a few scattered articles, most of them in the Graduate Faculty journal *Social Research*. He had planned to write his magnum opus on Weber after his early retirement, but he only succeeded in producing some fragments. Thus his influence, in almost archaic fashion, was only from his teaching, confined to the memory of a handful of students.

Mayer's analyses of religion were purely Weberian. They revolved around the interaction of religion and society without assuming that either was the determinant. Mayer exhaustively conveyed Weber's key categories in this area—the "elective affinity" (*Wahlverwandschaft*) between specific religious movements and social forces; charisma and its "routinization" (*Veralltäglichung*); the social structures of church and sect; and, of course, the huge issues connected with his seminal work on the relation between the "Protestant ethic" and the origins of modern capitalism (to which Mayer devoted a full-semester course).

Mayer had a real empathy for religious experiences and theological ideas, but in his teaching (Weberian in this too) he never gave a hint about his own convictions. In conversation with me he did, rather reluctantly, tell me a little. Unlike Salomon and Schutz, he was not Jewish (his wife was). He was Protestant, from the German province of Baden, where Protestants were Reformed (Calvinist) rather than Lutheran. Mayer indicated that he considered himself a Christian, but he did not go to church. He once said, without going into detail: "If I did go to church, it would be to an Episcopal one. I might feel comfortable there."

If Mayer was reticent about his theological beliefs, he was anything but reticent about his Weberian ones. He certainly made a convert of me. Thus I early on identified with the core elements of a Weberian approach: society as constituted by actions inspired by human meanings; sociology as the attempt to understand these meanings (*Verstehen*); the use of "ideal types"—theoretical constructs that only approximate social reality; the relation among meanings, motives, and actions; the institutionalization of the state, the economy, and class; and sociology as "value-free." There were two pieces of Weber's work on which Mayer did become almost passionate—the essays on science and the essays on politics as vocations. In the former, Weber rejected the role of the scholar as propagandist; in the latter, he developed his distinction between two types of ethics—the "ethic of attitude" and the "ethic of responsibility," strongly endorsing the second as a guide for political actors.

Mayer did not easily open up to his students in a personal way. He

did to me, at least up to a point. I was invited twice to his house in Westchester County. Shortly after he retired to Italian-speaking Switzerland, my wife, Brigitte, and I visited him once in Brissago. Here he had bought a house, which had unending problems that kept him from his scholarly intentions. He and his wife, Trude, visited us at least once in Ascona, a short drive away, where we had rented a house. I recall the four of us sitting in our garden, as the late afternoon merged into evening, looking out over the breathtaking beauty of the landscape around Lago Maggiore. I cannot recall what we talked about.

Looking back on my period of graduate study at the New School, I conclude that I took away with me three theoretical perspectives that were very helpful for the work I did in subsequent years—from Salomon, an understanding of the place of sociology in the history of ideas and a good grounding in the French tradition of the discipline; from Schutz, a sense of how phenomenology could enrich sociological theory, especially the sociology of knowledge, and an introduction to the American tradition of social psychology derived from George Herbert Mead; and from Mayer, a basic approach to the sociology of religion and a quite thorough knowledge of the work of Max Weber. Mayer, who was my advisor and doctoral supervisor, was most relevant to what I did in the early stages of my career. But all three teachers had a lasting effect on my thinking. When Thomas Luckmann and I sat down to plan and then write *The Social Construction of Reality*, the central part of our argument was a synthesis of the three aforementioned theoretical strands. Earlier I had called my approach to sociology "humanistic." I would now question whether this was a felicitous adjective, though I would not quarrel with the basic intention. I had intended two meanings: One was to stress the contribution of sociology to a *humane* society, based on its debunking of the myths legitimating cruelty and oppression. I suppose that this came out of the Enlightenment roots of the discipline. But more relevant was the second meaning, sociology as one of the "humanities" (or *Geisteswis-*

senschaften), closely related to history and philosophy but also to the intuitions of the literary imagination.

These, then, were the quite rich fruits of my New School education. I don't want to suggest that I learned nothing else. There was a very useful course on the history of American sociology by a young lecturer recruited from outside the Graduate Faculty. Among other things, the course introduced me to the then-fashionable schools of "structural functionalism" and "symbolic interactionalism." A principal lacuna was in the area of quantitative methods. I took a course in statistics with a very competent teacher, but his well-meaning efforts foundered on the rock of my stubborn ineptitude in anything involving mathematics. (I liked to say that I had the measles every time that arithmetic was taught in my primary school in Vienna.) Years later I took a summer course in statistical analysis at the University of Michigan. It was a disaster. Not only was the course taught by a woman in the final stages of pregnancy—the students were distracted by mounting anxiety that she would give birth in class while explaining the mysteries of multiple correlation. But also I had the worst ever attack of hay fever. I was told that the area around Ann Arbor was famous for inducing this condition in the summer, though I cannot discount the suspicion that it was also psychosomatic in my case. Be this as it may, I left the course early, with stuffed nose and itching eyes, the instructor (as far as I knew) still pregnant.

VENTURING BEYOND TWELFTH STREET

In order to leave the New School with full doctoral credentials, I had to produce two texts, a thesis for the master's degree and a dissertation for the doctorate (the second text supposedly differing from the first in terms of length and degree of sophistication—the former requirement did apply in my case, the latter probably not). The first exercise was an

original empirical investigation about religion in the burgeoning Puerto Rican community in New York. The second was a study of the transition of the Baha'i faith from a nineteenth-century messianic movement in Iran to a rather sedate community in twentieth-century America; it had an empirical component, but most of the study was historical. In academic ideology these exercises are supposed to be important tests of competence, the second also making "an original contribution to knowledge." I rather doubt whether my case fulfilled either aspiration. However, these exercises were important learning experiences, and they adumbrated work I would do much later. Most important, they made me get my "hands dirty with research" (in the words of Louis Wirth, one of the founders of the so-called Chicago school of sociology), and that was very exciting.

I was looking around for a thesis topic that I might finish in one year (I was still eager to start my theological studies). Coincidentally, I had met a Protestant church official who mentioned in passing that his interdenominational agency, the New York City Mission Society, had come on an interesting fact—that many Puerto Rican migrants, who were then streaming into the city in large numbers, were Protestant. He said that very little was known about this. This struck me as a manageable topic for my thesis, and, when I said that I would like to investigate this, he offered to put me in touch with other church officials (both Protestant and Catholic) who could be helpful to me.

I quickly discovered that there was virtually no previous research to look at—just a few references to religion in general writings on Puerto Ricans in New York and some unpublished papers by church organizations, and very few in either category. I was both intrigued and a little scared by the realization that I really had to start from scratch. It turned out that my initial informants, the church officials my acquaintance introduced me to, were indeed helpful. Mainly they put me in touch with Catholic clergy and with Protestant clergy from the mainline denominations. But I realized soon that the most dynamic group on this religious scene was the one I categorized as "sectarian" (not a very helpful term; I got it from the church officials)—essentially, this was the group of Pentecostal churches.

My "official" informants did tell me useful (though rather prejudiced) stories about Pentecostals. By their very nature, these churches were hard to find; they could not be looked up in the telephone directory. I did my best to find them, but my efforts, as I can see now, were only partially successful. I interviewed and listed most, if not all, pastors of Spanish-speaking mainline Protestant churches and of Spanish-language Catholic parishes in Manhattan, Brooklyn, and the Bronx. I did find out some interesting things during these interviews, such as the fact that, with one exception (an Argentinian), all the Protestant pastors were Puerto Ricans, while none of the Catholic ones were. A few of these informants suggested (probably correctly) that some Puerto Ricans were already Protestant on the island but that a larger group had converted after arriving in New York. Yet, in retrospect, most of these interviews were a waste of time. This was not where the action was. My time would have been much better spent by chasing down Pentecostals wherever I could find them, interview those preachers and lay leaders, and engage in a lot of "participant observation" in the best ethnographic tradition.

Well, I did *some* of this. And that is where the material becomes more interesting, even when read all these many decades later. In any case, work on the thesis allowed me to realize my Balzacian fantasy—roaming the streets of the city and discovering its secrets, mostly at night. The streets were mainly in East Harlem; walking them at night was safe at the time (at least compared to later years). I did some of those rather useless interviews, but most of the time I visited one Pentecostal place or another—storefront churches, garages, some private apartments. I interviewed preachers and laypeople, and I attended services. In my text is a long, detailed description of a typical Pentecostal service—remarkably accurate, given the fact that this phenomenon was completely new to me.

I should mention two factors that enhanced my ethnographic exercises. During the year of this research I lived with my parents and had almost no income of my own. I took a part-time job with the East Harlem Protestant Parish, an interdenominational venture that combined church outreach and social work. The organizers encouraged male staff to wear clerical collars, both so as to allay suspicions and to reinforce personal safety. I acquired such a garment, wearing it mostly at night. I felt awkward at first—sharply so when, on a couple occasions, nuns nodded to me on the subway—but the collar probably facilitated contacts with people understandably suspicious of a visiting *gringo*, and it probably made my nocturnal excursions safer. In the course of the research I also acquired a reasonable command of Spanish. I never took a formal course in the language. I worked through a Spanish grammar and read Spanish newspapers with the help of a dictionary. I made friends with a recently arrived young Puerto Rican actor, a very pleasant individual who wanted to learn English; we exchanged English and Spanish lessons. But mostly I picked up Spanish on the street, no doubt with something of a Puerto Rican accent. It has served me well ever since. I also developed a definite empathy with Puerto Rico, and when I first visited the island, years later, I had a feeling of homecoming.

Needless to say, my presentation of the Pentecostal phenomenon was very inadequate. I could make no real effort to determine its size. I quoted a figure of 5 percent from the chapter on religion in a study of Puerto Rican migration by a team from Columbia University. That figure was undoubtedly much too low. The vast explosion of Latino Pentecostalism was yet to come, but I would think that a figure somewhere around 20 percent would probably have been more correct even then. I did say that, by all indications, the phenomenon was large and growing.

However, the qualitative findings on the Pentecostal churches I could observe were surprisingly accurate. I understood the motives that led many Puerto Ricans to convert to "sectarian" Protestantism. Here was a population recently transplanted from a still quite traditional society into the turbulent environment of New York. These churches provided strong community, mutual aid, spiritual and (so they believed) physical healing. These churches (even the mainline Protestant ones) were "Puerto Rican places," unlike the Catholic churches where even the Spanish-speaking priests were Americans or Europeans. As one woman I interviewed said: "The Catholic church I went to, the priest didn't even know my name. Now, if I don't attend for two Sundays, the pastor visits and asks if anything is wrong."

The God presented in the Pentecostal church is close, accessible directly without any priestly mediation, a loving and comforting presence. The most common inscription in front reads "*Dios es amor*" ("God is love"). The services, which often take place every night of the week, are emotionally cathartic—the music is stirring, and all can freely express themselves in singing, dancing, testifying, and from time to time "speaking in tongues." What is more, the church, while it is not at all censorious, teaches a firm moral code—something much needed by people uprooted from taken-for-granted traditional norms.

Given the fact that I was steeped in Weberian texts at the time, it is curious that I never spoke about the "Protestant ethic" in the thesis. I understood this connection much later. I had a hint of it. I remember being struck by a sign I saw in a storefront church, which read (in Spanish of course): "Spitting on the floor is an offense against this holy place and a sign of bad manners." Although I was struck by this odd combination of religious awe and bourgeois etiquette, I did not find it necessary to include this little fact in the text.

Night after night, in addition to Sundays, the Pentecostal church was a refuge, a place of being at home, a place that belonged to ordinary people in a way that a Catholic church never could. The church provided a very strong community indeed. This came home to me in an incident that I described in full in the thesis. I was attending a service in a storefront church. About halfway through the service, an obviously drunk American woman stumbled in and started shouting in English—in the context, a potentially threatening disruption. The reaction of the congregation was remarkable. The woman shouted: "I don't belong to no church. I am a stranger around here, just like everybody in this room. Why don't somebody speak to me in English? I want somebody to speak to me in English." The pastor said to her, in very halting English: "We will sing a song just for you." (For some reason the pastor's response, which I remember very well, was left out of my final draft.) The congregation, in equally bad English, then sang, "You pray for me and I'll pray for you." The woman calmed down, evidently pleased by all this attention. Then an elderly Puerto Rican woman, who apparently could not speak a word of English, sat down with the intruder, smiling at her, patting her. I described this incident, correctly I think, as an illustration of communal strength; this tight-knit community was able to embrace a stranger who could very easily have been perceived as a threat.

In discussing the non-Pentecostal Protestant churches with Puerto Rican membership, I made the point that their services bore certain resemblances to the Pentecostal ones, though of course they were more sedate and would not tolerate the more exuberant manifestations of "being filled with the Spirit." Their services too were informal, with children running around freely and adults talking and coming and going. Some of the music was similar (though less loud!). Perhaps most important, the sermons were based on a literal reading of the Bible and emphasized the importance of personal conversion. I did not use the term (I'm not sure whether I even knew it then), but what I observed, correctly, was that these services were profoundly *Evangelical.* Although I did not understand the full implications, I stumbled on the very important fact that almost all Latino Protestantism—and indeed almost all Protestantism in the global South—is distinctly Evangelical.

It would be very surprising if this piece of work, submitted as a thesis in 1950 when I was all of twenty-one years old, could be read today as a serious work in the sociology of religion. It did serve as a useful finger exercise in empirical research. And it adumbrated a number of themes that have continued to occupy me—the relation of faith and social context, especially the faith of people on the margins of society, and the empirical (as distinct from the theological) differences between Catholicism and popular Protestantism. But above all, the powerful impression I then had of Pentecostalism has lingered in my mind ever since. It came to the foreground of my attention when I became aware, decades later, of the veritable tsunami of Pentecostal Christianity sweeping across Latin America, sub-Saharan Africa, parts of Asia, and other unlikely places. When in 1985 I started the Institute on Culture, Religion and World Affairs, I decided to make Pentecostal studies an important part of its research agenda. The institute supported the pioneering research in Latin America of David Martin, the "dean of Pentecostal studies." His work continues to be a major interest of the institute, though by now there is a mass of other literature on the subject.

Before I turn to the other credentialing text, my Baha'i dissertation, I should mention another experience, which, with a little stretch, could also be described as an exercise in field research. In the summer of 1950, my master's degree (so to speak) in my pocket and perennially short of money, I took a job with the "church extension" office of what was then the United Lutheran Church in America. Putting it bluntly, this was a project of market research. I was paired with another young man, a beginning theological student. We were sent to a number of localities in the Midwest, all newly founded suburbs (this was the era of the great postwar suburban explosion). We went from house to house, identified ourselves as representatives of the office of church extension (no mention of Lutheranism up front), and basically asked two questions: (1) Did the interviewee (usually a woman) or her family belong to a church? If the answer was yes, we said thank you and moved on. (2) Would she or he be interested if a Lutheran church were established in the community? If the answer was no, we would also move on. But if interest was expressed, we would take down basic contact information. Reams of these data were sent from each locality to the office at the denomination's headquarters (which was then in New York). I have no idea whether our research led to any Lutheran church implantations. That summer, though, was a rather useful learning experience: I learned how to interview people who, very possibly, might rudely close the door in one's face. And, for a change, I was interviewing people who understood English.

My main memory of this summer is of trudging along endless, often still unpaved streets in blistering heat, pursued by dusty winds and barking dogs. I fell violently in love with a young woman in a Chicago suburb (this episode led nowhere), and on the train from Chicago to Saint Louis we heard about the outbreak of the Korean War. But neither of these events is relevant to these pages.

"HOW CAN ONE BE A PERSIAN?"

In one of Albert Salomon's classes, I wrote a term paper on Montesquieu's satirical novel *The Persian Letters*. Through the lens of fictitious letters sent home by a couple of Persian visitors to Paris, Montesquieu tried to undermine the taken-for-granted assumptions of his society. Parisians kept asking, "How can one be a Persian?" What Montesquieu really wanted to ask was "How can one be a Parisian?" Be this as it may, as I embarked on the next phase of my graduate studies, I was about to compose my own "Persian letter." For my dissertation I chose a topic very far indeed from Puerto Rican Protestants in East Harlem— "The Baha'i Movement: A Contribution to the Sociology of Religion." The methodology too was completely different. The earlier study was based entirely on empirical research. While the dissertation had a very small empirical component (a couple of interviews and the distribution of a questionnaire to members of the Baha'i community in New York), almost all of it was based on historical materials, from the beginning of the movement in mid-nineteenth-century Iran to its character in contemporary America.

I had come across the Baha'i movement before, but my choice of this topic for my dissertation came from an accidental meeting with an elderly Iranian gentleman by the name of Ahmad Sohrab. I was interested in visiting as many religious groups as I could. In these peregrinations through American religious pluralism I came across a small center of Baha'i dissidents on the Upper East Side. Called the Caravan of East and West, it was led by Sohrab, with the support of a wealthy American widow. The center as such held little of interest. But Sohrab had been an interpreter of Abbas Effendi, the son of the Baha'i founder, from 1912 to 1915. During those years Abbas made a number of missionary journeys to Europe and America. Sohrab had kept a diary, in English, recording from day to day what Abbas did and how people reacted to him. I was allowed to read this diary, which was contained in eleven handwritten notebooks. It made for fascinating reading, and I could indeed make good use of it. In the end, though, most of the dissertation was based on published sources.

Perhaps following the example of my earlier experience with Spanish, I started to learn Farsi. But I soon discovered that all I needed for my purpose was available in English and French books, and I gave up on Farsi. Instead, I spent many hours in the Oriental section of the New York Public Library (a treasure trove in this as in so many other fields). In preparing to write the present chapter, I read my thesis and dissertaion one after the other (probably the first time ever that I have done this); I was struck by how very different they were from each other.

The dissertation was a detailed application of Max Weber's theory of the "routinization of charisma"—the process in which a passionate movement led by an extraordinary leader mutates into a formal organization administered by bureaucrats. In order to apply the theory to the Baha'i case, I had to follow the history of the movement in some detail. That history is full of dramatic incidents, especially in its early period.

That period went through two stages. The first consisted of the career of a prophetic figure who called himself the Bab ("the Gate") and his disciples, who started an armed uprising with the aim of overthrowing the shah of Iran and establishing a messianic theocracy. It ended in a bloodbath, the Bab himself executed and the disciples cruelly killed wherever they could be found. One of these disciples, who later called himself Baha-ullah ("the Glory of God"), escaped to the Ottoman Empire and eventually proclaimed himself (rather than the Bab) the prophet of a new era. In this transition the movement gave up its violent character and became essentially pacifist. This change became much more pronounced after Baha-ullah's death, when the aforementioned Abbas Effendi carried the movement to the West.

After Abbas's death the "routinization" followed a strictly Weberian trajectory, with the establishment of the institution of the so-called Guardianship, a very formal ecclesiastical construction. In the same process the religious content of the movement was also transformed. Most of its esoteric elements were left behind, and Baha'ism, at least in America, became a sedate, respectable, "progressive" community—a sort of Unitarianism with a slight Persian accent. (The course of Baha'ism in Iran was quite different, and much less sedate, especially after the persecutions in the wake of the Islamic Revolution.)

Contrary to the academic ideology, which claims that every doctoral dissertation must make an original contribution, very few dissertations actually do so. This one, in fidelity to its subtitle, did make a modest contribution (original if only because, to my knowledge, no one had previously imposed Max Weber on this drama of the Persian religious imagination). I made use of the concept of "motif research" (coined by a school of Swedish religious scholarship)—searching out core themes of a religious tradition. I argued that one can understand any religious history as the changing interaction between such motifs and their institutional embodiments—in the Baha'i case I identified the motifs as "chiliastic" and "gnostic." Making sense of the fact that, in the early history of

Baha'ism, different individuals kept popping up and claiming to be the dominant messianic leader, I coined the phrase *charismatic field*: In the wide heat of an incipient charismatic movement, there is room for more than one charismatic leader. This may well be a useful notion. Looking at the struggles for succession following the deaths of the Bab and Baha-ullah, I ventured the hypothesis that, before "routinization" sets in, the most radical version of the movement's message will win out over more moderate ones. This may be wrong, but taken as a hypothesis it may be worth exploring.

More interesting is the way in which I redefined the sect/church typology. Max Weber and Ernst Troeltsch had defined the two types in strictly sociological terms—the sect is a voluntary group set aside from the world, the church an established institution that becomes part of the world; in sum, one joins a sect, while one is born into a church. Carl Mayer, in his little book *Sect and Church* (published in German in 1933—as far as I know, his only book-length publication), accepted the Weber-Troeltsch typology but criticized it for not taking the respective religious contents seriously enough. I tried to take it from there (he must have been greatly pleased!).

I suggested that the two types could be understood through their different relations with the "spirit" (that is, the object of religious faith): proximity, in the case of the sect; remoteness, and therefore in need of mediation, in the case of the church. Also, I coined a term in my discussion of conversion—*alternation*—a shift, not necessarily irreversible, from one reality to another. This concept was really inspired by the work of Alfred Schutz and turned out to be useful in my later work.

Looking at this dissertation from my present vantage point, I find most interesting a number of observations that adumbrated my later formulations in the sociology of knowledge. I discussed the claim to superior knowledge typically made by sectarian groups, and I extended the discussion beyond the area of religion. In this context I coined the term *epistemological elite*, applying this not only to sects, but also to certain churches, notably Roman Catholicism, and to Marxism and psycho-analysis. Any epistemological elite, religious or secular, must develop a system of cognitive defenses to defend its claims against outside criticisms but also, very importantly, to assuage the doubts harbored by insiders. Thomas Luckmann and I made use of these insights in our later work on the sociology of knowledge.

One incident during the time I was working on the dissertation vividly illustrated the notion of cognitive defenses. Albert Salomon told me that he had a Baha'i student in one of his classes. He had mentioned my work to this individual, who wanted to meet me. Would I mind if Salomon gave him my phone number? I agreed and almost immediately received a call, suggesting a meeting. The individual was evidently a fairly recent convert (I cannot recall his name—I think it was Jewish). He lived with his parents, which is where I visited him. I should emphasize that he only knew two things about me: that I was working on a doctoral dissertation and (I had said this on the phone) that I was not myself a Baha'i. When I arrived, he led me to a coffee table on which he had laid out a number of pamphlets, the kind that one would give to a first-time visitor to a Baha'i service—"What Is Baha'ism?" and the like. He said that I might find these useful. I was struck by the inappropriateness of this offering: anyone writing a dissertation on Baha'ism would surely know all this. I correctly interpreted this incident (which is recounted in a footnote): my interlocutor could deal with an unbeliever, and he could deal with someone who was ignorant of the faith; he could *not* deal with someone who was not ignorant but still not a believer.

He then asked me what my work was about, and I gave him a summary. This was followed by a curious question: He knew that I was not a Baha'i, but if I were, was there anything in my findings that would disturb my faith? I first responded by muttering something about "value-free social science" in good Weberian fashion. But then I said that, on second thought, there *was* something that would disturb me. After Abbas took over the leadership of the movement, he ordered the systematic search for and subsequent destruction of an early history that contradicted the official interpretation of the Bab. The campaign almost succeeded. But then a British scholar discovered one copy of the book that Abbas's operatives had overlooked; he published the Farsi text with an English commentary. I thought this was a rather distressing episode; of course my interlocutor had never heard of it. He said nothing for, at the most, three or four minutes. Then he gave me seven (!) reasons why this could never have happened. In other words, the cognitive defenses went up instantaneously!

Another incident connected to my dissertation was rather funny. Immediately after I finished my doctoral studies, I was drafted into the US Army, where I spent the next two years, most of the time in Fort Benning, Georgia. (I will later on discuss the unexpected contributions this period made to my development as a social scientist.) I made the acquaintance there of a young man from Chicago, who was a physical therapist at the base hospital. In the course of a conversation, he mentioned that he was a Baha'i, I mentioned my dissertation, and he expressed a desire to read it. It so happened that I had a copy with me; I was writing a summary article for a sociology-of-religion journal. He borrowed the copy and returned it a couple of weeks later, without any comments. I did not know this individual well, and I lost track of him for several months. Then I met him on the street. He was accompanied by a woman, whom he introduced as his wife. When she heard who I was, she embraced and kissed me, saying "I'm so glad to meet you. I must thank you for saving my marriage!" In the ensuing conversation (naturally, I was curious!) it was revealed that religion had been a major source of friction in the marriage: The wife could neither understand nor accommodate the husband's Baha'i faith. As a result of reading my dissertation, he had lost his faith, thus ending the friction between them. I did not know what to say, mumbled my congratulations, and quickly excused myself. I did not learn any intellectual lessons from this incident, except perhaps about the unintended consequences of scientific endeavors.

However, there was another incident during the time I worked on the dissertation, this one providing a secular example of cognitive defenses at work. I had met an attractive young woman named Ruth; as I recall she was a nurse. This relationship did not go very far, mainly because of politics: She was an avowed communist. I was not politically engaged or even very interested in politics, but I did detest every form of totalitarianism. I asked her how she could possibly be a communist, given the awful things that the Soviet Union had been doing in its sphere of influence. She asked me if I had personally experienced these things; I said no, but I knew people who had. She then said something careless: She would like to meet such people. I said that this could be arranged. And arrange it I did.

I knew a couple from Latvia who had recently arrived in America. I called them up, explained what Ruth had said. They avidly agreed to a meeting and invited us to dinner. They lived far out somewhere in Queens, and Ruth and I took a long subway ride to their apartment. The atmosphere at the dinner was rather awkward, with conversation staying trivial. But after dessert and over coffee, my Latvian friends began to tell us what had happened after the Soviet occupation—one horror story after another. This went on for maybe forty minutes or so. Ruth said nothing, but she showed signs of becoming more and more upset and even became quite pale. Then, abruptly putting her hands over her ears, she said, "I don't want to hear anymore!" The Latvian couple wanted to go on, but I said that perhaps we should continue this some other time, and we quickly made our departure.

There followed a very strange conversation on the long walk back to the subway. I asked her whether she thought these people were lying. She said no, they didn't impress her as people who were lying. She paused, and then she said something truly interesting: "You know, I think there is something, if only we knew what it is, that would completely change what they said." Much later I understood that she was expressing a deep longing for a transforming magic. Alfred Schutz wrote about this in the essay "Don Quixote and the Problem of Reality." Quixote invokes these magicians who have the ability of switching from one reality to another—in his case, from the reality of everyday life, the world of Sancho Panza, to the reality of Quixote's world of knights and giants and damsels in distress. The two realities are incompatible, but with the help of the magicians one could manage to live in both.

Ruth said that she would "check out" what the Latvians had said. I said: "You mean, check it out with your communist sources." She nodded. "Fine," I said, "but then check out what *they* said by looking at other sources." She nodded again. Nothing else happened that evening. *I never saw Ruth again.* I phoned several times, spoke with a roommate, but Ruth was out, or sick, or otherwise unavailable.

There is one more episode I should mention before I leave, somewhat reluctantly, my life as a graduate student in New York. Carl Mayer had, improbably, received a sizable grant from an American foundation for a study of religion and politics in postwar Germany. There were funds for three junior researchers, and I was hired to do the Protestant part of the research. I never got to Germany. Instead I was drafted, and Thomas Luckmann took my place in the team. But by then I had done a lot of preparatory reading, which came in very handy when I did go to Germany for another research project after my military service.

What, finally, did I take with me from my student career at the New School? Evidently, a lot. As outlined in this chapter, I received a solid grounding in classical sociological theory and in the sociology of religion, and I began to learn how to apply this to concrete empirical and historical phenomena. Despite the heavily "Eurocentric" orientation of the faculty, I did obtain a fairly adequate knowledge of the history of American sociology. My education was deficient in terms of quantitative methods of research, a deficiency that I really never overcame. My approach to sociology was established as "humanistic," in the sense of being close to historical and philosophical perspectives. Perhaps most important, I early understood that most important problems had to be addressed in an interdisciplinary manner.

This last understanding was institutionalized at the Graduate Faculty in the so-called "General Seminar." This was a regular meeting of the entire body of professors and students, usually introduced by a paper written by one professor. The discussion was often very heated, sometimes becoming downright unpleasant. And here were sociologists arguing with political scientists, economists, and philosophers. I remember attending a session during my leave from basic training in the army. The discussion was particularly heated that day. I cannot remember the topic. But I felt very much at home. At the same time, I did not have a clear overall picture of sociology as a field. Probably I'm not alone in that I only acquired a comprehensive perspective when, a few years later, I had to teach introductory sociology to undergraduates who wanted to know what this field was all about.

One thing I definitely learned was to strictly separate my work as a social scientist from my religious concerns, which greatly preoccupied me during those years. This, of course, was an instance of applying the Weberian notion of "value-free" social science. Carl Mayer was a good role model for this position. It was impossible to deduce his religious views from either his lectures or his (sparse) writings. Only in a few personal conversations did he give some hints on these views, and even then with obvious reluctance. I was reassured that I had indeed learned this lesson a few years later, also when I was teaching undergraduates: I found out that the prevailing opinion among the students was that I must be an atheist. (Graduate students, who knew me through conversations outside the classroom and who often read my writings as a "lay theologian," were usually better informed.) I have throughout my career rejected the role of "prophet of the lecture hall" (Weber's *Katheder-prophet*). When pressed to take on this role, I have usually refused by saying that the university pays me to teach sociology, not to engage in religious—or for that matter political—propaganda. No university is paying me to write this book. But, in the same Weberian notion of kosher cooking—keeping fleshy science separate from milky religion—

it seems appropriate to keep my religious journey out of an account of my adventures with sociology (unless there is an immediate connection, which I think is mostly not the case).

I undertook another journey, which began a couple of years before I started my graduate study—my mental journey into America, following my physical arrival in the country. But, apart from my initial mistake about the kind of sociology I would learn at the New School, I cannot really call this period a typical immigrant's story of discovery. I had spent a year attending college in Ohio, and during that year I hitchhiked all over the Midwest (hitchhiking was safe then, unless one was picked up by a driver who was drunk, which happened to me once). Thus I did not arrive at the New School innocent of all American experiences. But these experiences had nothing to do with sociology, and my academic studies can hardly be said to have contributed significantly to my Americanization. That process received a big push during my military service, and that push did have a somewhat bizarre connection with sociology. I will get to that in the next chapter.

But then (although there are people who deny this) New York is America too—a very special America, to be sure, but America all the same. I did discover New York, and in the course of that discovery I acquired a cosmopolitanism of a distinctive sort. The discovery had a physical aspect. For a year, while I was working on my dissertation, I had a curious job at the American Bible Society. This organization published the several books of the New Testament in a magazine format reminiscent of *Time* or *Newsweek*, presumably with the (almost certainly mistaken) assumption that this format would induce people to read the Bible. My job was to find photographs to illustrate the text, pictures not of works of art but of places and artifacts; I was also to write an explanation under each picture. I went in pursuit of suitable pictures all over town, to photo archives, museums, some individual collectors. But this activity could usually be finished in the morning. This left the rest of the day for reading in the New York Public Library—or, if I felt like it, exploring Manhattan from one end to the other. The intellectual ferment of my time at the New School occurred in the wider context of the sheer excitement of being in New York. It was a very powerful emotional mix, with an unavoidable erotic tinge. Once, in a Balzacian mood, I said that I was acquiring *une éducation newyorkaise* (very different from the education I would have received in, say, Paris or Oxbridge). In my memory New York has become, and remains the city of my youth. And all of us were so touchingly young!

2

IMPROBABLE HORIZONS

My student days at the New School ended abruptly. As soon as I finished my studies, I lost my student deferment from the draft. Instead of sailing off to Germany, as planned, to begin working as a researcher for Carl Mayer's project, I reported to an induction center in Lower Manhattan and soon thereafter began basic training in Fort Dix, New Jersey. My military career, such as it was, spanned 1953 to 1955 (I was already in uniform when I received the doctoral degree in 1954). Needless to say, the time in the military opened unexpected horizons to me, most of them disagreeable. But, looking back, the following eight years, from 1955 (when I was discharged) to 1963 (when I returned to the New School, this time as a member of the faculty), also propelled me into a series of horizons, most of them quite unexpected and some downright improbable. Of course, much that happened during these years had nothing to do with my having been formally accredited as a sociologist, nor did much of what I learned (such as how to assemble an M-1 rifle in the dark). All the same, this period also developed, often without my being aware of this at the time, my understanding of the possibilities of being a sociologist. I moved out beyond Twelfth Street in more ways than I could have imagined.

RELUCTANT SOLDIER AND FAKE PSYCHOTHERAPIST

I hated the army. The basic-training phase was not only physically exhausting but psychologically degrading. I experienced it as a massive assault on my dignity as a person. Things improved after that, but even now I would not want to say that I was wrong in my reaction to the military institution (though surely my middle-class and academic background made the reaction especially violent). Nevertheless, looking back, I am amazed at how much I learned while I ran around in uniform, much of it definitely contributing to my development as a sociologist.

Most important was an encounter with the manifold reality of America, a learning experience that would have been difficult in any other setting. It is important to recall that this was a period in American history in which a draft was in effect. There was some class bias, as in the draft deferment from which I benefited as a student. Still, the army reflected the social diversity of the country in a way that ended sharply when conscripts gave way to volunteers. The result for me was simple: I only now learned what I had wanted to learn when I decided to study sociology at the New School. In the most literal sense of the word, I rubbed shoulders with every conceivable sort of American. Most of my fellow trainees in Fort Dix were from the New York area, and among them were a good many college graduates (who, to a man, felt about the army the way I did). But this changed when I was sent to Fort Benning, Georgia, where I spent the rest of my military service.

In my first barracks there, I lived with a shoe salesman from Oklahoma, a recent immigrant from Eritrea, a former Mormon missionary from Utah, and a former male prostitute from just about everywhere. I suppose that I experienced the American melting pot with a vengeance—not a bad experience for a budding sociologist. But this experience became greatly enhanced, and so to speak officially certified, in what happened after a few months in Fort Benning: As the result of a bureaucratic mistake, I became a psychotherapist and, ipso facto, an undercover researcher into various dark corners of American society.

The sergeant who took down my personal information when I was inducted asked me: "What is your civilian occupation?"

I proudly replied, "I am a sociologist."

He retorted, "What's that?"

I don't remember what I said, but evidently it made no sense to him. "Is that like social worker?" he asked.

I said, "Well, not really."

He shrugged and said, "Never mind, that's close enough," and registered me as a social worker. This bureaucratic mistake turned out to be a stroke of luck.

At Fort Benning I was first assigned to a unit called the Allied Liaison Section. This was a unit within the huge Infantry School, which among many others was attended by officers from foreign armies allied with or at least not hostile to the United States. Our unit was supposed to take care of these officers in any way not directly connected with their training. We were selected on the basis of our language skills. Actually these skills were completely unnecessary; with the exception of the South Koreans (who brought their own interpreters), the foreign officers spoke pretty good English. Once in a while we had to drive one of our charges to some destination in town, but those occasions were very few. As a result, most of the time we were immensely bored, sitting in the kitchen of the small hut that housed us, drinking coffee, chatting, or reading. Once in a while the command of the Infantry School would assign us to other duties, such as unloading stuff from trucks or standing guard somewhere. These tasks were even more boring than sitting around in our hut and unpleasant to boot.

By chance, I had met another sociologist who had also been falsely classified as a social worker and was now working as such in the psychiatric clinic of the base hospital—Benton Johnson, a recent doctor of philosophy from Harvard. (The discrepant reputations of our two academic institutions may possibly be responsible for the fact that he made it to corporal, while the highest rank I attained in the military was private first-class.) He told me that there was a vacancy for a social worker in the clinic and that working there in this capacity was as close as you could get to civilian life. I mentioned this to my favorite fellow linguist, a streetwise New Yorker who spoke Spanish. He advised me on what to do, and, with some trepidation, I followed his advice.

I got an appointment with the officer under whose jurisdiction our unit fell. Dressed in my best uniform, I stepped in front of his desk, saluted smartly, and requested a transfer to the base hospital. Then I said exactly what my friend had advised me to say: "Sir, with my skills I could take care of sick American soldiers, rather than serve the needs of foreign officers." He nodded. A few days later, I received orders to report to the clinic for duties in accordance with my officially listed occupational specialty.

Johnson had not exaggerated. It was indeed a very pleasant job. No more sweaty work details, no more guard duty. I never wore fatigues again. I received permission to live in town. Basically, except for wearing a uniform, I had a nine-to-five office job. That of course was what I had hoped for. What I had not anticipated was that my new assignment would turn out to be a unique learning experience—not about the actual business of the clinic (though that too was quite interesting), but about America. Thanks to the US Army, I received precisely the education that I had sought in studying sociology and that the New School was unable to provide. As a result of the draft, patients came to the clinic from the most diverse sectors of American society. And, one by one, this incredible diversity marched through my office!

The staff of the clinic was small—three psychiatrists, two psychologists (who did testing), and four social workers (two real ones, with master of social work degrees, and Johnson and myself). The social workers did the intake of everyone who came to the clinic. We were not only supposed to register the reason for the visit, but also to get a full life history, usually in one session, occasionally in more than one. This was the unique learning experience I got on this job.

After we had obtained the life history, we would make appointments for the patient to see one of the psychiatrists (who might then order psychological testing). But sometimes a psychiatrist would come to one of us and say something like this: "Look, there is nothing I can do for this person. His problem does not lend itself to psychiatric treatment. Why don't *you* see him for a while." And thus, mirabile dictu, I became a fake psychotherapist. And (if I may say so) I was not a bad one.

Of course (except for a few intake cases) I did not see full-blown psychotics. My patients were either run-of-the-mill neurotics, much like the rest of us, or people with ordinary social problems. Needless to say, I learned even more from these extended interactions. I was fascinated by the stories I heard. *I really listened.* I think that this is what most therapy is about. A few times I made some commonsensical suggestions. Mostly I just listened, asking for clarifications or more details. I'm quite certain that I did not harm anyone. In a few cases, I think that I helped.

I worked in the clinic for about a year, at the end of which I was discharged from the army. Over these months I assembled a thickening dossier of case histories, adding up to a treasure trove of Americana—actually a belated replication of Balzac's "human comedy"!

I recorded the life history of an individual about to be court-martialed for a string of burglaries; our psychiatrists were to decide whether he was sane enough to be tried.

I had several interviews with an officer and his wife, recently married and with a vague sense that something was wrong. It turned out that the husband, a model military type, had asked an army doctor how often he was supposed to sleep with his wife. He was told twice a week (nothing indecisive about army doctors), whereupon he put up a weekly calendar in their home, similar to the training schedule of an infantry company, with Tuesday and Friday marked in red.

I established a good relationship with an African American military policeman—he had a sexual problem, but our breakthrough came in a conversation about race.

All told, I would have had to take many semesters of American Studies, with far-ranging field trips, to learn as much about the country as I did in this year of my military service.

I had a couple very instructive experiences of what sociologists call "role conflict."

The first was after I had met the head of the local branch of the University of Georgia, who asked me to give a series of public lectures and then a semester course on the sociology of religion. This was my first regular teaching assignment. It began when I was still with the Allied Liaison Section. One day a group of us had been detailed to unload some equipment from a truck. We took a rest break and were sitting on the grass, dressed in fatigues and drenched in sweat. One soldier had a portable radio. An announcement came on, an invitation to attend a lecture by "Dr. Peter Berger, a specialist on the sociology of religion, currently serving in the US Army at Fort Benning." No rank was mentioned.

The other experience occurred after I had started my career as a therapist. I walked into my first class. Naturally, most of the students were army people. Sitting in the first row, grinning from ear to ear, was the major who commanded the hospital detachment—in other words, my military superior. I was rather disconcerted, then rallied and successfully performed my professorial role. The students had to write term papers, which of course I had to grade. Johnson asked me whether I would pass the major even if he wrote a bad paper. I immediately replied that, of course, I would pass him (an answer that shocked Johnson, and actually rather shocked myself). Fortunately I was spared this Shakespearian dilemma: The major wrote a quite good term paper.

All this took place in the context of my first encounter with the American South, which then struck me as a different country (it would hardly do so now). Johnson and I had organized an informal seminar on sociological concepts that might be relevant to psychiatry and psychology. Johnson was from North Carolina, and many of his examples came from the South. The seminar resembled an interfaith project: Both of us had worked on the sociology of religion, but Johnson was a disciple of Talcott Parsons, while I was a devout Weberian. That could have been an instructive dialogue at any university.

The Southern context was powerfully illuminated one day when the chief psychiatrist, who hailed from Michigan, walked in and turned to Johnson: "I had a patient this morning. He told me that he talked with Jesus every morning. Back home I would say that he is schizophrenic. But maybe in the South it's different. What would you say?"

Johnson replied, "Maybe he *is* schizophrenic. But down here we have many quite normal people who talk with Jesus every morning."

But of course the most startling difference was in the matter of race. This was after the Korean War, when President Truman had dramatically desegregated the military. There was a fully integrated society within the boundaries of Fort Benning. But as soon as one stepped outside the post, the old segregation system was fully in force. I found it very disturbing indeed. To learn more about it, I visited Wilberforce College, a black institution, and became friendly with a faculty member there. The more I learned about this matter, the more repulsive I found it. This first encounter with Southern racism shaped my attitudes in this matter for many years to come.

The last few pages may give the impression that this was a happy period for me. It was not. My first marriage began to fall apart (at least in part because my then wife found it intolerable to live as the spouse of an enlisted man in Columbus, Georgia—even if, or perhaps because, it proudly described itself as the Peanut Capital of the World). My life after I escaped from the Allied Liaison Section became much more pleasant, but I still hated the army and chafed at the restrictions my place in it forced on me. Only in retrospect did I understand that this was an important period in my life, both as a social scientist and as a person. (If there is a thesis in this book, it is that the two are related.) It is only a slight exaggeration that it was then that I became an American. Among other things, I had a, or perhaps *the*, prototypical American experience: I bought my first car.

"YOU ARE NOW IN THE SERVICE OF THE PROTESTANT CHURCH. BEHAVE ACCORDINGLY."

I was discharged from the army three months early under a legal provision that I happened to hear about—as a "seasonal worker." I imagine that the provision was inserted into the law by a legislator from an agricultural state, so that, say, peanut farmers could get out in time to help with the harvest. I obtained an invitation to teach a summer course at the New School and applied for an early discharge. To my surprise, the application was approved. It might be said that, as a result of bizarre bureaucratic fictions, I entered the army as a fake therapist and left it as a fake peanut farmer. Perhaps a sort of sociological lesson may also be drawn from these facts.

There was nothing fake about the course I taught that summer. I think it was on the sociology of religion. In the meantime I had received an invitation to undertake a research project at the Protestant Academy in Bad Boll, Germany. And so, almost exactly two years after the draft prevented me from going to work for Carl Mayer's study on German religion and politics, I sailed for Germany on yet another project on the sociology of religion. The prospect was exciting both professionally and personally; it was my first study as a fully accredited sociologist in my very own field, and it also happened to be my first return to Europe as an adult. The year I spent on the project was formative, again both professionally and personally.

A word about the Protestant Academy (*Evangelische Akademie*— *evangelisch* in German does not mean what *Evangelical* means in English; it just means Protestant): This was a brand-new institution founded right after the end of World War II. It came out of conversations among a number of people, mostly theologians, associated with the so-called Confessing Church, the movement that had resisted the inroads of Nazism within German Protestantism. The conversations revolved around two questions: (1) What should be the role of the church in a democratic postwar Germany? And (2) How could the church help ensure that never again would a horrendous regime like the Third Reich come into power? The new institution was to be an answer to both questions. It was envisaged as having two functions—to educate laypeople about matters of public concern and to provide a space in which representatives of different interest groups could come together and talk in an atmosphere of civility about the issues that concerned them. It was the second function that constituted a very new understanding of the church's role in society.

The institution of the Protestant Academy still exists. About twenty centers are scattered throughout Germany, varying in size and importance. The institution, with conferences and seminars attended by some one hundred thousand people annually, has become an established feature of German Protestant church life, and a distinctive one—there are Catholic and non-German imitators, but nothing quite like it. Of course the institution has changed in the half century since its founding, yet its core purpose has not. Very importantly, though, it now lacks the exciting novelty of its early years—as one would expect if one had read Max Weber's theory of the "routinization of charisma"!

The academy in Bad Boll was the first to be established and is still a major one. It is located in the southwest of Germany, near Stuttgart, in the tranquil countryside of the so-called Swabian Alps. The village of Bad Boll, in addition to containing a well-known spa, had an interesting history in the nineteenth century. It was the parish of the Blumhardts, father and son, Protestant pastors famous for two reasons. First, they were important in the creation of the Inner Mission, a Protestant institution engaged in extensive social services. Second, in a number of dramatic incidents, they engaged in exorcising demons. It might be said that the Protestant Academy continued both activities!

The founder of the Bad Boll academy, Eberhard Müller, had been a member of the original group that during the war had envisaged the new institution. He started his academy in the summer of 1945. A friend of mine, a lawyer, attended the first conference. The postal service did not function yet; invitations were carried to local churches on bicycles. The topic of the conference was "How can Germany become again a state under law (*Rechtsstaat*)?" Apparently the participants felt that they were attending a historic event.

I had met Müller a few years previously, while, as a student, I did some translation work for Lutheran World Relief. He had come to America on a first visit and did not speak English, and I had gone around with him as an interpreter during the few days he stayed in New York. I was very impressed by him, and he evidently liked me. We stayed in intermittent contact until the end of his life. Sometime during the summer of my "seasonal work" he wrote me, asking me whether I would like to work for him for a year or so. He said that he could use a sociologist who spoke German to do some research of interest to the academy—on how different occupational groups related to the church. I accepted at once, enthusiastically. I arrived in Bad Boll in the fall of 1955, after some exhilarating days in Paris rediscovering its delights, from the taste of fresh baguettes to the splendor of the Place de la Concorde.

Müller must then have been in his mid- or late thirties. He was a very tall man with a large square face, deeply etched, resembling a portrait by Dürer. He had a commanding presence, somewhat mellowed by the folksy Swabian accent of his speech. As I was waiting outside his office for our first conversation upon my arrival, I could hear him shouting at what was evidently a government official. "And you can go and tell your *Herr Minister. . . .*" I could not hear the rest. He did not shout at me. He received me with great warmth. We discussed what he had in mind concerning the research and the financial arrangements, then sent me on my way with an admonition: "You are now in the service of the Protestant Church. Behave accordingly." I doubt whether my behavior lived up to this standard.

As a research site he suggested Reutlingen, a medium-sized industrial town about an hour's drive from Bad Boll. Since the research was located in Reutlingen, I lived there, but I frequently came to Bad Boll to attend academy events. To facilitate my movements, Müller actually bought me a car (if that is the word for it)—a vehicle named Isetta, a small, completely round death trap. It had one door, which opened from in front, with the steering wheel swinging out with it. I still shudder when I recall that I drove this contraption on the Autobahn, the superhighway, which then had no speed limits. My Isetta was bright red, and I drove it all over the region with the insouciance of youth.

Of the events I attended at the academy, the one that interested me most was a conference discussing what form the chaplaincy should take in the new army then being planned by the Bonn government. The conference was attended by church officials and theologians, people from the Bonn planning office, former Wehrmacht chaplains, and, most interesting, US Army chaplains. These came in uniform, with the army insignia on one collar and a cross on the other. One of the Germans asked an American chaplain whether he ever felt any contradiction between the two symbols. The American simply failed to understand the question. Years later, during the Vietnam War, I was at a conference discussing the role of military chaplains who felt that the war was wrong. Everyone there understood the question.

The conference at the academy, as all other events there, closely adhered to Müller's motto that the institution was "a forum, not a factor"—that is, it was a place for free discussion, after which participants could draw their own conclusions, but the academy would not take a position or make recommendations. Nevertheless, academy events indirectly had practical consequences. In this case the shape of the chaplaincy in the new West German Army was greatly influenced by the conversations that had taken place in Bad Boll. Thus German military chaplains are employed by the church, not the government; do not hold officer rank; and wear uniforms only in the field and then without military insignia.

I settled down in Reutlingen in a small apartment (I was a bachelor again). For the first time there was no role ambivalence—I was officially defined as a sociologist, period. I enjoyed this. How much I enjoyed it came home to me in an incident that did not show me in a favorable light. I regularly had breakfast in the same restaurant around the corner. As I came in, the owner would say, "*Guten Morgen, Herr Doktor,*" as did the cashier and the waitress when she came to my table. Thus, my first social interaction of the day was a ritual ratification of my academic status. Then, one morning, something terrible happened: Neither the owner nor the cashier happened to be around, and the waitress was new and did not know me. No "*Guten Morgen, Herr Doktor*"! I felt offended, indeed, angry. I can only say in exculpation that, immediately afterward, I felt ashamed of this reaction.

The research consisted of interviewing a sample of residents who were legally registered as Protestant. The names and addresses were obtained from the church tax records. (Then, as still today, the government collected this tax on behalf of the church, though the tax is voluntary in that individuals can opt out by declaring themselves to be religiously unaffiliated.) The interviewees were asked a number of very simple questions, mostly about their occupation and degree of church participation. I hired some students from the nearby University of Tübingen to do the interviews and tabulate the results. While the students fanned out to conduct the interviews, I would sit myself down in a café to receive their reports and deal with any problems, like a general with a (very small) army. The results of this research were less than earthshaking. Basically, we found what we had expected—individuals with middle-class occupations were more likely to be actively engaged with the church than working-class individuals, women more than men, older people more than younger people. The one surprising finding concerned women: The above-named differences between men and women only held when the women were not in the labor force; if they were, their engagement resembled that of their male colleagues. In any case, Müller was quite satisfied. Later I published an article about the research in a German Protestant periodical, thus beefing up my curriculum vitae. What is more important is that I got my "hands dirty with research" in a totally different environment.

I had two instructive encounters with totalitarianism, one current and one past. When the research was completed, Müller said he wanted to reward me—he paid for a brief vacation in Berlin. I enjoyed West Berlin, but the more dramatic experience was visiting the eastern part of the city, which I did a couple times. This was long before the Berlin Wall, and one could still cross the border by subway. The train lingered for a long time in the last station in the West. A loudspeaker kept repeating that this was the last station in the West. All Western newspapers were thrown out. Berliners tend to be a noisy lot, but as the train moved out of the station, all conversation ceased. There was an eerie silence. At the next station, officers of the People's Police got on, walked through the train, and asked some passengers to produce identification. I rather nervously held on to my American passport (which authorized me to visit any part of the city). I had a few conversations in the East, did some sightseeing, and had someone take my picture in front of the Socialist Unity Party of Germany headquarters.

The other encounter was with the Nazi past. I had met the editor of a church-related weekly, a man who must have been in his forties or fifties then. After a lively conversation, he asked me to write a couple articles, my first venture into journalism. The editor liked what I had written. Shortly before my departure from Germany, he asked me whether I could be their "man in America." I agreed. The offer intrigued me—it opened up the possibility of an alternative career. Then a German acquaintance showed me a book that the editor had written during the Nazi period. It made for shocking reading—full of Nazi propaganda, including gross anti-Semitism. I wrote him a note, asking him how he now looked upon what he had written then. He replied that we ought to meet.

We met in an elegant Stuttgart restaurant. He was friendly, rather avuncular. His basic message was that I was too young to understand what things were like but that he saw no reason to apologize. I was a bit overawed and only said that I would think about it. Then I wrote him a letter, which I still have somewhere. I said that people sometimes make political mistakes but that he could not write things today on the assumption that people did not know what he wrote in the past and that public mistakes had to be retracted publicly. Under the circumstances I had to withdraw my agreement to write for his paper from America. In reply I received a brief note, saying that he hoped that I would become more tolerant when I was older. I was still young when this happened and at first did not know what to do, but looking back I think I did quite well.

I did not realize this at the time, but the most important thing that happened to me during this year in Germany was that I met Brigitte Kellner. She was then a student of sociology, working in a research center in Stuttgart. We got married four years later. We had some good conversations after we met, but we did not get seriously interested in each other until she came to America, independently of me. When we met she was engaged to an older sociologist who worked in the same center she did. At our first meeting, when the three of us were going to go out to eat, he asked me whether I could first accompany them to a department store where he wanted to buy an overcoat. He was a vain man. He kept us there for a long time while he tried on different overcoats. He kept asking me whether I thought that he looked good in them.

BACK TO DIXIE: BELLES AND THUGS

I returned from Germany to New York in the summer of 1956, too late
to go on the academic job market. I applied for a number of nonacad-
emic jobs, falsifying my curriculum vitae downward as no one wanted to
hire me (finally claiming no degree beyond the bachelor of arts). I was
even rejected as "overqualified" for a job as a store detective. I finally did
get a job, which provided another research experience of sorts. I spent
several weeks as a field worker for a market research firm.

One assignment was to visit a sample of bars and count the brands
of beer on offer, evidently on behalf of a beer company. The other assignment was more unpleasant: I had to ring doorbells, carefully random-
ized, in apartment buildings and offer people cartons of unmarked boxes
of cigarettes on condition that they said how they liked them. New
Yorkers are much less friendly to unsolicited salespeople than the mid-
westerners to whom I had offered Lutheranism a few years earlier, and I
left many buildings pursued by maledictions and threats in a glorious
pluralism of angry accents.

Then I got lucky. Benton Johnson, my buddy from my social-worker
days, was teaching in his native North Carolina but wanted to leave for
a job elsewhere; he thought I could succeed him if I had a successful
interview. The job opening was at what was then the Woman's College
of the University of North Carolina, usually called "WC" (an unfortunate abbreviation for anyone who first learned English from British
people); it has since become coed and is now just known as
UNC–Greensboro. I flew down and was interviewed by the chair-
woman of the Sociology Department, Lyda Gordon Shivers ("call me
Lyda Gordon"), a formidable upper-class Southerner from Mississippi. I
must have made a good impression, because she hired me on the spot. I
arrived on campus a few weeks later, suffering from ferocious heat and a
very bad case of hay fever.

I stayed at WC for only two academic years, but they were important ones for me. Among other things, this was my first experience teaching large numbers of undergraduates, forcing me to organize my rather unorthodox sociological lore so as to be understood by young students who had never heard of Balzac, let alone Weber. WC was a state college, and a great majority of students were from North Carolina. For quite sensible pedagogical reasons, it was thought that students were best introduced to sociology by using information with which they were familiar. Thus the introductory course was called "Southern Regions," and I had to teach it with only a couple weeks to prepare. All through that first semester I was just one step ahead of my students. But I learned a lot about the history of the South and its present society, and I managed to use this material to illustrate key concepts of sociology. I was a popular teacher.

While this may not fit well into a book dealing with an intellectual trajectory, the social context of WC should at least be mentioned. Here was an agglomeration of 2,500 women, all just a few years younger than me, cooped up on campus from Monday through Friday. (On weekends men from Chapel Hill and Duke invaded, or the WC students went there in quest of male company.) As far as I can recall, there were five unmarried young men on the faculty. One was gay and correspondingly unaffected by the erotic undertones that this situation had for the rest of us.

The situation was dramatically clarified for me by a little incident occurring early in the first semester. A topic in the introductory course was family and sexual behavior. The Kinsey reports were just coming out, and I made reference to some of the alleged statistical findings. One charming young woman, with a magnolia-dripping Southern accent, asked a question when I mentioned the (almost certainly misleading) statements on the incidence of virginity: "Professor Berger, what do you think is the percentage of virgins among WC students?" I mumbled something about the absence of data but then said that there must be differences between freshmen and seniors and that most students came from what was a conservative part of the country. I then opined that the overall percentage might be 85 percent. The student demurely thanked me. The next day I found a bouquet of flowers in front of my office door with a card inscribed "From the 15% club."

I will not elaborate on how our little band of unattached males responded in different ways to what, at first glance, seemed like an adolescent fantasy come true. But I will allow myself a quasi-sociological observation: If you live long enough, everything comes back. In the 1950s, if you slept with a student, you were fired. In the late 1960s and the 1970s, if you did *not* sleep with a student, you were called a fascist. Today, if you sleep with a student, you are again likely to be fired, though of course the ideological reasons for this sanction have changed.

I was mostly busy building up a set of courses; in addition to the aforementioned introductory course I added more specialized ones on theory and religion. But I did find time to get my "hands dirty with research," for the first time in collaboration with others. One member of our little heterosexual fraternity was Robert Radlow, a psychologist. We had some conversations about a hypothetical relationship between self-esteem and gossiping behavior. We hypothesized that people who gossip indiscriminately are lacking in self-esteem. The reasoning behind this hypothesis was complex and is really not worth repeating here. We undertook a very modest quantitative study, which gave (barely significant) statistical support to the hypothesis. But we published an article in an obscure psychological journal, thus following the principal imperative for junior faculty—publish, *anywhere*, and build up your curriculum vitae.

The more interesting study was in collaboration with Richard Lieban, an anthropologist. He and his wife, Ruth, frequently had me over for dinner. We became good friends. Evelyn Waugh's satire on the American funeral business, *The Loved One*, had just come out. We studied the professional ideology of funeral directors, our main focus being the way in which the stark reality of death was avoided by the language and the practices of the directors. We did a content analysis of the several professional journals then in existence (including one with the memorable name *Casket and Sunnyside*, the latter being the euphemism for cemetery), augmented by in-depth interviews with funeral directors around the state. It was very much a descriptive study (Lieban would say an exercise in ethnography), probably the first of its kind in America. We published an article in a sociological journal. We enjoyed the research and each other's company. I also heard the most ghoulish jokes ever in the course of the interviews.

By way of an example: The funeral director has laid out the body of a man to be viewed by the mourners before the funeral. He asks the widow if she approves. She says yes, but she notices that her husband is wearing his gray suit; she would prefer if he wore the dark blue suit. "No problem," says the funeral director. "Just step outside. I'll only be a minute." And indeed, he is back in just sixty seconds and asks the widow to step back to the coffin. She expresses satisfaction with the change but asks how he could make the change so quickly. "Easy," says the funeral director, "just switched heads."

At Fort Benning I had lived in the bubble of the military; the South had been present, disturbingly so, but in the background. In Greensboro I lived *in* the South. Several people, including Benton Johnson, assured me that North Carolina was not the Deep South, that it had a progressive tradition, especially in its state university system. All the same, the Southern racial situation was all around me; I felt it to be oppressive.

I was teaching a community course and invited speakers from several sectors of local society (including a funeral director!). I had met the chair of the local branch of the National Association for the Advancement of Colored People (NAACP) and planned to invite him. I thought it prudent to get Lyda Gordon's approval, which she gave immediately: "I think that's a right progressive thing for you to do." I had the speaker already in mind, but pro forma I asked her whether she had any suggestions. Her reply rather took away the "progressive" flavor of her approval: "Well, I don't know too many people in the 'Nigra' community. But here's what I'll do. I'll ask my cook."

Two incidents, within a few weeks of each other, contributed to my understanding of the sociology of religion, in addition to offering sociological vignettes of the South in the late 1950s. The civil rights movement was in its very early stages (a little later Greensboro was the locale of the first sit-ins). Martin Luther King came to speak at an NAACP rally right after his participation in the Montgomery bus boycott. Lieban and I attended the rally, which took place in a church. What impressed me most was that it had all the characteristics of an old-fashioned Protestant revival meeting, though with a distinctive black quality—King's rhetorical style, the jubilant participation of the congregation (*amen*s, *halleluja*s), and the hymns that were sung ("Rock of Ages," "Down by the Riverside," "The Old Rugged Cross").

A short time after that rally, the Ku Klux Klan (KKK) announced one of its own. Lieban and I, with some trepidation, decided to attend that one too. It took place at night in an open field some distance from town. The KKK contingent appeared dressed in their notorious white hoods, spouting their notorious racist rant. Here also there was enthusiastic audience participation—*amen*s and all that. The climax of the proceedings was the lighting of the cross. As the cross blazed, a hymn was sung. It was "The Old Rugged Cross."

For me the lesson was dramatic: The identical symbols of a religious tradition could be deployed in the service of two diametrically opposed political movements, one morally admirable, the other morally loathsome. I have never forgotten the lesson.

I was an observer, not an actor, at these events. In my second year at WC, briefly and futilely, I tried to act in a racial matter. A black man, Ross McAfee, was sentenced to death for "first-degree burglary." I think this crime is defined as a felony in the course of which another felony is committed. In the course of the burglary, it seems, McAfee had sexually assaulted a white woman present in the house. I had learned enough about "Southern Regions" to assume that it was the assault rather than the burglary that led to the sentence. The state supreme court had sustained the sentence; only an act of clemency by the governor could halt the execution. I tried to get a number of organizations to appeal to the governor. The council of churches would not; neither would the NAACP. They explained that they might have if McAfee were innocent, but he had actually committed the acts that were charged. Only the local Quaker church agreed to write to the governor, but only, as they explained to me, because of a general opposition to capital punishment and without reference to this particular case. I wrote a letter to the governor, but of course that had no effect whatever. On the day after McAfee's execution, I read to my class two newspaper stories—one detailing the execution (McAfee declared that he had found Jesus and was ready to die), the other reporting on a state Baptist convention, full of self-congratulations. I thought of this as a sort of requiem. Most of the students did not understand my attitude.

About the same time there was a widely reported trial for "sodomy" in the local court. A married man, belonging to a prominent family in town, was caught having sex with a fifteen-year-old boy. No coercion was charged, and this was a first offense. There were eloquent pleas for clemency by the man's lawyer and family members, which were rejected by the judge: "In my book this is a right terrible crime." I was in court when the man was sentenced to twenty to fifty years in prison. As sentence was pronounced, I happened to see the expression on the face of the man's mother.

These experiences help to explain why, a few years later, I wrote about sociology as having a "humanistic" purpose in unmasking the murderous ideologies underlying the death penalty, racism, and the persecution of homosexuals. I should stress that this view did not contradict my embrace of the Weberian ideal of "value-free" social science: Of course the analytical enterprise of sociology should be "value-free," but its practical application is morally justified by its contribution to a more humane society.

On a personal level, it was during these years that my relationship with Brigitte Kellner deepened, as I understood the degree to which both our intellectual interests and moral convictions converged. She once came to visit me in North Carolina, and I frequently went to see her in New York. Ever since she has been my principal interlocutor, critic, and collaborator. We were married in 1959, a year after I left the South. There actually was a moment of flashing insight into Brigitte's character in connection with one of the above-mentioned episodes. I knew that she knew a young lawyer who worked for the NAACP. I phoned her, asking that she should help me get in touch with him. I only told her the gist of the McAfee case in a sentence or two. She asked no questions whatever, only said "Of course." In the event, the NAACP was not interested either.

EMBRACED BY THE PROTESTANT SMILE

While the University of Carolina in general and WC in particular had a generally deserved reputation for liberalism in matters of race, there were limits. I crossed one limit when I invited a group of students from a nearby black college to visit one of my classes. Their arrival on campus naturally attracted attention, some of it decidedly unfavorable. I was asked to see the dean, who was taken aback when I brought a student along for the interview (I think she was chairing the sociology club). Still, he was very friendly, assuring me that he was sympathetic to my views about race but explaining that, as a sociologist, I had to be aware of the mores of the region. I responded with what in retrospect was a rather silly homily on the immorality of those mores (I may have wanted to impress the student). At that point the dean became visibly irritated and said, "Well, this is one reason why some people prefer not to teach in the South."

I took him up on the suggestion and started to look for a job north of the Mason-Dixon Line. I found one quickly, though it was hardly a conventional one for a career-minded sociologist (which I definitely was not). After a brief visit, I was hired as an associate professor of social ethics at the Hartford Seminary Foundation in Hartford, Connecticut, where I taught from 1958 to 1963.

It was a friendly, laid-back place. It had been founded in the early nineteenth century by a group of conservative Congregationalists who felt that the Yale Divinity School was getting to be too liberal. But that was far in the past. In the meantime, Hartford had become theologically liberal itself. It was marked by what someone once called "the Protestant smile"—a pervasive niceness, which an outsider might at first judge to be insincere but in fact was the outward sign of an inner worldview of moderation. I had encountered it before when, shortly after coming to America, I had worked as an office boy at the Methodist headquarters in New York. I was such an outsider, not only ridiculously young and self-consciously European but a neoorthodox Lutheran and a self-styled existentialist. I had not liked all this niceness then, and I did not like it when I encountered it again in Hartford. It seemed to lack the passion to which I aspired. Nevertheless, perhaps reluctantly, I enjoyed the pleasant atmosphere. Without my noticing this at first, it influenced my thinking. I too mellowed.

The Hartford Seminary Foundation had three divisions—the theological seminary proper (ecumenical though loosely linked to the United Church of Christ, into which the Congregationalists were then merging), a school of education, and an entity called the Kennedy School of Missions. The latter, though its name was misleading, was by far the most interesting part of the institution. It was in fact a place where returning missionaries as well as others could study for advanced degrees in three fields—linguistics, anthropology, and Islamics. The linguistics originated in an interest in Bible translations, the anthropology in the need of missionaries to understand the exotic environments in which they were to do their work. The original impetus for the Islamic program undoubtedly came from the desire to convert Muslims to Protestantism—an inauspicious undertaking at any time and more than ever now. In any case, as the Protestant smile replaced the Protestant scowl, even among the descendants of New England Puritanism, the desire to convert morphed into an interest in understanding and engaging in dialogue with Islam. The journal *Muslim World*, which is still published today and enjoys a scholarly reputation, reflects this shift.

The campus at Hartford was small and compact. Almost all the faculty lived in campus housing, as did most of the students, creating a quasi-village community (with both the advantages and the disadvantages of such a habitat). In the center of the campus was a truly excellent library. Its main holdings were, of course, in theology, world religions, the social sciences, and linguistics, but there were books on other subjects as well. Since the number of library users was small, the books one was looking for were usually available and instantaneously accessible—a rare luxury.

One of my first problems was to define the field I was appointed to teach—"social ethics." What was that supposed to be? No one was really interested in clarifying this for me; I was left free to find my own definition. I read about the history of the name chair (I was soon promoted to full professor, with tenure, and holder of the chair). It was founded in the late nineteenth century, at the time of the Social Gospel, with which Hartford (by then evolved far beyond its Calvinist roots) strongly identified. I really could not. I assumed that teaching the sociology of religion was part of my assignment, and this I could certainly do. But "social ethics"? It seemed to me that all ethics was necessarily social; the only nonsocial activities on which one might reflect ethically were masturbation and suicide.

My search for a plausible definition of my alleged field was facilitated by an unexpected discovery. Attached to the chair was something called the Institute on Church Social Service; I was to be its director, in which capacity I was entitled to a secretary (another luxury). It had a faculty of one, an elderly gentleman who taught a course on social work and understandably resented me. I left him undisturbed but changed the name of the center to Institute on Church and Community. With that I defined my mission: I was going to set up an American replica of Bad Boll! As a start, I developed a program to study the human and moral issues in the workplace. When the elderly gentlemen soon retired (resentfully), I could appoint an assistant director—Joseph Duffey, who before that had been a very young pastor of a Congregationalist church near Boston.

We organized a number of seminars for people in different occupations. Some of the papers written for these seminars were later published in a book edited by me (the book was not reviewed and had very few sales, and I have lost my copy). I recall papers on moral issues in advertising and the human challenges in being a janitor. In the former field the main moral issue seemed to be having to formulate convincing lies about products and services. I remember being surprised by the paper on janitors. I expected a tale of marginality and humiliation. Instead, the paper alleged, janitors of large apartment buildings derived a sense of power because of their knowledge of various secrets pertaining to tenants, secrets discovered by rummaging through the garbage.

We also cultivated relations with labor unions. In pursuit of this I became friendly with an American Federation of Labor and Congress of Industrial Organizations (AFL-CIO) official, a woman who had one consuming interest in her private life—bird-watching. Brigitte and I spent a miserable day accompanying this woman and her husband on an expedition in a woodland area, looking for some rare species of bird. There were very active mosquitoes, and I had a violent allergic reaction to the local flora. But in consequence I attended an event that greatly impressed me and ever since has influenced my understanding of labor relations.

It was a mediation session between management and the union at the Underwood typewriter company. The issue was work rules—which workers were supposed to do what. The various tasks were colored differently in a large diagram of the work process. I happened to sit next to the main management representative. His union counterpart turned to him and said, "I forgot my copy of the diagram in my office. Could I have a look at yours?"

My neighbor replied, "No. Get your own damn diagram."

The union man got up and only came back some twenty minutes later; his office was on the other end of the plant. I thought that my neighbor's reaction was unnecessarily rude, and I asked him why he did this. He replied, "So no one gets the idea that we are one big, happy family here." An insight that applies to many institutions other than typewriter factories!

I did undertake a modest empirical research project during this period, in collaboration with Dennison Nash, an anthropologist at the University of Connecticut. This was the time of a so-called religious revival in America, suggested by data on increasing church participation. Some had criticized the phenomenon on theological grounds as being somehow inauthentic. Social scientists cannot make judgments as to whether a religious phenomenon is or is not "authentic," but they can explore the empirical shape of the phenomenon. So we interviewed new members of a number of mainline Protestant congregations in the Hartford area about their motives in joining. Most of the data were hardly exciting, with one exception: We found a major motive to be the provision of moral education for children. Indeed, many adults joined a church *after* their children had begun to attend Sunday school there, a curious sociological footnote to the biblical sentence that "a little child shall lead them." We published two articles about this little project, a popular one in the *Christian Century* (then, as now, a leading mainline Protestant publication) and a self-consciously scholarly one in the *Journal for the Scientific Study of Religion*. The former article was titled "A Second Children's Crusade."

Three colleagues at Hartford were important interlocutors for me: Paul Leser, an anthropologist; Ford Battles, a church historian; and Malcolm Pitt, who taught Hinduism.

Leser was a so-called diffusionist, studying how cultures borrowed from each other (he was the author of a definitive history of the plow). One of his main theoretical concerns was to debunk all functionalist theories of society; he argued that much of the time what one culture borrowed from another was profoundly *dysfunctional*—say, a tribe borrowing a particular type of hoe that was sure to destroy the soil. I took a course with Pitt, gaining a much better knowledge of the religious traditions of southern and eastern Asia.

But the most intriguing lesson came from a seminar jointly taught by Leser and Battles. It was called "Critique of Sources," and somehow its two teachers had persuaded the faculty to make the seminar compulsory for all doctoral students. Mostly it consisted in having the students detect plagiarism on the (probably correct) assumption that this was the best way to acquire a critical approach to texts. The students began by hating the seminar; it required more work than all their other courses combined. But in the end they had to admit that they would never look at a text in the same old way. The basic lesson was very simple and very useful: *Distrust all texts!*

It was the Kennedy School that provided most of the color to the institution and most of the exceptions to its pervasive Protestant smile. Paradoxically, it was the same moderate Protestantism that made the place a tolerant haven for various very un-Protestant types who somehow found their way to Hartford. There was a Pakistani who had converted from Islam to Christianity, with catastrophic consequences for himself and his family. In the same year arrived an Italian Franciscan monk who had written a book arguing that Catholics should accept the prophetic status of Muhammad and who had gotten into serious trouble with his order as a result.

There was also a middle-aged Russian Orthodox theologian with his aged mother; the latter spoke only French and smoked cigarettes from an elegant holder. The pair had spent years in a refugee camp in Germany, then lived in a Russian monastery in America (where they claimed to have been beaten and starved), and were deposited in Hartford by an ecu-menical agency. No one knew what to do with them. The son was given a more or less fictitious job in the library. Finally a theological institution in the Midwest invited him to its faculty. They were going by train. My secretary, a kindly soul, helped them and their ramshackle luggage to the train. Just before boarding the son stumbled over a suitcase, which opened and spilled a large number of pornographic magazines.

One of the seminary's few claims to fame was the fact that it was the undisputed world center of Schwenkfeld studies. Schwenkfeld was a minor figure in the so-called left wing of the Reformation (Luther called him "Stinkfeld"). His movement disappeared in Europe, but a small group of followers came to America. A few congregations survived in Pennsylvania, and they subsidized the Schwenkfeld project at Hartford, which was directed by a church historian on the faculty. The main activity of the project was the publication of Schwenkfeld's collected works in German and Latin, which had been started by a Hartford scholar about the time of World War I and was still going on during my time there. The books were edited at Hartford and published by the Schwenkfeld publishing house. If I remember correctly, seventeen vol-umes were in print when I arrived (the whole set has since been com-pleted). I was told that every new faculty member was entitled to receive all these books. I had neither use nor space for this "Corpus Schwenk-feldianorum" and declined the offer.

On a visit to Hartford after I no longer worked there, I remarked to the director of the project that I never received my set. A couple of weeks later, a delivery truck arrived at my house in Brooklyn and dis-gorged this full supply of theological esoterica. I placed the books on a prominent shelf in my library, making it possible for me to magnificently one-up visitors: "What! You *don't* own the Corpus Schwenkfeldianorum?!"

But, speaking of books, my time at Hartford saw the beginning of a big change in my intellectual life: *I started to write books myself!*

THE ONSET OF "BIBLIORRHEA"

Quite a few years ago there was a film with the title *The Pumpkin Eater*. It was about a woman who only felt happy when she was pregnant; once her children were born, she was only mildly interested in their subsequent fate. Ever since the early sixties I, too, could be described as a "pumpkin eater." My "pumpkins" are books.

In 1959 I published a lengthy article in the *Christian Century*. The article compared Albert Camus and Dietrich Bonhoeffer in terms of their view of religion in the modern world. Theologically I was still in my neoorthodox phase, much taken with Bonhoeffer's idea of a "religionless Christianity." (A few years later I gave up this idea as an implausible oxymoron.) Soon after the article was published, I was contacted by an Englishman with the improbable name of Clement Alexander, an editor with Doubleday. He asked me whether I might be interested in developing the article into a book. The prospect of writing an entire book was somewhat intimidating, but also exciting, and I agreed. The result was my first book—*The Precarious Vision: A Sociologist Looks at Social Fictions and Christian Faith*, published by Doubleday in 1961.

The book is organized in a way that became a pattern for much of my later work on religion: I start with a sociological argument, which intends to be theologically "value-free" (my colleague Anton C. Zijderveld has used the term "methodological atheism" to describe this approach; the scholastic phrase for it is *etsi Deus non daretur*—"as if God were not assumed"). And then, putting on a different hat, I make my theological points. That exercise, in the second part of the book, does not belong here. (If, in a further development of "bibliorrhea," I write a book on my theological trajectory, I might take it up there.) But the first part of *The Precarious Vision* sketches out a sociological perspective that I would still affirm today, albeit with some modifications.

In this early version it is a very youthful perspective, strongly influenced by existentialism. Society is a structure of fictions. These fictions are embodied in the roles that society assigns to individuals. As individuals identify with their roles as a result of socialization, the fictions become moral alibis. Put differently, the fictions make possible what Jean-Paul Sartre called "bad faith" (*mauvaise foi*): Individuals act but pretend that they are not acting. Sartre has a raunchy example: A man puts his hand up a woman's thigh, and she acquiesces but pretends not to notice; in fact, she is a willing participant in the seduction, but she is pretending that it is just happening to her without her participation. That particular fiction may be deemed fairly harmless. But fictions can be murderous.

In the book I describe in some detail the fictions involved in the imposition of capital punishment. The judge who pronounces the death sentence is, supposedly, not acting as an individual but is only the agent of the law—that is, the judge is not acting; only the law is acting via the role society has assigned to the judge. There follows a chain of similar fictions all the way to the executioner, who also has the alibi of not acting at all; it is the role that is acting. In the end, a human being is killed—and there are no killers.

Religion may enter this murderous drama by providing its ultimate legitimation.

This social function of religion has a grisly illustration in the inscription on an executioner's sword displayed in the Tower of London: "Thou Lord Jesus art the Judge." In other words, the execution is performed not by the man wielding the sword but by none less than God—the man is only the passive instrument in God's hand. A perfect alibi indeed! I summarized this argument in one sentence: "Religion is needed in society because men need bad faith."

Sociology is akin to comedy because it debunks the social fictions. By the same token it is potentially liberating. It shows up the "bad faith" by which individuals hide behind their roles and forces them to confront the reality of their own freedom. In the same process sociology must debunk the religious legitimations of the social fictions. And I go on to argue that Christian faith is similarly debunking. The argument of course is helped if Christian faith is not religion, but it does not depend on that particular tour de force. Much later I put it this way: The law absolves the executioner from personal responsibility for his action. But God is "illiterate." He does not read the law books. He only sees what one human being is doing to another.

While I was waiting for the publication of *The Precarious Vision*, the National Student Christian Federation (a mainline Protestant organization) approached me, asking whether I would write a book on the American religious situation that could be used as a study guide by its students. The Federation was in a hurry, and I complied by writing the book very quickly. It was published before *The Precarious Vision* so that, on any list of my publications, it is misleadingly listed as my first book. With the title *The Noise of Solemn Assemblies: Christian Commitment and the Religious Establishment in America*, it had the same structure of sociological description followed by theological critique.

The sociology, in retrospect, was not bad. I argued that one should not let the constitutional separation of church and state obscure the fact that religion was *socially* established, despite its legal disestablishment. In this capacity religion served to legitimate what I called "the okay world" of American society. This view was much influenced by the so-called religious revival of the 1950s. It significantly ignored the Evangelical community, which would have been more difficult to squeeze into the notion of "the okay world." I went on at some length to say that American society was indeed morally "okay" if one compared it with any number of other societies. But what was wrong here, from a Christian point of view, was that religion ought not to legitimate *any* society.

I don't think that I quite realized how fashionable my ideas were at that time, from the *Christian Century* article through these first two books. There were any number of books arguing that the seeming revival of religion during the Eisenhower years was not genuinely religious at all. Very influential was the 1955 book *Protestant—Catholic—Jew* by

Will Herberg, a Jewish writer strongly influenced by the neoorthodoxy of Reinhold Niebuhr. One reviewer described me as "prophetic." I suppose I was asking for this: The phrase "noise of solemn assemblies" is taken from the prophet Amos, who proclaimed that God took no delight in Israel's "solemn assemblies." I felt it necessary, though, to write a short piece, also in the *Christian Century*, disclaiming any "prophetic mantle"; rather I was doing my job as a sociologist and then trying to figure out as a Christian layperson what the sociological findings meant. All the same, it was not unpleasant to bask in the favor of the zeitgeist. I should have taken to heart Dean Inge's famous statement that "he who marries the spirit of the age soon finds himself a widower."

The "bibliorrhea" did not stop. In 1962 I wrote my next book, *Invitation to Sociology: A Humanistic Perspective*. It took me about three weeks to write it. Published in 1963, it had only one review in a sociology journal, a very negative one. (I may have been in step with the zeitgeist but definitely not with the *Geist* of early sixties sociology.) Despite this, it became a bestseller almost immediately. It has been that ever since. The American Anchor Books edition reached its one million mark in 1981; I have no idea how many copies it has sold by now. To date there have been twenty-one translations into foreign languages—not just into the obvious major ones but, among others, into Basque, Lithuanian, and Bahasa Indonesia. I keep running into people who tell me that this book induced them to become sociologists. This is often said in an accusatory tone, because they discovered that what most sociologists do today has little to do with the picture of the discipline conveyed by the book.

In preparing to write the present chapter I did something I had never done before: I reread my first three books in sequence. What struck me was that *Invitation to Sociology* was a sort of secularization of *The Precarious Vision*—a certain view of sociology, minus the theological commentary. And the earlier book was much more interesting and indeed original.

The term *humanistic* in the subtitle of *Invitation to Sociology* had two meanings. It suggested that the methodology of sociology should place the discipline close to the humanities—specifically literature, history, and philosophy. Of course that is the sort of methodology I obtained at the New School. But the term also suggested that the discipline could serve a liberating purpose—to free individuals from illusions and to help make society more humane. This was, so to speak, the existentialist aspect of the argument, which had been made with considerable passion in *The Precarious Vision.*

The newer book presented sociology not so much as a scientific discipline but as a form of consciousness, a distinctive look at the human condition. I formulated here, in much simpler language, what in later writings I analyzed as the basic dialectic of social reality: man in society—society in man—society as a (precarious) drama. Sociology derives its moral justification from its debunking of the fictions that serve as alibis for oppression and cruelty. Significantly, I singled out racial persecution, the persecution of homosexuals, and capital punishment, the ultimate cruelty. Sociology liberates by facilitating a standing outside one's social roles (literally, an "ecstasy"—*ekstasis*) and thereby a realization of one's freedom. At the end of the book I use a metaphor that has become widely known: Sociology suggests that we are puppets of society, but unlike puppets we can look up and discover the strings to which we are attached, and this discovery is a first step toward freedom.

I wanted out of Hartford, not because I was unhappy there but because (perhaps misguidedly) I wanted to be in a proper Sociology Department, with graduate students in sociology. Thus *Invitation to Sociology* had a subtext, a plea to fellow sociologists: *Please invite me!*

They did, promptly. Or rather, my old *Doktorvater* Carl Mayer did. I was invited to the Graduate Faculty of the New School and started teaching there in 1963. The department had moved to a new building around the corner on Fifth Avenue, but metaphorically I was back on Twelfth Street.

The Hartford years were biographically important both personally and intellectually. I started life with Brigitte, and our two sons were born there. I learned much from Brigitte's writings at the time—her master's thesis on the Duc de St. Simon, whose voluminous memoirs from the court of Louis XIV she interpreted as expressing the consciousness of a declining class, and her doctoral dissertation on Vilfredo Pareto, ingeniously interpreted as a father of the sociology of knowledge. Toward the end of my stay in Hartford I finally left behind my neoorthodox theology and defined myself (as I have ever since) in terms of a liberal Lutheranism. Put differently, I gave up any chance of becoming a fanatic of any description, and the only orthodoxy to which I continued to adhere was a Weberian understanding of the vocation of social science.

3

FROM A CLIQUE TO A FAILED EMPIRE

And so, in the fall of 1963, I was back in New York as a full member of the Graduate Faculty of the New School. It was a double homecoming: to New York, where I had first arrived in America—a city that seemed magical to me then and once again enchanted me with its magic; and to the New School, which had been a place of great intellectual excitement in my student days and which seemed to promise more of the same again. It was exactly ten years since I had been forced to leave New York for the military. I was now thirty-four years old, a husband and the father of two boys. Yet, in a way that I would not call an illusion in retrospect, the homecoming experience was rejuvenating. I taught at the New School until 1970, and these seven years were the most productive of my entire career. I wrote books and articles, with rabbitlike frequency. But, more important, I fleshed out a distinctive approach to sociology, which of course had been adumbrated a few years earlier but which now was undergirded by a strongly formulated theoretical foundation. What is more, I did not have to do this by myself. I had a clique to help me.

BACK TO TWELFTH STREET

The New School, of course, had changed over the decade of my absence. Many of the European scholars who had constituted the founding members of the Graduate Faculty were no longer around. Alfred Schutz had died in 1959. But Carl Mayer, my old mentor, was not only still around but also was chairman of the Sociology Department. My friend Thomas Luckmann also was teaching in the department. Most important, the atmosphere of the place had not changed—there still were evening classes, lively and intellectually stimulating students, and the ambience of Greenwich Village with the cafes and bistros to which one could go after class. All in all, it was quite intoxicating after the Protestant sedateness I had left behind in Hartford. I am reminded of that most New York statement by Woody Allen: "The question about the hereafter is not whether it exists. The question is how long it stays open, and whether one can get there by cab from midtown Manhattan."

Most important, I now had, for the first time, what could best be described as a clique. At the core were Luckmann and myself; we saw each other almost daily. There was Maurice Natanson, a philosopher on the faculty at Chapel Hill but a frequent visitor to New York. Then there were two younger individuals—Hansfried Kellner, Brigitte's brother, who was now a sociology doctoral student at the New School, and Stanley Pullberg, also working for a doctorate at the New School but in philosophy. Both Kellner and Pullberg lived in the Village. Also, very importantly, there was Brigitte, in the final phase of her doctoral work, and Benita Luckmann, Tom's wife, a budding political scientist. With the exception of Natanson, we were all within easy reach.

Never before, and (alas) never since, did I participate in an ongoing conversation of comparable sophistication and liveliness. The memory of Alfred Schutz hovered over this conversation. Most of us had been students of Schutz, and those who were not had been greatly influenced by his thought and, more generally, by the old New School approach to the social sciences.

Even before I left Hartford, Luckmann and I had been talking about a project to reformulate the sociology of knowledge. In January 1963 we put the idea on paper. Our group (needless to say, we did not use the word *clique*) would collaborate in the composition of a book that would undertake the reformulation. We envisaged a completion of the project—that is, a completed volume in hand—by 1967.

I still have the paper that launched the project. It began with a somewhat grandiose sentence: "The project is designed for the purpose of theoretical codification in the sociology of knowledge." The codification was to realize an observation that Schutz had made without much further elaboration: "If the sociology of knowledge is going to be true to its name, it will have to deal with everything that passes for knowledge in everyday life." This sentence calls for an explanation.

The *sociology of knowledge* is a rather marginal subdivision of the discipline. The term was invented in the 1920s by Max Scheler, a German philosopher interested in the way society influences thought. The term was subsequently adopted by a small group of scholars in Britain and America. Essentially, it was a sort of sociological footnote to the history of ideas. Schutz had no quarrel with this area of study, but he pointed out that what "passes for knowledge" is not just ideas, theories, and products of high culture but what ordinary people (who don't write books and in many cases have not read any) think they "know." Put differently, Schutz "democratized" the sociology of knowledge. This shift, of course, would greatly expand the area of study. And since there are many more ordinary people than producers of ideas, the expansion would make the sociology of knowledge much more significant.

The project cooked up by our little clique thus began rather modestly. It became clear to us early on that the logic of the project led to something much more ambitious—to wit, a basic reformulation of sociological theory. Specifically, we came to undertake a synthesis of several strands of theory that have often been understood as contradictory: the so-called voluntaristic approach commonly attributed to Max Weber, which emphasized that society is created by the meaningful acts of individuals; the approach, strongly represented by the Durkheimian school of French sociology, that emphasized social institutions as facts that resist the acts of individuals; and, finally, the tradition of American social psychology, mostly deriving from George Herbert Mead, which studied the way in which individuals are socialized into their roles. As the project became more grandiose, we began to dream of an academic empire, centered of course at the New School, that would change the character of sociology. Things did not go that way. In academia as in other fields of human endeavor, dreams of empire most often end pathetically.

Our empire failed to happen, for reasons I will come to presently. But we did produce a vision of society that was original and turned out to be useful in any number of empirical investigations. The outline of the projected book closely resembled the organization of the book *The Social Construction of Reality*, which Luckmann and I ended up writing. Two major portions of the book were headed "Society as an Objective Structure of Meaning" and "Society as a Subjective Structure of Meaning." There was to be an opening chapter dealing with some anthropological and phenomenological presuppositions and a concluding portion dealing with historical variations in the social organization of meaning. That last segment turned out to be impossible to include in our book. Other than that, Luckmann and I followed the original outline closely, though of course we developed it much further.

FINGER EXERCISES

With the 1963 manifesto in hand, the clique went into action in a productive frenzy. One article after another was written and promptly published in a variety of journals. (The variety is interesting. Academic journals were more open-minded than they are today.)

Luckmann and I wrote "Sociology of Religion and Sociology of Knowledge," published in *Sociology and Social Research* (1963). We argued that, in a plausible organization of subdisciplines, the sociology of religion should be understood as belonging under the sociology of knowledge—religion is also something that people "think they know."

Kellner and I published a rather entertaining article, "Marriage and the Construction of Reality" (*Diogenes*, 1964). We coined the phrase *marital conversation*, the vehicle by which spouses fabricate their own distinctive view of things, including the reinterpretation of their individual pasts.

Luckmann and I again collaborated in "Social Mobility and Personal Identity" (*European Journal of Sociology*, 1964)—a first step toward a theory of identity based on our view of society.

I collaborated with Pullberg on "Reification and the Social Critique of Consciousness" (*History and Theory*, 1965). We tried to incorporate his idiosyncratic use of Marxist concepts in our joint outline. I think the exercise was not terribly successful, but the article has the most obtuse language of anything I ever wrote.

That is not all. I wrote, by myself, "Toward a Sociological Understanding of Psychoanalysis" (*Social Research* [the New School quarterly], 1965)—even now, in retrospect, a delicious piece of chutzpah, debunking psychoanalysis as an unsuccessful attempt to respond to modern society. Again by myself, I published "Identity as a Problem in the Sociology of Knowledge" (*European Journal of Sociology*, 1965)— another exercise of replacing psychology with sociology.

Kellner and I wrote "Arnold Gehlen and the Theory of Institutions" (*Social Research*, 1965)—probably the first presentation in English of the work of this important German social theorist, then as now little known in this country.

And finally, once again jointly with Luckmann, there was "Secularization and Pluralism" (*International Yearbook for the Sociology of Religion*, 1966)—a first statement of our later separate analyses of contemporary religion (in retrospect quite flawed ones—but about that later).

This list may read like a tedious rendition of a collective curriculum vitae. But I reproduce it here to show that we were indeed a bunch of busy little boys (the little girls, Brigitte and Benita, were busy with their dissertations). All of these furious scribblings were very useful finger exercises for the work all of us did later on, some together, some separately. I for one know that I learned a lot from all this activity.

Our clique did not survive for long. Natanson went to teach in California, Kellner returned to Germany, and Pullberg went to France to study with various Marxist theorists there. Natanson and Pullberg effectively disappeared from the scene. Kellner, naturally, did not, and he and I collaborated later in several ventures. But Luckmann too left New York to take up a professorship in Germany, and the final work on our book took place in an intercontinental mode, a strenuous form of collaboration. As for the project launched in 1963, Luckmann and I remained the only two members of the clique ready to write the book we had envisaged then.

"YOU ARE REALLY A LITTÉRATEUR."

Or so that professor of French told me years ago (he meant it as a compliment). In the middle of the 1960s, in between all this activity of sociological theorizing, I lived up to this prophecy to the extent of writing two novels. Both were singularly unsuccessful. Both (as I only realized much later) were important to me in my quest to define my theological position. But the first of the two novels (as I did realize then) was also a sort of literary illustration of the Schutzian concept of "multiple realities," which was important in the reformulation of the sociology of knowledge. (As I look back on those years, I find it hard to understand how I found the time to do all this writing. Perhaps a supernatural explanation is the most plausible: I was possessed by a demon—hopefully a benign one.)

Both Brigitte and I were teaching now (Brigitte was on the faculty of Hunter College in New York), and for the first time we had an adequate income. We went to Europe with the children in the summer of 1964, renting part of a house in the village of Ronco in the Ticino (the Italian-speaking canton of southern Switzerland). The village is perched precariously on a steep hill overlooking Lago Maggiore. The view is breathtakingly beautiful. It was very restful.

It was also (at least for me) very boring. As all exorcists know, boredom provides an opportunity to demons. It seems that one of them landed in my head. I sat down and wrote the novel. Its title was (I suppose, still is) *The Enclaves*. It was published a year later under the pseudonym Felix Bastian. I decided to use the pseudonym precisely because I did not want to be categorized as a "litterateur." I had realized by now how marginal I was to the mainstream of American sociology, and, after all, I was nursing dreams of building an empire with our new approach to sociological theory. Yet the novel, in a curious way, mirrors the argument of *The Social Construction of Reality*.

I had read somewhere that all first novels are autobiographical. I decided to write about social settings that I had never experienced or that did not exist at all. Attila, the protagonist of the novel, is a middle-aged Hungarian refugee, a historian teaching at a Catholic women's college "roughly equidistant from an oil refinery and the New Jersey Turnpike." That depressing milieu dominates Attila's "paramount reality" (as Schutz called the massively real world of everyday life). He escapes from it into a series of alternative realities (Schutz's "finite provinces of meaning"). One such province centers on the parochial conspiracies of the Magyar section of the New York Public Library (no such entity exists), a scholarly universe of discourse revolving around an obscure controversy over the legend of a lost realm of eastern Hungarians. Another involves an erotic underworld of master-slave fantasy. Attila shares a house with a psychologist whose work, consisting of bizarre laboratory experiments, explores how many realities can be tolerated by different types of individuals. Attila must devote a lot energy keeping his different "provinces of meaning" going and, most important, keeping them separate.

I am not sure whether writing this novel helped my sociological theorizing. I certainly had a lot of fun writing it (and it certainly helped me cope with the summer's bucolic idyll). Doubleday agreed to publish it; perhaps they thought, mistakenly, that it could replicate the surprising success of *Invitation to Sociology*. It did not. Its sales were close to nil, and it was soon remaindered. There was one, not very favorable review. The reviewer did say, much to my satisfaction, that the pseudonym obviously points to a Hungarian author.

In this connection I might mention an idea I had when I was coming up with the pseudonym: I don't know where "Bastian" came from, but "Felix" occurred to me as an allusion to Thomas Mann's novel about one Felix Krull—a confidence man. I suppose that a sociologist writing a novel under a pseudonym could reasonably be described as a confidence man. Still, if one is teaching a course on Schutz or on sociological theory inspired by him, it would not be a bad idea to assign *The Enclaves* as supplementary reading. Too bad that it is out of print.

I have always been doubtful about the Freudian notion of the unconscious, tending to agree with the view of the Austrian satirist Karl Kraus that "psychoanalysis is the disease of which it pretends to be the cure." Reflecting on this novel gets me as close as I have ever been to giving credence to a notion of the unconscious. I was writing it at a time when my emancipation from my youthful neoorthodoxy had made me consider seriously whether I would now have to define myself as an agnostic if not an atheist. The first sentence reads, "Hungary is located almost exactly halfway between the North Pole and the Equator" (it goes on to describe Hungary as a geographical and linguistic enclave in central Europe). The last sentences, following a description of the text that finally disproves the legend of the eastern Hungarians, read as follows: "There is no brotherly kingdom in the east. There are no other Hungarians. We are alone on the earth." It struck me years later that the first sentence alludes to Pascal's description of the human condition, halfway between everything and nothing. And the last sentence reminds me of what I believe is spoken by a character in a novel of Albert Camus, that there are only human beings. In other words, the novel ends with a sentence denying any reality beyond the empirical human world.

The following year, in the summer of 1965, we returned to the Ticino, this time renting a house with a garden in Ascona, the lakeside town lying below Ronco. Being in town was less boring than sitting on top of a mountain, so I only began a novel there and finished it in New York a year later. But this time Doubleday would not publish it, and I did not feel like making an effort to find another publisher. I showed the novel to my friend Richard Neuhaus ten years later, and he encouraged me to submit it to the Seabury Press, a religious publisher. Seabury brought it out in 1975 under the title *Protocol of a Damnation*. This time I put my own name on it. I felt sufficiently established as a scholar not to hide under a pseudonym. Not that it helped. The sales were again negligible. It did get some favorable reviews, including an enthusiastic one by Noel Perrin (who generously compared it to Walker Percy's *The Moviegoer*). But the overall fate of both novels has discouraged me ever since from writing another one.

It was the question of theodicy that had brought me close to abandoning my Christian faith: How can a God who is both all-powerful and all-good permit evil and suffering in what is supposed to be His creation? The novel, in a roundabout way, addresses this question. It adumbrates an idea I developed a few years later in the book *A Rumor of Angels*. I suggested an "argument from damnation," referring particularly to the trial of Adolf Eichmann: Some evils are so horrific that no human condemnation of the evildoer will suffice—the very certainty of our moral judgment points to a metahuman judge, who alone can effect the damnation that such evils call for.

This time the setting is Ascona; I thought that a respectably executed novel should have some freshly experienced local color. The story, which need not be detailed here, concerns the discovery of a vacationing Nazi criminal who, shortly before being mysteriously murdered when his garage is turned into a gas chamber, is ritually sentenced to death and damnation by a character who makes this prophetic utterance after we first encounter him in the role of a gigolo. In a postscript, appended to the novel at the time of its publication, I refer to this theological theme as rooted in the "subterranean network of connections" (a phrase used by the novel's narrator, a Dutch children's photographer with a huge, grotesque tattoo on his back). I then go on to say that this hidden theme could be described as "the apparent inevitability of some sort of Christianity."

As I have had occasion to say several times in the preceding pages, the present book is not intended to deal with the trajectory of my religious positions. Telling the story of an accidental sociologist is complicated enough. However, the two stories obviously interlink at many points, and these linkages must be mentioned if either story is to make sense. My less than brilliant career as a novelist touches on both stories.

THE MANIFESTO

As the sociology of knowledge project morphed into a much more ambitious theoretical enterprise, and as the fantasies of our little clique took on imperial scope, the book that was to be the end product of the project became a kind of manifesto. It was seen as such by others. In the years since its publication in 1966, *The Social Construction of Reality* has often been referred to as the opening statement of a new school of social-scientific thought, so-called "constructivism." More of this unfortunate development in a moment.

The subtitle, *A Treatise in the Sociology of Knowledge*, nicely reflected an ambivalence in the minds of Thomas Luckmann and myself. Describing the topic simply in terms of the sociology of knowledge was an understatement—the book had turned into something much more ambitious. Yet the word *treatise* is pretentious, worthy of cofounders of an imperial undertaking. Well, the empire never happened. Yet this book was successful far beyond anything we could have imagined when our clique began. It has been described as a "minor classic," a phrase that combines a congratulatory noun with an adjectival putdown. In any case, the book has engendered a whole literature of commentary, both positive and negative. Its influence has gone far beyond sociology.

Someone suggested that it was the most read sociology book written in the twentieth century. That is doubtful. But the book was widely noticed right after publication in America and elsewhere as foreign translations appeared. The American edition is still in print at this time of writing and is still selling well. To date there have been eighteen translations, most recently into Bulgarian and Greek.

Some ten years after the book's first publication I was in Rio de Janeiro, standing in line with my hosts, waiting to enter a concert. A young man came over to say hello. My hosts introduced me to him, just giving my name. He beamed and said, "Ah, *The Social Construction of Reality*" (of course naming the title in its Portuguese version). Luckmann has had similar experiences. I think that both of us have managed to avoid delusions of grandeur that such experiences can induce by a pervasive sense of the ridiculous. After all, both of us come from Central Europe, where the delusions of empire are part of the collective memory, perhaps best expressed in an old joke: After a battle on the eastern front in World War I, the German Army bulletin describes the situation as serious but not hopeless, the Austrian bulletin as hopeless but not serious. Probably this same attitude of detached irony helps explain the ease with which we collaborated, chapter by chapter, in the writing of the book. All the same, we were very pleased with the book, and we have remained so. We have a number of times asked ourselves whether we would change anything if we were to rewrite the book. Apart perhaps from using simpler language here and there, we always concluded that we would leave the text as is.

It is not an easy text, not to be recommended as bedtime or bathtub reading. As pointed out before, it contained a synthesis of different strands of social theory, essentially reformulating the sociology of knowledge as a *sociology of consciousness* (a term we actually used in other writings). That is, our "treatise" tried to explain the overall relation of society and consciousness. We described this relation as a "dialectic," an ongoing interaction of three processes: externalization, by which human beings jointly "think up" a social world; objectivation, in which this social world attains a seemingly "hard" reality over and beyond the individuals interacting within it; and then internalization, which is the process by which this objective "outside" world is retrojected into the consciousness of individuals through various experiences of socialization, beginning in childhood but continuing throughout life.

Another old joke: An American couple is adopting a six-month-old boy from China. They take intensive Chinese language lessons. They want to be able to understand the little boy when he begins to speak. One way of describing our theory is to say that it explains why this joke is absurd (and therefore funny). Can this be put in simple terms? Let me try.

Language is the most elementary vehicle of interaction among human beings. As Americans, we continuously use the English language to communicate with each other. The language is only kept alive by our speaking it; if we ever stopped, it would cease to live and would, literally, become a "dead language," like, say, ancient Assyrian. In other words, the English language is the product of its ongoing externalization by living human beings. In yet other words, it is not a fact of nature, handed on from one generation to another by way of genes (which is why the little boy will not sit up and speak Chinese in his playpen in Cleveland). At the same time the English language has achieved an objective reality over and beyond the people who speak it. If it is our first language, we will take this reality for granted. If we learn it as a foreign language, we will be forced to accept its reality—even if we don't like it. We can tell our teacher that the pronunciation or the grammar is absurd, only to be told that, absurd or not, this is what English is, and we had better use it accordingly if we wish to be understood.

Put differently, objectivation means that what was once "inside"—in the consciousness of individuals who used and kept changing the English language ever since the Battle of Hastings in 1066—becomes something "outside." But it does not stay "outside." It becomes internalized, "inside" again, by all the processes of socialization, be it from childhood or in later developments. The language then shapes individual consciousness—we "think in" English.

Language is the most fundamental human institution. It is paradigmatic of all other institutions. It is thus paradigmatic of the relation between society and consciousness. We "know" the world through the language and all the other institutional programs that society has instilled in us.

The quotation marks here are important: Whether our "knowledge" of the world is valid by this or that philosophical criterion is beyond the method of empirical social science. Mark Twain put it nicely: "The trouble is not what people don't know. The trouble is what they know, which ain't so." Or, in the words of W. I. Thomas (the famous "Thomas's dictum" memorized in every sociology introductory course): "If people define a situation as real, it is real in its consequences." Thus an individual in one milieu "knows" that he is possessed by a demon; an individual in another milieu "knows" that he suffers from a neurosis. The empirical sociologist can only look at the contents and the consequences of each "knowledge."

Some other discipline—perhaps philosophy or neurobiology—may feel entitled to remove the quotation marks or to replace "knows" with "operates under the delusion of," thus respectively validating or invalidating the cognitive assumptions at issue. The sociologist of "knowledge" is condemned to operate within the quotation marks. Needless to say, this is especially important for the sociologist studying religion: The gods cannot be studied empirically, but what people "know" about them and what consequences ensue from this "knowledge" is precisely what a sociological analysis will be all about.

What happened after the manifesto?

Most of the early American reviews were favorable, though of course it was noted that our argument leaned heavily on European sources away from the mainstream of the discipline in this country. There was a veritable explosion of reviews after the German translation was published in 1969, with a friendly foreword by the influential philosopher Helmut Plessner and excellent translation by his wife Monika Plessner. Unlike what happened to me in America, Luckmann succeeded in establishing something close to a school of sociological theory, especially after he moved to the University of Konstanz.

On the twenty-fifth anniversary of publication, the newsletter of the theory section of the American Sociological Society asked me to reflect on what had happened to the book: "Did you mean to found a school of social theory, in which case why did you decline to lead it?" To the first question, I said that our initial aim had been modest (I did not own up to our imperial fantasies). But in response to the second question I observed: "One can only decline an offer that has been made. No one offered." I went on to say that for just a few years after 1966 there was a narrow window of opportunity for our approach to sociology, since especially younger colleagues were disillusioned by the double dominance of so-called structural-functional theory and quantitative methodology; hence the initially favorable reception of the book.

But then, almost immediately afterward, there occurred "an orgy of ideology and utopianism" with which neither Luckmann nor I could identify. In the cacophony of this cultural upheaval the sober tone of our book could not be appreciated: "It is not possible to play chamber music at a rock festival." But the book, by and large, was not repudiated. Rather, it was incorporated into the ascendant ideology, the peculiar mix of neo-Marxist and countercultural discourse that came to dominate the social sciences and humanities on both sides of the Atlantic. (In that context, Luckmann's "Konstanz school" acquired an almost underground flavor.)

In 1999 Luckmann presided over a symposium in Essen on the occasion of the thirtieth anniversary of the German edition. He was asked very similar questions, and his answers were very similar to mine. But he commented on two intellectual trends that are frequently interpreted (both by advocates and critics) as having been influenced by *The Social Construction of Reality*—"ethnomethodology" and "constructivism." Both developments are impressive illustrations of the unintended consequences of publishing one's ideas. Werner Stark, who wrote an interesting book on the earlier authors in the sociology of knowledge, taught for many years at Fordham University. He was an erudite and somewhat eccentric scholar. I once asked him how a book of his that had just been published was doing. He replied, "About books of mine that have been published I feel like Calvin felt about the dead: There is nothing more we can do for them. They have gone on to their doom."

Ethnomethodology was the name chosen by a small of group of sociologists, most of them on the West Coast. The key figure in the group was Harold Garfinkle, who taught at the University of California–Los Angeles. The group claimed to have been initially inspired by the work of Alfred Schutz. They did use some Schutzian concepts, though they also developed a vocabulary of their own. Apparently there was some correspondence between Garfinkle and Schutz, but I never saw that. I read some of the group's writings. I did not quite understand what the theoretical import was supposed to be, though I found some of the empirical studies interesting. It seemed to me that there was a strong affinity with the so-called "symbolic-interactionist" school in American social psychology. But, frankly, I was not terribly interested (though, when I joined the faculty at Boston University very much later, I discovered an East Coast outpost ensconced there, and I had some good conversations with George Psathas, one of the group). Luckmann was decidedly less friendly. He wrote a scathing review of a number of ethnomethodology works, describing the school as a "provincial orthodoxy." As far as I know, not much is left today of this subdiscipline.

Much more important has been the intellectual movement known as "constuctivism." It is a diffuse phenomenon, covering a number of disciplines in the social sciences and the humanities. It is (correctly, I think) subsumed under the heading of "postmodernist theory" (somewhat a misnomer). There is really a bundle of theories here, what might be described as a tendency rather than a coherent school of thought. The immediate originators of this tendency were two French writers, Michel Foucault and Jacques Derrida, though there is behind all this the long shadow of Nietzsche and the philosophical method he recommended— the "art of mistrust." This is not the place to delve into the complex trains of thought of these thinkers, but the connection with *The Social Construction of Reality* should be clarified.

The argument goes something like this: Since all reality is socially constructed, there is no objective truth or at least none that can be accessed. Indeed, there are no facts, only "narratives." There is no objective way to make epistemological judgments as between the "narratives." But what one can do is to "deconstruct" them—that is, to unmask the interests that they invariably express. These interests are always expressions of the will to power—of class, or race, or gender. And here, of course, postmodernism links up with various ideologies of the Left— Marxism, "postcolonialism," "Third Worldism," and all the various strands of identity politics (notably radical feminism and "queer theory").

This amalgam of theoretical trends has become enormously influential in American academia over the last few decades, and in many places it has become an oppressive orthodoxy. But these trends have been popularized far beyond academia. They have a pronounced affinity with a widespread relativism (which, by the way, can be explained by a sociology-of-knowledge analysis of modern consciousness, as I have tried to do in my recent book with Anton C. Zijderveld, *In Praise of Doubt*).[1] It is a widely diffused worldview, in which the only real virtue is "tolerance" and the only real vice is "being judgmental."

The disastrous intellectual and indeed political implications of this type of nihilism cannot be followed up here. But it should be clear why Luckmann and I have felt constrained to say repeatedly, "We are not constructivists" (perhaps imitating Marx's statement "I am not a Marxist"). Our concept of the social construction of reality in no way implies that there are no facts. Of course there are physical facts to be determined empirically, from the fact that a particular massacre took place to the fact that someone stole my car. But the very concept of objectivation implies that there are social facts as well, with a robust reality that can be discovered regardless of our wishes (Durkheim: "Consider social facts as things"). Reality indeed is always socially interpreted, and power interests are sometimes involved in some interpretations. But not all interpretations are equal. If they were, any scientific enterprise, not to mention any medical diagnosis or police investigation, would be impossible. As to the most radical formulation of this "postmodernism"—that nothing really exists but the various "narratives"—this corresponds very neatly with a definition of schizophrenia, when one can no longer distinguish between reality and one's fantasies.

Luckmann and I would place ourselves in a tradition of sociology rooted in the Enlightenment project of seeking to understand the world by exercises of reason. Many "postmodernists" have proudly described their purpose as the end of the Enlightenment project. We understand our sociology as a defense of that project.

To sum up: *The Social Construction of Reality*, when it was first published, was in tune with the cultural atmosphere, the zeitgeist, at the time. That goes quite some way toward explaining its success. But the zeitgeist changed very soon afterward. The book did not die as a result. But many of those who now rode the crest of the new cultural wave annexed the book for their own purposes, translating its language into their own conceptualization. Luckmann and I were, so to speak, *post-*

modernized—a somewhat ironic fate. It took both of us some time to understand this.

I got a first inkling sometime after the Spanish translation was published in Argentina in 1968. I was then editor of *Social Research*, the New School quarterly (a fun job, by the way). I had a small suite, two offices, in the basement of a brownstone adjacent to the New School on Twelfth Street. The front office was occupied by my secretary, a sassy New Yorker not easily intimidated. That afternoon she came in, clearly shaken. There were two bearded, possibly dangerous men who wanted to see me. I asked them in. They were indeed quite wild-looking. One clutched in his hand a copy of the Spanish translation. He told me that they came from a country in Latin America (I forget which one) and that they had been sent by their leader, who was currently in hiding. He then added: "We are revolutionaries. You write about the construction of society. We want to *re*construct society. Our leader thinks that you might give us advice for our revolutionary project." We spoke in Spanish, not too fluently on my part. As best and politely as I could, I explained that this book was a theoretical exercise and that I had no useful advice to give. They were clearly disappointed and soon left, to my (not to mention the secretary's) relief.

"ONCE A GODDER, ALWAYS A GODDER."

In the period before the writing of *The Social Construction of Reality* and during it, Luckmann and I had often talked about the relation of the sociology of knowledge and psychology. We were probably influenced by the fact that psychoanalysis was at the height of its influence in America (before it receded in the face of less expensive methods of the cure of souls); virtually everybody we knew around the New School was in analysis, was thinking of going into analysis, or had completed several years of it. We were going to collaborate on a book formulating what we were going to call a "sociological psychology." Other interests then diverted us from this project. I did propose a first axiom for our putative theory: "Any identity is better than none." Actually, I think that this axiom will take you quite some way.

Instead of dethroning Freud and replacing him with Schutz (thus at least retaining a Viennese accent), Luckmann and I, separately, wrote books on religion, both published in 1967—Luckmann, *The Invisible Religion*; I, *The Sacred Canopy: Elements of a Sociological Theory of Religion*. As far as I know (we were always discreet in this area), Luckmann was not struggling with any theological obsessions at the time; I was. Once during my time in the military I had said to a buddy (a very sharp character, who, among other colorful activities, had worked as a pimp in New Orleans) that I had done theology in the past but was now doing other things. He commented: "Once a Godder, always a Godder."

Whatever differences there were in our personal stances on religion, Luckmann and I differed in our social-scientific conceptualization of religion. He operated with a very broad, essentially functional definition of religion as consisting of an intrinsically human propensity to transcend the immediate concerns of the empirical situation. This definition (a quite ingenious synthesis of Emile Durkheim's sociology of religion and various strands of philosophical anthropology) thus subsumed under the category of religion every conceivable overall ordering of meaning—including, say, science, or nationalism, or for that matter the mythic constructions of psychoanalysis. I thought that this definition was too broad. I once asked Luckmann who would *not* be religious by his definition. He replied, "A dog." I have ever since preferred a narrower, substantive definition, consisting of a specifically supernaturalist worldview. I spelled out this difference in an appendix to *The Sacred Canopy*.

Both our books applied the theoretical perspective of *The Social Construction of Reality* to religion in general and to the contemporary religious situation in particular. Logically enough, *The Sacred Canopy* was divided into two sections. The first section presented religion as a crucially important factor in the construction and maintenance of social worlds. Religion provided a sacred cosmos to serve as a legitimating "canopy" for the institutional order. The sociology of knowledge shows just how precarious all institutions are, dependent for their plausibility on people going on acting *as if* the institutions are real. This of course is the basic message of W. I. Thomas's famous dictum quoted earlier. But we know how often people change their minds. Religion powerfully reinforces the "reality" of institutions by anchoring them cosmologically, as it were: "It's not just us people who choose to act this way. *The gods command it.*" This basic service of religion to social order is to make people forget that institutions are of their own making and thus highly contingent in character. *Religion changes contingency into necessity*. It now seems as if society has an invulnerable place in the ultimate order of the universe.

In this connection I found the early Marxian categories of "alienation" and "reification" useful (without thereby agreeing with the later body of Marx's writings). I followed Max Weber in his concept of *theodicy*—a term derived from Christian theology (dealing with the question of how God can permit suffering and evil) but that Weber used more generally to denote any socially established explanation of the negative aspects of human existence. Religion always provides some version of theodicy: Suffering and evil now make sense in the supernatural order of reality and therefore do not threaten the plausibility of the social order. A neat trick, one may say.

The second part of the book discussed secularization—that is, the decline of religion both in society and in the consciousness of individuals—as a necessary concomitant of modernity. In this I conformed to what was at the time the prevailing view not only among sociologists of religion, but also among historians, philosophers, and, last but not least, religious thinkers (many of whom deplored this, some of whom actually welcomed it, and all of whom thought that one had to accept it as a fact). Later in this book I will describe why and how I changed my mind about so-called secularization theory. In *The Sacred Canopy* I again leaned on Weber, who had proposed that "rationalization" (his term for modernization) had its roots in the radical "disenchantment of the world" already implicit in the religion of ancient Israel, further radicalized by the Protestant Reformation. I added an argument derived from the sociology of knowledge: Modernity brings about a weakening of consensus about collective beliefs and values and in this process weakens the plausibility of these. Simply put, modernity produces pluralism, which in turn produces secularity. This does not make religious faith impossible, but it makes it much more difficult. Believers become a "cognitive minority."

To get ahead of myself for a moment: I later realized that I had been quite right that modernity produces pluralism, but pluralism does not necessarily produce secularity. What it does produce, pretty much necessarily, is a situation in which no worldview is any longer taken for granted so that individuals have *to choose* among the different worldviews on offer. But some of these choices may well be religious—and, in fact, in most of the contemporary world they are. This situation presents religious faith with a great challenge—but it is not the challenge of secularization.

The "doom" that Werner Stark ascribed to books that one has let loose on the world in print can last for a long time. In the summer of 2008 I was in China with some colleagues, laying the groundwork for a seminar on contemporary religion at two Chinese universities. In Beijing we were received in a somewhat surreal ceremony at the State Administration of Religious Affairs (SARA), the agency by which the government seeks to control religion (happily with limited success). The director of SARA welcomed me warmly as the author of *The Sacred Canopy* and thus as one of the greatest proponents of secularization theory. I don't think he quite registered my statement that I had changed my mind about this since writing the book.

The Sacred Canopy was a success too, both academically and commercially. It too is still in print, with twelve foreign translations thus far. Another "minor classic," so to speak. However, if I were to rewrite it, I would not leave the text as is. Of course I would have to radically change the part on secularization. But I would also rewrite the first part. The language is unnecessarily complicated. I would translate it into English.

I had carefully announced that *The Sacred Canopy* was strictly an argument within the boundaries of sociology, an empirical science, and that it had neither theological nor antitheological intentions. But I was nevertheless worried that it could easily be read as having the latter—that is, that the adjective *methodological* could be overlooked in my approach of "methodological atheism." To forestall such a misreading I added another appendix, in which I indicated how a theologian might deal with the ideas of the book.

Briefly, the book depicts religion as a gigantic projection of human desires into reality, especially the desire for a meaningful world allowing for hope. This is a correct picture, within a very specific way of looking at the world without religious prepositions, "as if God were not given." The idea of projection goes back to Feuerbach, who purported to translate theology into anthropology. Fair enough. But if one switches to the perspective of faith, one, so to speak, stands Feuerbach on his head. Anthropology is translated into theology. One can then say that human beings can project meaning into the universe because they themselves were projected into being by God who created them. The two perspectives are not contradictory, but they are strictly discrete. I also said that such a cognitive exercise would be in the spirit of liberal Protestantism, thus confirming the break with the neoorthodoxy of my youth.

I felt that these ideas were too important to be confined to an appendix. So I sat down and wrote another book, *A Rumor of Angels: Modern Society and the Rediscovery of the Supernatural*, which was published in 1969. I made it clear that I was not speaking here as a sociologist but as a layperson without formal theological credentials. This stance gave the book the great advantage that it is generally free of academic jargon.

The title was suggested by the statement of a French Catholic priest, who described his mission in the contemporary world as making sure that the rumor of God did not altogether disappear. In other words, my theological argument continued on the assumption that secularization theory was valid. Religious believers are a "cognitive minority." The theological task then is to show how even in this secularized world the supernatural may be "rediscovered." This task cannot be undertaken with the tools of sociology (or, for that matter, any other empirical science). But sociology is relevant because it can help to "relativize the relativizers" —the secular worldview, just like any religion, has a specific "plausibility structure," which, when analyzed, loses its pretension of conveying absolute truth.

The theological argument I then go on to make does not belong here. Suffice it to say that it was my first succinct statement identified as belonging in the tradition of liberal Protestantism and its attitude of "relentless honesty" in the face of uncomfortable truths. I cite as a significant example of this that liberal Protestantism was the first religious tradition in history to apply the tools of modern critical scholarship to its own sacred scriptures—a feat of unique intellectual courage, most poignantly in the so-called "search for the historical Jesus." I then sketch the outline of what could be a theological method, with two characteristics. First, it would proceed inductively from ordinary human experiences, which I termed "signals of transcendence" (significantly including both the experience of the comic and the right to utterly condemn certain acts of cruelty). Second, it would construct Christian theology in an ongoing dialogue with the other religious traditions thrust by pluralism on our attention.

A Rumor of Angels was my last truly successful book of the sixties (and, to date, of any subsequent period). It too is still in print, with nine foreign translations, including (surprisingly for a book of Christian theology) into Japanese and Bahasa Indonesia. Most of my major books have appeared in the latter language, published by a Muslim publishing house. I did not understand this, until I met the publishers on a visit to Jakarta. As believing Muslims they were intrigued by an author who looked at religion from an empirical perspective and nevertheless affirmed his own religious faith (never mind that it was Christian).

My status as a "Godder" intellectual received as solemn ratification as one could possibly wish for in 1969—by the pope, no less. In the wake of the Second Vatican Council, the Curia had set up three agencies devoted to ecumenical and interfaith dialogue to talk with "separated brethren" (that is, non-Catholic Christians), with Jews, and with non-Christian religions other than Jews (who of course had a special relation with Christianity). It then dawned on somebody in the recesses of the Roman bureaucracy that an important group had been left out—those who didn't believe in anything! But then, how could one talk with them, if one did not know who they were? An agency had been set up to develop this additional dialogue. It went under the ponderous name of Secretariatus Pro Non Credentibus and was headed by Cardinal Koenig, the archbishop of Vienna, who, it happened, had read my works. An emissary of the archbishop, one Monsignor Antonio Grumelli, an Italian priest who held a sociology degree, visited me in my house in Brooklyn (where we had come to live a couple years after our return to New York). Grumelli asked me whether I would be willing to organize and chair a conference that would try to define just what "unbelief" meant and thus to help locate the people with whom the Church should talk. I was to select the social scientists or historians; the Vatican would select the theologians.

The conference met for five working days at the Vatican. It was quite a gathering. Among the social scientists were, naturally, friends of mine—Benton Johnson (my army buddy and fellow fake social worker), Siegfried von Kortzfleisch (a Lutheran theologian who had been on the staff at Bad Boll), and Thomas Luckmann (our wives, Brigitte and

Benita, though not formally invited, came along). I had also invited Talcott Parsons, the Harvard professor who might reasonably be described as the pope of American sociology. The most prominent theologian was Henri de Lubac, the French Jesuit who had previously had some difficulties with the Church authorities. Curiously, they also invited Harvey Cox, the Protestant theologian who had gained some notoriety from his book *The Secular City* (one of the works that welcomed secularization from a theological point of view). At the opening session there was a large crowd, including five cardinals in full regalia, and a swarm of media people. The conference ended with a formal audience with Pope Paul VI, who shook everybody's hand and blessed a small crucifix that Cox had brought along (for his Irish maid, he explained).

I don't think that any profound insights came out of this conference (the major papers were subsequently published as *The Culture of Unbelief*, coedited by Grumelli and another Catholic sociologist). But it was a fascinating event. We could observe the impressive machinery of the Vatican in full gear. Since we had been invited by the Vatican, members of the Roman elite believed that we must all be important people.

On a couple evenings we were invited for dinner at decaying palaces of the "black nobility" (that is, old papal aristocracy, not to be confused with the upstarts ennobled in recent times by the Savoy dynasty). I had invited a Hungarian sociologist, who was rudely inspected by a lady from those circles who said that she had never before seen a real communist, only some Italian communists who didn't count.

But my favorite incident took place at one of these parties when a leading politician of the Christian Democratic Party paid a visit. He wanted to know what the conference was about. "Secularization" (*secolarizzazione*), Grumelli explained.

"What is that?" asked the politician.

Grumelli gave a succinct, quite adequate definition.

The politician listened attentively, then said, "We will not permit it!"

A DOUBLE EXILE

The sixties ended with a double fiasco that finished the dream of establishing a new sociology empire with its headquarters at the New School. The first fiasco took place at the New School itself. The second had an immensely larger scope.

I was becoming increasingly unhappy about the changed character of the New School Sociology Department. The tradition of European sociology, which had attracted me to the field in the first place, was fast disappearing. I played with the idea of looking for a job elsewhere. Then, in the fall of 1969, I was elected department chairman. I decided to use this position in a make-or-break effort to change the direction of the department. The effort failed completely and very quickly.

I went about it in a singularly inept fashion. I issued a memorandum on the state of the department, dealing with some practical matters (mainly the inordinately high faculty-student ratio) but also stating that the department had lost its distinctive character and consequently its niche in the academic market. The memorandum began with the sentence, "The Department, in my opinion, is . . . on the verge of bankruptcy as an intellectual enterprise"—not exactly diplomatic language in a situation in which the supposedly bankrupt intellectuals would have to vote on one's proposals. I'm not sure just what I expected, perhaps intervention by the administration or by the increasingly active students. Be this as it may, the negative reaction of my colleagues was vehement and instantaneous.

The immediate issue to be voted on was that of new appointments, obviously needed to improve the faculty-student ratio but intended by me to help restore the lost tradition. I proposed three names—Hansfried Kellner (Brigitte's brother and of course a member of our clique), Anton C. Zijderveld (a Dutch sociologist, whom I had met some time ago and who was very much up our alley intellectually), and Diane Wilkinson (an African American woman teaching at the University of

Kentucky, whom I had met briefly and who struck me as a reasonable person in the rapidly radicalizing subdiscipline of "critical sociology"). The opposition to Kellner and Zijderveld was led by Arthur Vidich, a more or less "critical" sociologist whom I had originally recommended for the department. He made some counterproposals, which I rejected—I thought that this was an all-or-nothing situation. All other members of the department joined Vidich in opposition, with the exception of Deborah Offenbacher, who, like me, had received her doctorate under the *ancien regime*. The administration, after a half-hearted attempt at mediation, approved the Vidich opposition. Some of the students took my side, but most of them at that point were too much involved in the burgeoning cultural revolution to pay attention to this storm in an academic teapot.

My Battle of Twelfth Street had begun just after Labor Day. It ended on November 25, when the department asked me to step down from the chairmanship, which I promptly did. I vacated my office in the department and holed up at *Social Research* for the rest of the academic year. I started an active job search. It was a good time for this. The academic job market was booming, and I had several offers. I took the one that seemed (and turned out to be) most appealing, from Rutgers University in New Brunswick, New Jersey (across the Verazzano-Narrows Bridge from our house in Brooklyn). I started teaching there in the fall of 1970. Five of my graduate students followed me across the river, three of them ending up with degrees from Rutgers. It was a fairly mild ending to a turbulent set of events. All the same, it felt like going into exile. I had lost the one academic institution with which I had a strong identification.

Although the fiasco at the New School had nothing to do directly with the cultural tsunami that at that time was gaining its maximum force, the latter was its larger context and eventually was more important in influencing my intellectual career. The vast impact of what was happening became clear only gradually to many of us living through it. Those who were swept off their feet by the alleged revolution of course look back on this time as a high point in their lives, and they have influenced many younger people to hold a romantic view of what (not altogether accurately) has come to be called "the sixties." It is interesting to observe that sociologists and other observers of the cultural scene have done a poor job of explaining this enormously influential development and its enduring consequences. This is not the place to attempt such an explanation.

At first I was quite sympathetic to "the Movement." My previous experiences made me look favorably on a political development that emphasized racial justice and recognition of the rights of homosexuals. I even felt a certain affinity with the debunking of authority. After all, it was just these themes that I had identified as characteristic of a "humanistic sociology." I was opposed to the war in Vietnam, though I could not go along with the increasingly shrill anti-Americanism and pro-socialism of the antiwar campaign.

Also, the last years of the 1960s saw the beginnings of my friendship with Richard Neuhaus, who was at the time passionately "Movement" oriented. He had marched with Martin Luther King Jr. in Selma, had been arrested at the 1968 Democratic convention in Chicago, and briefly ran as an antiwar candidate in the fourteenth Congressional district in Brooklyn. He convinced me to join the national steering committee of an organization called Clergy and Laymen Concerned about Vietnam (CALCAV). But along with Neuhaus and a good many others, I was progressively repelled by the leftward thrust of "the Movement." I had definitely *not* signed on to a project of replacing democracy with some version of Marxist ideology.

This disillusionment took some time to develop. However, I can recall an experience that crystallized my doubts in one moment of sharp intuition. In true "postmodern" fashion the experience was virtual rather than actual: I saw it on television. It was in 1968, during the student riots at Columbia University. The scene was a confrontation between a crowd of students trying to storm the campus and a police cordon blocking them. The students were chanting, "The streets belong to the people! The streets belong to the people!" It reminded me of something, at first I did not know of what. Then, in a flash I remembered. It was a memory from my childhood in post-Anschluss Vienna: the first line of the second verse of the "Horst Wessel Lied," the Nazi anthem—"*Die Strasse frei den braunen Batallionen! Die Strasse frei dem Sturmabteilungsmann!*" Freely translated: "The streets belong to the brown battalions! The streets belong to the storm trooper!" The intuition was searing: *This* is *that*! Not completely, of course, but in important aspects—the mob psychology, the mystique of the street, the rage against all institutions of liberal democracy, and, last but not least, the militant antireason impervious to argument.

Not much later I resigned from CALCAV and registered as a Republican (I wanted to vote in the primary against Nixon in favor of a more liberal candidate!). Neuhaus took a little longer to move away from "the Movement"—he had a bigger chunk of his biography invested in it. When he did, he moved much farther to the right than I ever did.

What all this had to do with me was simple but far-reaching. The zeitgeist shifted dramatically in the intellectual culture, not only in America, but also in much of the world. The moment, in which it seemed that my thinking was congenial with the temper of the times, ended in a big bang. The window of opportunity closed. And this, as I mentioned some pages back, had much to do with the fate of the books I wrote subsequently. I would not want to interpret this estrangement "victimologically" (to use a term that has come into use in the politics of identity since the sixties). I was not persecuted. By any reasonable standard I made a good career. My books were read, even if they did not become best sellers. As the years went by, I was even assigned the role of a grand (even if definitely out-of-style) old man. But I became an exile, not only from my parochial alma mater but from the wider elite culture. Given the nature of the latter, this has not been such a bad thing.

4

GLOBE-TREKKING SOCIOLOGY

So, in the fall of 1970 I crossed the river with my little band of New School graduate students—not so much like Moses crossing the Red Sea with the children of Israel but more like Napoleon on the way to Saint Helena. Rutgers University was certainly no Promised Land, but it was not a prison colony either. The New Jersey location did not help. I had described this location (perhaps in a prescient hallucination) in my novel *The Enclaves*: "roughly equidistant from an oil refinery and the New Jersey Turnpike. . . . [W]ith the poignant odors emanating from these two sources . . . serving as a counterpoint to the overall aroma rising like a miasma of evil from the Jersey swamps, favored by New York gangsters for the dumping of their victims' bodies and deeply repressed from the consciousness of the politicians who had thought up the motto 'Garden State' for this territory."

Of course this is a near-slanderous exaggeration, proof of the degree to which I had come to think of myself as a New Yorker. (As in the old joke, which, I think, is not by Woody Allen but should be: Why are New Yorkers so often depressed? Because the light at the end of the tunnel is New Jersey.)

I taught at Rutgers from 1970 to 1979. If it was exile, it was a comfortable exile. The university was organized into colleges, which was convenient for avoiding ideological conflicts. My college was Douglass College. All the leftists were cloistered at Livingston College, quite some distance away, and one did not often meet them. Harry Brede-meier, the department chairman at Douglass, was a genial, open-minded individual who presided over a relaxed environment and who went out of his way to make me feel welcome. I could teach whatever I wanted, and I had some good students who wrote interesting dissertations and some of whom went on to make significant contributions to the field. Among those who came with me from the New School were John Murray Cuddihy, who later wrote some brilliant books on intellectual history, and Egon Mayer, who became a leading sociologist working on American Jews. Among interesting students who came to Rutgers directly to study with me were Michael Plekon, who has become an expert on the Russian Orthodox diaspora in the West; Judith Balfe, who before her premature death did some pioneering work on the sociology of art; and James Davison Hunter, who has created an innovative center on the sociology of culture at the University of Virginia.

We continued to live in Brooklyn, and I commuted to Rutgers, usually two days a week. As a result, I did not develop a social life around the university. I still recall the pleasure of driving home across the Verazzano-Narrows Bridge in the early evening, with the lights of the city before me—an experience I described in an article about New York as a "signal of transcendence."[1]

Rutgers as such had no direct influence on my intellectual trajectory. It was a base. But the 1970s saw a vast expansion of the geographical scope of my thinking, both physically (I crisscrossed the globe with maniacal frequency) and intellectually. An alternative title of this chapter could be "The Globalization of Berger." In the meantime, though, there was a journalistic episode that came directly out of my political turn in the wake of the "sixties" revolution.

A JOURNALISTIC EXCURSION

It began with some conversations with Brigitte, Richard Neuhaus, and a few others (mostly in our living room in Brooklyn). We thought that it would be a good idea to start a periodical, which would be in favor of civil rights and opposed to the Vietnam War but would *not* be on the left. Some moderately right-of-center foundations soon funded the idea, and we started a monthly that we called *Worldview*. Other people did the day-by-day editorial work, but the central person in the venture was clearly Neuhaus, who was then at his sparkling best, full of new ideas and exuding enormous energy. He and I got along very well (tension between us developed later, mostly for theological reasons as he moved steadily toward conversion to Roman Catholicism). I did not mind playing second fiddle. And, for the first time since my abortive relationship with the German journal run by the previously mentioned ex-Nazi, I could write in a journalistic vein.

Worldview came out from 1972 to 1984. I rather doubt whether we had much of an influence. The publication made one contribution that, at the time, was unusual: We published some articles describing the horrors of the Maoist regime, which were widely ignored by the liberal media in America.

I was an active member of what was in effect an editorial board. We had offices at what was then called the Council on Religion and International Affairs (CRIA), located on East Sixty-Fourth Street between Lexington and Third Avenues. Andrew Carnegie had founded CRIA in early 1914. Its mission statement, on the role of religion in fostering world peace, began with the not exactly prescient observation that this was an important topic, since war between "civilized nations" had now become unthinkable!

I usually went there once or twice a week, enjoying the fact that once again I had a pied-á-terre in Manhattan. The area, of course, was full of excellent restaurants. Our favorite was P. J. Moriarty's, a pleasant establishment on Third Avenue. This was the era when one could still smoke in public places. Our conversations took place over many cups of after-lunch coffee, with lingering effects from the before-lunch martinis and the comforting sensation from the cigarillos ("between the acts") that Neuhaus and I were smoking. (As I recall, he got the habit from me. The Austrian writer Heimito von Doderer, in one of his novels, tells of a man who adopted the same brand of cologne that had been used by a friend: "It is not a small matter," he writes, "when a person takes on the smell of another.")

I had a column and I could write whatever I wanted. I wrote something in many issues of the monthly and wrote on a great variety of topics. I commented on the moral implications of events in different parts of the world. I wrote a more philosophical piece on patriotism (we had all agreed that *Worldview*, though critical of some American policies, was patriotic). Brigitte and I wrote in defense of class as the most open form of social stratification.

One column of which I am still proud (it has been reprinted since) was called "In the Valley of the Fallen." It was about the *Valle de los Caidos*, the gigantic cemetery, hewn into a mountain, that Franco had built outside Madrid for the Nationalists killed during the Spanish civil war. I had just visited the place and had been moved by it to a reflection on the fact that, as things were turning out, neither side was the winner in the end. (As I put it some years later, the Nationalists had wanted to turn Spain into a suburb of Fatima. It has become a suburb of Brussels.)

One piece I wrote was called "Gilgamesh on the Washington Shuttle" (Gilgamesh is the protagonist in the ancient Mesopotamian epic of that name, a man who journeys in search of the plant that can bestow immortality). The piece was inspired by an incident I had witnessed on an airplane, when a passenger became very angry when the only free seat was in the nonsmoking section and the flight attendant told him to put out his cigarette. The flight attendant was evidently outraged, reflecting the moral passion of the antismoking movement that was then just beginning. I opined that this passion was rooted in a quest for immortality: Stop smoking and you will live forever. The column was read by a consultant for the Philip Morris company and led to my entanglement with the tobacco industry, which I will report on in a while.

Politically, I began to define myself as a "conservative," though my definition of this label was highly idiosyncratic. Neuhaus defined himself as a "radical," which, if anything, was even more idiosyncratic than my own self-definition. He and I published a small book in 1970, *Movement and Revolution*, in which we (somewhat painfully) spelled out these categories and related them to current issues in American politics.

The 1970s was also the period in which the so-called neoconservative movement came into being. Brigitte and I, just like Neuhaus and Michael Novak (another escapee from CALCAV), developed ties with that movement and to a degree began to identify with it. We developed a friendship with Norman Podhoretz and Midge Decter, and I published some articles in *Commentary*. For a few years this affinity made me feel less homeless politically. In 1986 Brigitte and I published an article in *Commentary*, "Our Conservatism and Theirs," in which we explained our affinity with neoconservatism. The affinity waned for Brigitte and me as neoconservatives became allied with social conservatives on such issues as abortion and homosexuality, issues where our views were very different.

Before getting to the globalization experiences of these years, I want to mention one little episode that gave me a rather shocking insight into the underworld of academic publishing. For the only time in my career I decided to write a book with no other purpose than to make money (we wanted to buy a summer house to get away from the heat in New York). Brigitte and I proposed to write an introductory textbook in sociology. One publisher (whose identity I will mercifully leave unmentioned) expressed an interest.

We met in a restaurant with an editor from the publisher and a middle-aged woman who was not at first identified. The editor explained that the publisher had conducted a national survey among instructors of introductory sociology to find out just what they would like to see in a textbook. The woman was then introduced, in effect as a ghostwriter: As she proudly announced, she had already written the book, taking bits and pieces from other textbooks to conform to an outline composed on the basis of the survey findings. The ghostwriter had no background in sociology, but she informed us that she had previously written other textbooks, in several fields, using the same "scientific" method.

It became clear that all they wanted from me was to lend my name to the book, though they assured me that, of course, I could suggest changes in the text that had already been written (as I recall, they had brought along a copy). I informed them that this was not a project with which I wanted to be associated. (A couple years later the publisher in question did come out with a textbook under the name of a sociologist I knew. I don't know whether a less "scientific" method was used to write it.)

Brigitte and I then proposed the textbook to Basic Books, who offered a contract with the understanding that we would actually ("unscientifically," if you will) write the book ourselves. It was published in 1972 under the title *Sociology: A Biographical Approach*. I don't think there was anything really original in it, except for the format—topics were introduced in the sequence in which they would be encountered in the biography of an individual. Textbooks tend to have a short life span, unless they are continually revised, which we were not willing to do. But the venture had fulfilled its purpose: We received a respectable amount in royalties, and this was helpful for the purchase in 1973 of a lovely house in the Berkshires of western Massachusetts.

NEW THOUGHTS IN DAZZLING SUNLIGHT

At the very end of the 1960s, amid all the personal and political tumults in my life, there occurred a sharp turn in my intellectual agenda, which had little, if anything, to do with either. It was a turn from theory to the empirical questions that have dominated my work as a sociologist ever since. Specifically two: What is modernity? What is a viable strategy for modernization and development?

In the spring of 1969, out of the blue, I received a phone call from Mexico. The caller said, "This is Ivan Illich. You probably don't know who I am." I said that I did know; I had read Illich's book *Celebration of Awareness*, but I had not been greatly affected by it and had had no previous contact with Illich. He went on to say that he had heard that I was going to be in Cuernavaca in the coming summer. This was correct. I had accepted an invitation to speak at a Catholic conference in that city, and, in our continuing search for escapes from the summer heat of New York, we had decided to rent a house there. Illich went on, "Come to CIDOC. We need you!" The invitation seemed irresistible and I accepted. I could not foresee the consequences.

Ivan Illich (who died in 2002) was a fascinating, indeed charismatic personality. Born in Austria, he was the son of a Croatian father from Dalmatia and a Jewish mother from Frankfurt. He was trained as a Catholic priest in Salzburg and Rome. Destined for the Vatican diplomatic service, he became proficient in several languages and obtained a doctorate in history. Presumably because of his knowledge of Spanish, he was sent to America. He worked in Latino parishes in New York, then became vice rector of the Catholic University in Puerto Rico. He had a run-in with the hierarchy, whose forays into politics he criticized. I'm not sure of his precise canonical status, but he was dispensed from all priestly duties, though (unlike many other dissidents) he remained a theologically conservative Catholic.

In the early 1960s he started a think tank in Cuernavaca, then a charming town not far from Mexico City (pollution and congestion have made it less charming since). His think tank had a rather vacuous name, Centro Intercultural de Documentacion (Intercultural Documentation Center), abbreviated to CIDOC. It did indeed collect documents, mostly about religion and social change in Latin America. But it served mainly as a gathering place for intellectuals from the region, the United States, and Europe, who served as an ongoing seminar on whatever issues interested Illich at the moment. His interests, usually connected with his work on a new book, ranged widely—education (on which he wrote his best-known book, *Deschooling Society*); health and medicine (*Medical Nemesis*); energy and the environment; the role of women; and the defense of what he called the "vernacular"—the language and culture of ordinary people. There was an underlying theme, which could broadly be described as a critique of modernity. Illich became a culture hero for different groups—liberal Catholics, leftists of all descriptions, the counterculture, environmentalists, and feminists. He disappointed them all, as, one by one, he refused to conform to their respective ideological prejudices. His wildly roaming spirit could not be imprisoned in any bottle.

CIDOC was a very peculiar place. It was located in a rented villa, with lovely grounds and a swimming pool (I never saw it in use), ironically called La Casa Blanca. CIDOC received no outside funding. It supported itself by running a language school, where mostly *gringo* students paid steep fees for total-immersion Spanish-language courses. Both physically and financially, this activity took place on the ground floor. On the floor above were seminar rooms, Illich's very Spartan living quarters, and a large terrace. Almost every day this was the locale for lectures, discussion groups, and many informal conversations.

Soon after my arrival there I understood what Illich had in mind when he invited me. He had read *The Social Construction of Reality* and intuited that here were ideas that he could use. He understood that all his interests were related to one very basic issue—the nature of modern consciousness. Could not this issue be explored using concepts from the sociology of knowledge? It did not take long for me to agree.

I gave some lectures at CIDOC (I think they dealt with the sociology of religion), but most of that summer was taken up with innumerable conversations with Illich and his shifting coterie of visitors—I recall a South American educational reformer, a French Protestant theologian, and a German leftist activist (who always went barefoot, exhibiting repulsive abscesses). Brigitte was an active participant in most of these conversations, as were Hansfried Kellner (who was to play an important part in what followed) and various friends of mine who came to visit during the summers (between 1969 and 1972) we spent in Cuernavaca—Richard Neuhaus, Michael Novak, and two graduate students of mine, Daniel Pinard and Jane Canning.

It is hard for me to separate the new ideas that flooded my mind during this time from the atmosphere in which this thinking took place. There were the dazzling sunlight and a warmth that, at this altitude, was never oppressive. There were the smell of tropical flowers, the sounds of Mexican music, and the sharp staccatos of the Spanish language. It was also a happy time for my family. We always rented the same house in a pleasant section of the town. It had a garden and a swimming pool. We had a car and made excursions all over the state of Morelos. My two sons went to a little nearby school, where the instruction was in English but where every morning the Mexican flag was run up and saluted by the children—my older son, Thomas, was worried that he might lose his American citizenship because of this salute. With the boys in school, Brigitte and I often went to eat in the center of town, in a small café near the palace of Cortez, the conquistador who had kept his Aztec mistress there. In the evening, on the main plaza, one could listen to roving bands playing mariachi music.

The intellectual atmosphere at CIDOC was one of unusual conviviality and openness. It was of course dominated by the personality of Illich, but it should be emphasized that his manner was not at all domineering. He liked to listen to the views of others; he presented his own ideas cautiously and tentatively; he was invariably courteous. His respect for the "vernacular" had a local focus in the person of the night watchman, a dignified gentleman in his eighties, who always carried a rifle, which he claimed to have used in the army of Zapata during the Mexican Revolution. From time to time Illich would ask him to express an opinion on whatever topic was on the table, serving as an incarnation of vox populi. In almost anyone else such a gesture would seem patronizing and false. Not in Illich's case; he really wanted to know what the old *zapatista* thought.

Early in the conversations among Illich, Brigitte, and myself a definite project emerged: The three of us would write a book together on the nature of modern consciousness. It would apply the insights of the sociology of knowledge to Illich's key concern—the defense of "vernacular" traditions and ways of life against their suppression by the large institutions of modernity. We then suggested that Hansfried Kellner be added as another coauthor, and Illich quickly agreed. During our first summer at CIDOC the project never went beyond many intensive conversations. No outline of the book or plan for a division of labor ensued. This was to happen during the following summer, when Kellner did indeed appear on the scene. The project then collapsed.

The ostensible reason for this was absurd. Illich insisted that Kellner should give some lectures; he claimed that this was a strict rule for people collaborating with CIDOC activities. That claim was false; I knew of quite a few people who did not follow this alleged rule, and in any case it was not clear just what "CIDOC activities" were supposed to be. Kellner said that he did not want to deliver any lectures, Illich (quite uncharacteristically) would not budge, and Brigitte and I decided to give up on our project.

This trivial disagreement cannot have been the real reason for Illich's strange demand of Kellner. I think that the real reason was Illich's discovery that there were fundamental differences in our respective presuppositions. When all was said and done, Illich did not like modernity. Contrary to what many admirers on the left thought, he was profoundly conservative in the full European sense of the term. His utopia, if any, was in the Middle Ages. Brigitte and I did, and do, like modernity. We were interested in a critique of modernity and in reform of its institutions but not replacing these with quasi-Gandhian arrangements in education, healthcare, and local government.

Our little family collective then decided to write the book without Illich's participation. We started working on the book in Mexico. *The Homeless Mind: Modernization and Consciousness* came out in 1973. More about this in a moment.

The early 1970s were consumed by my efforts to clarify my thinking about modernity and development, theoretically but also in terms of practical policies of development. I had made friends with a prominent Mexican anthropologist, Rodolfo Stavenhagen, and he invited me to lecture at the Colegio de México, the elite institution where he was located. This put me in contact with the prevailing intellectual trends, not just in Mexico, but in Latin America generally. These trends were overwhelmingly Marxist or neo-Marxist. I enlarged my knowledge of the region by traveling to Guatemala and Venezuela, and I read voraciously (in the process, incidentally, improving the Spanish that I had originally learned on the streets of East Harlem). I increasingly understood my intellectual agenda as one of understanding the causes of underdevelopment and finding strategies to overcome it, but without landing in the dead end of leftist ideology.

CIDOC did not fulfill the promise of its early years. In fidelity to his hostility toward formal education, Illich refused to impose standards or any other regulations. (An ultimate insult was scribbled on the wall of one of the toilets—"Ivan Illich runs a school!") He appointed his assistant, Valentina Borremans, as head of the center; she was an agreeable enough Belgian woman but had no scholarly or, for that matter, administrative qualifications whatsoever (her previous experiences included deep-sea diving with Jacques Cousteau and a stint as housekeeper for Helder Camara, the bishop of Recife in northeast Brazil and a friend of Illich).

All sorts of eccentric individuals came to lecture, and the place became an attractive destination for countercultural types from the United States. When their activities came to involve the overt use of drugs, the local police became interested. Illich then abruptly closed the place down. La Casa Blanca was evacuated, the language courses were terminated, and Borremans and the CIDOC archive were relocated to a village near Cuernavaca. Illich himself had a little house there, but he increasingly led an itinerant life holding meetings with a shrinking group of disciples in Europe and the United States. His writings became increasingly obscure, mainly dealing with supposed roots of modern thought in the Middle Ages. Illich died in Germany.

Despite our disagreement over the writing of a book, we remained on friendly terms. Illich came to visit me in Boston several times. He would call from the airport, then come to my house for an hour or so; on one occasion he had a taxi waiting outside. There was one episode that somehow seemed a perfect metaphor for the life of one of the most interesting individuals I have ever met.

Illich called me from somewhere and said that he would be coming through Boston. He had a request: He had forgotten a scarf in the office of his publisher in New York. It was a very unusual scarf, made of hair from both a llama and an alpaca. A Peruvian philosopher, Salazar Bondy (whom I had met myself on a trip to Peru), had given it to him. Illich had asked the publisher to mail the scarf to my house, where he would pick it up. Well, Illich arrived; the scarf had not. This was just before Christmas. Upon leaving again, Illich said that he was going to Atlanta "to dance in the New Year" with the widow of Erich Fromm (the psychologist and author of *Escape from Freedom*, who had lived in Cuernavaca for some time). Would I please forward the scarf to Atlanta? The scarf did indeed arrive, a few days after Illich's departure. As requested, I forwarded it to Atlanta. I did not know how long Illich was planning to stay there, but I calculated that, unless his stay was going to be a very long one, the scarf would miss him again. That was when I had this fantasy: The scarf would continue to chase after Illich, from one place to another, always missing him. Perhaps it still does?

WHAT IS MODERN CONSCIOUSNESS?

It seems that by the early 1970s I had become accustomed to writing first a book purporting to consist of "value-free" social-scientific analysis, to be followed by a value-laden argument about the implications of the analysis—except that now the second stage of such an exercise was political rather than theological. First my family team and I wrote *The Homeless Mind*; then I, by myself, followed up with *Pyramids of Sacrifice*.

The Homeless Mind, published in 1973, was introduced as an exercise in the sociology of knowledge. It applied the conceptual apparatus of *The Social Construction of Reality* to the question of the nature of modern consciousness. I think this application was quite successful, showing that these concepts could be useful in trying to understand complex empirical phenomena. Whether we were successful in all the details of this particular exercise is more debatable.

We tried to discuss the effects on consciousness of three central phenomena of modernity—technology, bureaucracy, and the pluralization of life-worlds. Thus technology induces a cognitive style we called "componentiality"—breaking up reality into separate components that can be analyzed and manipulated. The bureaucratic style is similar but much less related to empirical verification—it creates an artificial universe of pure abstraction. Pluralization forces individuals to live in different social worlds and to play different roles in each of them—we called this "multirelationality." Of course we went into much more detail, but the above terms give an idea of how we proceeded. In retrospect, apart from rather dubious contributions to the language of Shakespeare and Milton, I think we did a fair job of describing these structures of consciousness. But, also in retrospect, one must note a glaring omission in our list of modern phenomena—*we did not discuss capitalism*! I think this can be explained by the Mexican setting in which we designed the basic argument of the book: We were surrounded by Marxists of various descriptions, and while we did not agree with their ideology, we tried to construct an analysis that would avoid the ideological disagreements.

Be this as it may, we deployed a number of concepts that have been useful in describing the process of modernization. We used the classical Weberian concept of "carriers," a term reminiscent of medicine. One asks what are the "carriers" of a disease. Similarly, one can ask which groups or institutions "carry" modernization—say, an entrepreneurial ethnic group or an educational system. We then used a concept that we had heard Illich use, "packages," by which we meant clusters of behavior patterns and the structures of consciousness that go with them. We then made a useful distinction between "intrinsic" and "extrinsic" packages, the former being tied together in such a way that they cannot be taken apart if the behavior is to continue, the latter having come about more or less by accident and therefore being much more readily taken apart.

I can specify the incident in which this distinction became very clear to me. Shortly after we embarked on our Mexican adventure, I made my first trip to Africa (I will come to that in a while). I was taking an early flight from Entebbe, in Uganda, to Nairobi on what was then East African Airlines. I was groggy with sleep and only half awake. I sat down in the cabin, which was decorated to look like an African village. The flight attendants, dressed in African costumes, were serving tropical fruit. The public address system was playing African music, drums and all. The anxious thought occurred to me: "Who is flying this airplane?!" Then the voice of the captain came on—in clipped British accents—and I was relieved.

I don't feel the need to affirm that I am not racist. But it is important to note that, when I worried about the pilot flying the plane, I was not concerned about the pilot's skin color—I was concerned about his training. To be precise, I wanted his training to be exactly the same as that of a pilot of British Airlines (or United Airlines or Lufthansa). As soon as I heard the British accent, I could assume that the pilot was indeed British trained, no matter whether he was born in England, Uganda, or Kenya.

This little episode is a good metaphor for the logic of modernization. There is an "intrinsic package" that must be internalized by any individual who is to fly a modern aircraft—a way of behaving, necessarily linked to a way of thinking. For example, the pilot must think in terms of very precise concepts of time—"engineering time"—to be in control of the temporal dimensions of distance, speed, and fuel capacity. This temporality will be, must be, "British"—or, more accurately, "Western." Traditional African culture, by contrast, operates with a much more relaxed, less precise temporality. A traditionalist may say, persuasively, that this is a more natural, more humane way of experiencing time. If two villagers want to meet, it is enough to say, "Let us meet in the evening," which may be any time between, say, eight or ten by the clock. Any greater specification of time is unnecessarily constraining. Let it be stipulated that, in the perspective of some cultural philosophy, "African time" is superior to "Western time." But then let us add: *If the pilot flies by African time, the plane will crash.*

In other words, there is an intrinsic package linking behavior and consciousness in the activity of flying a plane. But there are also extrinsic packages, such as linking the activity of flight attendants with the uniform and the etiquette of Western airlines, which East African Airlines had decided to take apart and reassemble. Put simply, there is no leeway in terms of what goes on in the cockpit; there is a good deal of leeway in the cabin.

Take another matter: For obvious historical reasons, English has become the language of international aviation. Thus there is a linkage between knowing how to fly a plane and knowing how to communicate in English with flight controllers. But this linkage is extrinsic. It could be taken apart. Thus in the future English might be replaced by Chinese, or Spanish, or Swahili—or any language capable of absorbing the semantics of modern technology. What is more, our Ugandan pilot must behave and think in a tightly defined way while he is in the cockpit. When he is off duty, takes off his uniform and goes home, he may radically change his appearance, his behavior, his language, and, last but not least, the way he thinks. Recently there has been a powerful illustration of just this type of "multirelationality" when Jacob Zuma, the newly elected president of South Africa and a man proud of his Zulu heritage, made his first appearance in parliament, without embarrassment, accompanied by three wives.

The second part of the book discussed the dynamics of modernization through the transmission of packages and the ensuing collisions of consciousness. We discussed ideologies of modernization and countermodernity, including in the latter category many currents of the counterculture then sweeping across much of the Western world (we called these "demodernization"). In our conclusion we said that our analysis could not provide justification of either socialist or nonsocialist development policies. We pleaded for a "pedantic utopianism," an attitude that combines visions of a better future with careful attention to the empirical facts of modernity. The phrase did not inspire anyone, not even us.

"I HAVE BAD NEWS FOR YOU."

Overlapping with the last phase of my Cuernavaca period was an expansion into Africa of my perspective on the so-called Third World. This happened as a result of an invitation by an Austrian think tank, the Vienna Institute for Development, to direct an international working group on what was called "Alternatives in Development." It was based on an idea of mine that I had mentioned to an acquaintance connected with this think tank. The idea was simple: to explore a number of non-Western policies or institutions that had had positive effects on social or economic development. I assembled a rather interesting team for this project. The results were sparse, and the project was halted without any significant publication, largely because communications among the Vienna office, myself, and the team scattered over several countries proved to be cumbersome. However, the project was my first experience in directing an interdisciplinary working group.

Despite the fact that this one did not succeed too well (the reasons for the failure could be understood and avoided in the future), this type of working group became a favored modus operandi of mine. If one is to dignify it with the term *methodology*, it is based on a (naturally enough) distinctively Viennese principle. I call it the "coffee-house principle": If you collect the right people and have them sit together long enough, they are bound to come up with something interesting.

My first arrival in Africa was rather dramatic. Richard Neuhaus was going on a long trip through several African countries, so we planned to begin the journey together. We flew Air Afrique from New York to Dakar. On the plane the flight attendants spent all their time catering to the only passenger in first class, evidently an important Senegalese politician, paying little attention to the rest of the passengers. We arrived in Dakar while it was still dark. A wild-looking taxi driver grabbed our bags ahead of some competitors, threw them into the trunk, and drove at a dangerous speed through the pitch-black night. We could see nothing outside. He did deliver us to our hotel, where we were shown to our rooms by the night watchman.

I tried to get a little sleep, then got up to shower and shave. About an hour or so later there was a knock on the door. There was Neuhaus, with a very distressed look on his face. He said in a solemn voice: "I have bad news for you"—a sentence about which I kidded him for years afterward. When I looked puzzled, he explained that his testicles were rapidly and painfully swelling, saying that he had to see a doctor as soon as possible. It was then about seven in the morning. We had been in Africa about two hours. It hardly seemed likely that he had already contracted a tropical disease.

I went downstairs, but the night watchman spoke only Woloff, a language in which I was woefully incompetent. He only pointed to 8:00 on his watch and said "Madame." Sure enough, the manager, a French woman, arrived at that hour. Before her arrival I sat with Neuhaus, who kept going to the bathroom to inspect the alarming expansion of his testicles. I tried to calm him down by talking about other things. But I could not help thinking about what my obligations were in this situation. I remembered a picture I had seen of an African suffering from elephantiasis who had to put his enormous testicles into a wheel barrow, which he pushed ahead of him.

The episode ended with a big relief. The manager called an emergency number and made an immediate appointment with a doctor, who spoke English. He laughed as soon as he inspected the ailing member: This was a very common side effect of one of the many inoculations that Neuhaus had taken in preparation for his African trip. After one injection the testicles rapidly and reassuringly returned to their customary size. But my first sights of Africa were from the window of another taxi, racing on a Sunday morning through the deserted boulevards of Dakar to a *service d'urgence*. And Neuhaus's opening sentence that morning could be taken as a heading over much that I was learning about the Third World in those years, which later I called the years before my discovery of the economic miracles of East Asia.

The Viennese sent me on two trips, the aforementioned one to Africa and one to Latin America. I went to Peru and Brazil to look at two different approaches to slum rehabilitation. Peru had socialist policies of the leftist Velasco government; Brazil had very different policies of a right-wing military regime. The difference between statist and capitalist models of development was even sharper in Africa. I was to look at the program of *animation rurale* in Senegal, which was giving advice and training to small farmers, and at the program in Tanzania, which was carrying on an ambitious campaign of resettling farmers in so-called *ujamaa* ("solidarity") villages, which were socialist collectives. I don't think that, apart from some great tourist experiences, I learned much on these trips. But I had a startling "aha!" experience in Senegal and an instructive fantasy in Tanzania.

I was in a jeep in a rural area of Senegal, supposedly learning about the program of "animating" the local farmers. We drove through a village where the scene intrigued me. On a street corner a man stood on a wooden bench, speaking to a small group standing around him. I asked my guide whether this was a politician or a preacher. Oh no, I was told, this was a storyteller. I immediately had a very strong identification with this man: This is what I do when I teach! Ever since seeing this story-teller, I have had great self-confidence in doing without all those technical aids without which so many colleagues feel unable to teach. Whenever I hear that odious phrase "PowerPoint presentation," I see in my mind the Senegalese storyteller on his street corner.

In Tanzania I visited an allegedly exemplary *ujamaa* village. It was a pathetic place. I was taken to the "factory." Five guys sat on the floor of an empty warehouse, each equipped with a hammer. They cracked open the shells of some sort of nuts, which they then put in baskets—"for export," I was proudly told. A village official asked me whether I had any questions. I had a hard time thinking of any; my knowledge of agrarian affairs barely went beyond being able to distinguish between a donkey and a horse. I don't know what led me to this question, but I asked whether they had any festivals in the village. The official said, "Glad you asked," or words to that effect. He was happy to explain.

Some *ujamaa* villages were inhabited by people from only one tribe; others, like this one, had people from several different tribes. There was a committee with the task of encouraging intertribal solidarity. The tribes of course had different traditions, different dances. Once or twice a year the committee organized events in which each tribe performed its traditional dances, so that people would better understand and respect each other.

Much later I remembered this episode as perfectly illustrating the difference between tradition and neotraditionalism. A fantasy: Imagine two situations, a tribal dance performed in a traditional village and the same dance performed on one of the occasions that I had been told about. Imagine further that both dances are filmed. The two films are exactly the same; perhaps even the same dancers appear in both films. *Yet the two situations are totally different.* In the traditional village one danced at the appointed sacred days, one danced for the gods or the ancestors, and the purpose of the exercise was to retain a connection with the spiritual world. In the *ujamaa* village a committee scheduled the event: one danced for an audience and for a utilitarian purpose.

I did not learn much on these trips about urban or rural development policies. But the expansion of my vision from Latin America to Africa gave me more confidence in writing my next book.

Pyramids of Sacrifice: Political Ethics and Social Change was published in 1974. I now dealt directly with the political challenge that I felt as a result of my first encounter with Third World poverty, both in Latin America and in Africa. The challenge could be summed up in one question: What is an acceptable model of development? The book was reasonably successful upon publication in America, receiving some favorable reviews. It was nominated for a National Book Award in 1976. There were eight foreign translations, including one in Chinese (published in Taiwan) and one in Bahasa Indonesia (again published under Muslim auspices). The American edition did not stay in print for more than a few years.

In retrospect I don't look on this book as one of my better ones, though it was written with a good deal of passion. I think the best parts were a number of vignettes—short stories illustrating aspects of underdevelopment. The most searing one, entitled "Tableau in Garbage— Child with Vultures," tells of an experience I had in Bahia, one of the most romantic cities of Brazil that combines beautiful baroque architecture with the pervasive rhythms of Afro-Brazilian music. It also contains one of the largest slums in Latin America. I was taken there by a group of middle-class ladies volunteering as "social workers" for some government agency. We saw a gigantic garbage dump on top of which a half-naked little boy was chasing vultures; at the same time one of the ladies showed around photos of her little daughter, in a pretty party dress, at a birthday party. The account of this incident ends with the above question: What is an acceptable model of development?

The first vignette in the book is the one from which the title of the book is taken. It deals with the great pyramid of Cholula in the Mexican state of Puebla. Actually there is a series of pyramids, built one on top of the other as different Mesoamerican empires occupied this region— Olmecs, Toltecs, and finally Aztecs. Each destroyed the pyramid serving as a temple for the preceding rulers, then built a new temple on top of the ruins. This resulted in a veritable mountain, on top of which the Spaniards built a church. An agency of the modern Mexican government, which had an ideological interest in glorifying the pre-Columbian past, was excavating the site.

I made two points—that each incarnation of the pyramid was legitimated by a myth and that each required huge sacrifices by the people ruled by the mythmakers. The Mesoamerican civilizations believed that the gods needed to be fed by the blood of human sacrifices, which were ritually enacted on the top platform of the pyramid. The Aztecs were the most bloodthirsty of the lot. Then the Spaniards came, imposing their own sacrifices in the exploitation of the native population and in the fires of the Inquisition. And the myth of modern Mexican nationalism continued the sequence.

In using the metaphor of the sacrificial pyramid I borrowed from Octavio Paz, who, in his essay "Critique of the Pyramid," argued that the

Mexican state continued the Aztec myth of centralized power, requiring sacrifice in the name of a myth of development. His critique of all such myths used the wonderful term *syllogism-dagger*—a theory concocted by an elite and used as a weapon.

Most of the book is an analysis of what I called the *myth of growth* and the *myth of revolution*. The former myth, which I illustrated with Brazil under its dictatorship of the time, justified the suffering of the present with the promise of a better future to be brought about by capitalist growth. The latter myth, which I described in terms of Maoist China, justified present suffering by the promise of the socialist utopia that is to be the end product of the revolution.

I argued that both myths had to be rejected. In the Brazilian case, I used the realities of pervasive poverty as a moral argument against the capitalist ideology of the regime. To reject the claims of the Maoists, I described in some detail the successive bloodbaths, costing millions of lives. A negative view of the Brazilian military government was amply represented in the American media. But this was a time when the media and the majority of academic China experts did not give an adequate account of the horrors of the Maoist regime.

I did not come up with a new model for development policy. Instead, I described in some detail what I called the *calculus of pain* and the *calculus of meaning*. This meant that any acceptable model must try hard to minimize the suffering caused by social change and must also show respect for the traditional values that give meaning to human life. This message was widely misunderstood as advocating some version of social democracy or democratic socialism. That was not my intention. I was not enamored of socialism in any form. But I did present the two myths as being equally unacceptable—a notion of moral equivalence that I came to give up a few years later after the shock of my encounter with East Asia.

It is certainly true that the Brazilian regime of that time was a brutal one, particularly in its repression of all political opposition, possibly also in its insouciance in the face of abject poverty. But the Brazilian situation of the early 1970s is not typical of capitalism. All the same, the two promises under critique in my book were not equally false. Capitalism has lifted millions of people from dehumanizing misery to a decent standard of living. In other words, the myth of growth holds out a promise that, by and large, is empirically valid. By contrast, no socialist revolution has ever fulfilled its promise, not even in cases that were more humane than that of the Chinese Communists (such as the Tanzanian regime that undertook its program of "African socialism").

Thus I have mixed feelings in looking back on this book today. I cannot now write about capitalism and socialism in a similarly balanced fashion. What I have come to advocate in the years since then is not a more humane socialism but a humane, democratic capitalism—of which there are many examples. However, I would continue to affirm that certain levels of poverty are indeed morally unacceptable and that any acceptable development policy must be cognizant of the two calculi of pain and meaning.

GODDERS AGAIN

At about the same time I was instrumental in initiating an event that attracted a good deal of attention at the time. Richard Neuhaus was a coconspirator. The event was theological in character and thus, strictly speaking, does not belong in this book. But it was indicative of the overall cultural situation, and it clarified my own understanding of what it was to be a sociologist of religion.

Like much that I got involved in during this period, it began with a conversation in our living room in Brooklyn. Neuhaus and I thought it would be fun to make a list of the major themes in mainline Protestantism that irritated us. I should say that, even then, the two of us were not on the same wavelength theologically—Neuhaus was much to the

right of me in his theology and moving further to the right as he jour-
neyed toward Rome. But we could agree on, as it were, a negative list.
We produced such a list and circulated it among a small number of theologians who, we thought, would agree with it. Most of them did, and
with enthusiasm.

I then persuaded James Gettemy, president of the Hartford Seminary, to sponsor a meeting there in early 1975. After a lively discussion
and some follow-up correspondence, the group agreed to issue what was
called the "Hartford Appeal for Theological Affirmation." It was widely
distributed, then published a year later in a book edited by Neuhaus and
me, *Against the World for the World*, which also contained essays by some
of the drafters, elaborating their views and answering critics.

Despite its affirmative title, the appeal was based on a list of themes
that we deemed to be "false and debilitating." Of course in rejecting
these themes, we also stated what we accepted. The diversity of the
group would have made it difficult to use the opposite procedure.
Among the signers of the appeal were mainline Protestants (including
Episcopalians and Lutherans), Evangelicals, Roman Catholics, and Eastern
Orthodox Christians. Some were heavy hitters, such as Avery Dulles (Jesuit
theologian, later to become a cardinal), George Forell (a well-known
Lutheran theologian), Richard Myers (Episcopal bishop of California),
and Alexander Schmemann (one of the founders of the Orthodox
Church in America). Two of the signers came to feel that they had been
in the wrong company and withdrew from the group—Elizabeth Betten-
hausen (a bright, young Lutheran theologian who was on the way to
becoming a radical feminist) and William Sloane Coffin (the Yale University chaplain who was a hero of the anti-Vietnam campaign).

The themes repudiated by the appeal, thirteen in all (we were not
superstitious), ranged over a wide territory. What they had in common
was that they proposed an understanding of Christianity divested of its
transcendent (or, if you will, cosmic or supernatural) core. Conversely,
they reinterpreted Christianity as a moral code, a therapeutic instru-

ment, or a political agenda. All these themes were accommodations to a secularism dominant in elite culture. A good way of describing this is Thomas Luckmann's phrase "secularization from within" (within the churches, that is). In my essay in the volume, I described this as "a world without windows"; against this, I affirmed, faith opened up a window toward transcendence.

The appeal attracted a good deal of publicity. There were stories in the *New York Times*, *Time*, *Newsweek*, and of course any number of Protestant and Catholic publications. Needless to say, we made sure that *Worldview* covered the debate (including publishing the critics). There were some favorable responses. There were also very sharp criticisms, primarily by those who, correctly, felt that they were being attacked. A countermanifesto was issued by a group of left-leaning theologians who met in Boston under the leadership of Harvey Cox, the Harvard theologian who was an iconic figure in those circles. The "Hartford Appeal for Theological Affirmation" was interpreted as a "neoconservative" document, as a statement by religious and political reactionaries, even as a replication of the infamous *Syllabus of Errors* of Pope Pius IX. The Evangelical church historian Mark Noll wrote a largely sympathetic account ten years after the event, claiming that it was still significant. But it faded from public attention long before that. I doubt whether many people still remember it today.

Theologically, my participation in this event confirmed my view that being a liberal Protestant need not imply being part of the "secularization from within." As a sociologist of religion, I was helped to understand the place of religion in the cultural revolution then under way, its relation to class, and (which surprised me at the time) the role of Evangelicalism as a counterforce.

5

MANY GODS AND
COUNTLESS CHINESE

As the 1970s proceeded there occurred two major changes of mind in my career as a social scientist. Step-by-step I gave up my adherence to the so-called secularization theory. And also in steps, but at a faster rate, I came down clearly on the side of capitalism as the only viable model of development. Neither change reflected either theological or philosophical considerations. They were both due to my rethinking of what I considered to be the weight of evidence. As I often told my students, one of the advantages of being a social scientist is that one can have as much fun when one's theories are shot out of the water, or perhaps even more, than when those theories are supported by the data.

NOT TOO FEW BUT TOO MANY GODS

Secularization theory holds that the modern world suffers from an absence of gods. Max Weber used the haunting phrase "the disenchantment of the world" to describe this alleged situation. The enchantment is gone, and modern man is imprisoned in the "iron cage" of a pervasive rationality. It offends my filial piety to disagree with Weber (who, a bearded Germanic apparition, hovered over my formation as a sociologist)—alas, I must. I would now say that the modern world, with a few exceptions here and there, is not characterized by secularity but rather by *plurality*—not by too little but by too much religion. Modern man may have lost the one enchanted garden in which his ancestors dwelled, but instead he confronts a veritable emporium of such gardens, among which he must make a choice.

My conclusion that secularization theory will not hold up was based on three experiences—my encounters with the Third World, with the counterculture, and with Evangelicalism.

It is impossible to spend any amount of time in what was then called the Third World (now known, equally confusingly, as the Global South) without being struck by the pervasiveness of religion. In my case that impression began in Latin America. It was reinforced in Africa and later in Asia.

One of my first experiences in Mexico was the celebration of a folk mass in the cathedral of Cuernavaca. Our Lady of Guadalupe was every-where, and in the background still lurked the dark deities of the pre-Columbian past. I was struck by the fact that, to be plausible beyond the small world of the intellectual elite, even Marxism had to put on a reli-gious garb. Intellectuals, many of them quite secular, propagated Catholic liberation theology, but as an unambiguously religious move-ment it tried to attract people from the "popular classes." It was not ter-ribly successful in this attempt, but that is another story. Supposedly Christian socialism at least had a chance of inspiring the masses—Our Lady clutching a red banner. Marxist atheism had no chance beyond the universities.

The religious themes in the American counterculture were overt and impossible to ignore. Woodstock had the characteristic of a pilgrimage, and the much-vaunted sexual revolution was suffused with "spirituality," a curious reincarnation (literally!) of the archaic carnality of sacred orgies. As an experienced Godder, I could sniff out these themes quite early. I think my first statement of this insight came in an article pub-lished in 1974, in—of all places—the *Christian Century* (the ironically named flagship periodical of mainline Protestantism). The article was titled "Cakes for the Queen of Heaven—2,500 Years of Religious Ecstasy." The title is taken from a passage in the Book of Jeremiah, in which the prophet berates the women of Jerusalem for baking the cakes that were used in the cult of Astarte, the great mother goddess of the ancient Near East. I argued that what was happening around us was a return of sacred sexuality and that Jeremiah's rejection of it still made sense for the same reasons that he gave—both because it was idolatry in the perspective of biblical faith and because it detracted from the pursuit of justice for "the alien, the fatherless, or the widow." The more "spiritual" branches of the feminist and environmentalist movements also bought into the religious themes of the counterculture. The coming of the Age of Aquarius did not suggest a secularized culture, at least in America.

It is paradoxical that Evangelicals sprang into public awareness beyond their own subculture as a result of Jimmy Carter's campaign for the presidency. Never mind that this peanut farmer from Georgia, once ensconced in the White House, turned out to be less a born-again Christian than a born-again liberal. It was the famous White House Conference on the Family—or rather its renaming as the White House Conference on Fam*ilies*—that provoked social conservatives to walk out of the conference and that was an important impetus for the emergence of the Christian Right. In any case, Carter's political advent sparked interest in Evangelicals in the most secular locales of American culture, the intelligentsia and the media. Although I was hardly a typical denizen of either locale, it sparked my interest too; previously I had not paid attention to this religious community, nor had I been conscious of its very large numbers in the American population.

What happened is beautifully illustrated by an episode that Richard Neuhaus recounted to me. He had written about Evangelicals and was considered something of an expert. He was invited to speak to a meeting of the domestic news department of one of the major television networks. The head of the department, no less, asked the questions, which Neuhaus answered:

Q: "Now let me understand this. These people believe that in order to be saved, you have to accept Jesus as your lord and savior."

A: "That's right."

Q: "And they believe that the Bible is the authoritative Word of God."

A: "Yes, that's right."

Q: "And they also believe that history will end with the return of Jesus and a Day of Judgment."

A: "Yes, right again."

Q: "*How many of them are there?!*"

A: "Well, religious statistics are not very accurate. But there are probably between sixty and seventy million Evangelicals in America."

Q: "*Wow!*"

Since then I have had extensive and mostly very pleasant contacts with the Evangelical world. But beginning about then it became clear to me that a society with such a large, intensively religious population could hardly be called secularized.

My new understanding of the contemporary religious situation, which of course I have developed further since then, can be stated quite simply: *Modernity does not necessarily secularize; it necessarily pluralizes.* I had indeed mentioned pluralism as an outcome of modernization—the peaceful coexistence and interaction of diverse ethnic and religious groups in the same society. I had correctly argued that such a situation undermines the taken-for-grantedness of all beliefs. But I had incorrectly argued further that this must lead to a decline of religion. The mistake was this: Pluralism undermines *taken-for-granted* religion but not religion as such. There are other forms of religion, from religion as a superficial consumer preference to religion as a passionate leap of faith.

If religion is no longer a given, the individual must *choose* among different religious or, for that matter, nonreligious worldviews—some choices may well be secular. In most of the world, including America, most of the choices are religious ones.

These considerations led to a different intellectual agenda: Instead of a theory of secularization, what is needed is a theory of pluralization. What are also needed are explanations why some parts of the world (especially Europe) are more secularized than others (such as America). Both theories present challenges to faith, but they are different challenges. Secularization theory proposes that there is *a shortage of gods*; pluralization theory that there are *too many gods*. Put differently, it was thought that modernity would be an age of atheism; it turns out that, surprisingly, it is an age of polytheism.

I took a first step toward the new theory in a book published in 1979, *The Heretical Imperative: Contemporary Possibilities of Religious Affirmation*. The title was a pun on the word *heresy*, which derives from the Greek *haeresis*, which means selection or choice. The book (now out of print) was reasonably successful—quite a few reviews, five translations. The most recent translation was into French, published in 2005. It contained an introduction by a scholar (I think a Protestant theologian), who remarked that the book had been ignored in France but that now was the right time to pay attention to it. I am not sure why he thought so, but the increasing presence of Islam has made Europeans aware of the challenge of pluralism in a new way.

I described modernization as a gigantic shift in the human condition *from fate to choice* in everything from technology to institutions, lifestyles, beliefs, values—and, last but not least, religion. The reasons for this are not difficult to explain. Some basic processes of modernity—urbanization, mass migration, mass literacy, all the new media of communication—break up the kind of closed communities in which most human beings have lived through most of history. In the course of all this, modernity also breaks up the robust social consensus, which had allowed the basic definition of reality to be taken for granted. Before modernity, in most places, the gods in which an individual believed were a matter of fate, like so many other things determined by the accident of birth. Now the individual is compelled to choose among different gods made available in a market of worldviews.

I went on to analyze three ways in which religious traditions have responded to the pluralistic situation: reduction (translating the tradition into secular terms), deduction (defiantly reaffirming the pristine tradition), and induction (reformulating the tradition in an engagement with the plurality of alternatives). I illustrated these adaptations by means of selected Protestant theologians. Each adaptation has its dangers, but I concluded that induction, characteristic of liberal Protestantism, is the most plausible. In conclusion, the book discusses the new presence in the West of the great religious traditions of southern and eastern Asia—"the dharma is going west," as Buddhist missionaries have put it. For this reason Christian theology will have to engage the Asian traditions, notably Buddhism and Hinduism, in a serious dialogue.

I followed up on this suggestion myself. Employing my Viennese "coffee-house methodology," I put together a lively group of religious scholars from a variety of traditions—Jewish, Christian, Muslim, Hindu, and Buddhist. The enterprise received a small grant from a Jewish foundation, spent on travel. The project began while I lived in New York and went on after I moved to Boston. The papers of the group were published in a book in 1981 with me as editor—*The Other Side of God: A Polarity in World Religions*. I still think that this was an original contribution to the sort of interreligious dialogue I had called for. The polarity mentioned in the subtitle is between the divine to be found deep within the consciousness of human beings as against the divine encountered in a reality outside and beyond human consciousness. Everyone involved in this project understood it as a first stab at an immensely complicated task. Other concerns kept me from pursuing this task any further. From time to time I have been tempted to take it up again.

THE SKYSCRAPERS OF HONG KONG

The first city I visited in East Asia was Hong Kong. I arrived late in the evening and saw virtually nothing on the taxi ride from the airport to the hotel, where I checked in and promptly went to sleep. In the morning I got up early and drew the shades. The magnificent vista took my breath away—the harbor, with hundreds of Chinese junks at anchor, and all around the surreal cityscape of skyscrapers climbing up the hillside toward Victoria Peak. The juxtaposition of a classic Chinese scene with the artifacts of supermodernity remained with me as a metaphor for the economic miracles of East Asia. The encounter with these realities definitely changed my ideas about development and modernization.

I moved toward East Asia in stages. My first stop on the way was the Middle East. In 1976 I was invited to give a lecture in Tehran; it was published under the title "Toward a Critique of Modernity." I had some time for tourism and was greatly impressed by the culture. I don't think I learned much as a social scientist. In retrospect I was struck by the fact that, although every intellectual I met was (cautiously) opposed to the shah's regime and hoped for some sort of revolution, no one expected the Islamic revolution that was to occur two years later. In Iran, as elsewhere, intellectuals are typically unaware of the stirrings in the bazaars of the "unenlightened."

Later I visited India on a lecture tour that took me all over the country. I was drawn to India partly because of the ubiquity of religion. On a train trip I shared a compartment with a businessman who started the conversation by asking me about my views on reincarnation. However, again the experience did not have much effect on my positions as a social scientist, though (especially in Calcutta) I saw poverty more extreme than anything I had seen in Latin America or Africa.

When I first traveled to Hong Kong in 1977, again it was to give lectures. From the beginning it was this encounter that brought about a major shift in my view of the contemporary world.

The late 1970s and early 1980s were the most frenetic years of globe trekking. In one year, within months, I went around the world twice. I have just tried to figure out the chronology, did not succeed, and then concluded the obvious—that, in terms of this book, it does not matter. (No need for a chapter headed "What I Did During My Summer Vacation—Look, Mom, I Went to Tokyo!") I added Southeast Asia to my repertory, most memorably Indonesia and Thailand. In East Asia I went to Japan and what was then called the "Four Little Dragons"—South Korea, Taiwan, Hong Kong, and Singapore. I did not go to mainland China until later, after economic reforms were beginning to take hold there. The intellectual result of these peregrinations can be stated in one sentence: *I discovered capitalism.*

Subsequently it was no longer possible for me to deal evenhandedly with capitalist and socialist models of development, as I had done in *Pyramids of Sacrifice.* The encounter with East Asia made crystal clear that Brazil under military dictatorship (and for that matter other Latin American cases that called themselves "capitalist") was not a prototypical case of capitalism. East Asia demonstrates two very important points: that a capitalist model of development is uniquely capable of fundamentally improving the material conditions of life for huge numbers of people and that it can do so without destroying indigenous culture and traditions. In other words, it is possible to give passing grades to important cases of capitalism precisely on both tests that I had defined as morally crucial in *Pyramids of Sacrifice*—the calculus of pain and the calculus of meaning. No socialist case exists outside the utopian imagination.

Of course I did not reach this conclusion simply by trekking around Asia. I read voraciously about the history and the present situation of East Asia. But I would not underestimate the importance of visiting places that figure in one's theorizing—seeing, hearing, smelling, tasting them. I came to use the phrase *sociological tourism*—going to a place after one has read about it, planning one's stay so as to meet as many well-informed people as possible, and then just letting its reality seep into one's consciousness. If one proceeds like this, it is amazing how much one can learn from even a short visit. Insights augmented by living experience have a stronger persuasiveness than those gained in an armchair. As Goethe put it, "All theory is gray. How beautiful is life's golden tree!"

Figuring out the calculus of pain is not easy. It is clear that any program of development will involve a measure of pain. There are indeed no free lunches, especially in the earlier phases of economic growth. The moral question will always be what degree and what kind of pain is acceptable. Joseph Schumpeter's famous description of capitalism as "creative destruction" encapsulates the moral dilemma succinctly.

The calculus of meaning is even more difficult to figure out. One may add that it is much less congenial to economists and others who design development policy. As soon as one poses the question, one arrives at a central issue—the relation of development and culture. No culture can go through the modernization process without changes. Again, some of these changes will be painful. Which changes are morally acceptable?

The issue becomes more complicated when one must conclude that not all cultures are equally conducive to development. Traditionalists will be willing to sacrifice development goals in order to preserve this or that cultural value. There are also economists and other "developmentalists" for whom economic growth is the overriding goal and for whom cultural factors are evaluated simply in terms of their contribution to this goal. It seems to me that the term *calculus* is helpful because it pushes one toward a search for balance between the costs and the benefits of development policies.

Since in most of the world culture is inextricably linked to religion, thinking about the calculus of meaning quickly leads to territory explored by Max Weber. He is best known for his famous thesis about the relation of Protestantism and the culture of capitalism. But Weber's vast opus exploring the economic and social consequences of the major religious traditions is equally relevant. The East Asian economic miracles have led to an extensive debate of a quasi-Weberian nature: Were there cultural factors that can help explain these success stories? The so-called "post-Confucian hypothesis" gave a tentative answer. All the countries in question have a legacy of Confucian ethics—a moral system that encourages discipline, hard work, education, and respect for authority. Classical Confucianism did not allow these values to be economically effective. The Confucian elite, the mandarin class, despised commerce. But when Chinese people were torn out of the original context of Confucianism, the same values suddenly showed their economic potential. Not the Confucian ideology of the imperial bureaucracy, but the vulgar Confucianism of Chinese entrepreneurs in Hong Kong, Taipei, and Singapore can now be seen as a functional equivalent of Weber's "Protestant ethic." This is evident even more dramatically in places like Manila and Jakarta, where Chinese minorities have achieved economic success vastly disproportionate to their numbers. The same ethic can be seen at work in non-Chinese societies influenced by Confucianism, notably in Japan and Korea.

To get ahead of the chronology that I have followed more or less in this book so far, I have kept thinking about these matters ever since. In 1988 a book was published, coedited by me and Hsin-Huang Michael Hsiao (a Taiwanese sociologist), which attracted a good deal of attention—*In Search of an East Asian Development Model.* (The book contained papers from a conference hosted by the Council on Religion and International Affairs [CRIA], the outfit that had hosted our by-then-defunct periodical *Worldview.*) Like all empirical phenomena, this one gets more complicated the longer one looks into it. Neither Hsiao nor I are "culturalists." We did not, and do not, claim that culture is *the* explanation of the success stories of East Asia (which now, very significantly, include mainland China—a truly ironic case of a ruthless capitalist society ruled by a regime that still calls itself communist). However, I continue to be convinced that specific cultural values dominant in East

Asian populations are *an* important factor explaining their economic successes. To what extent these values are "post-Confucian" is another question. For example, a Chinese anthropologist I met through Hsiao has claimed that Confucianism is just an intellectual elaboration of themes endemic in Chinese folk religion.

The social scientist concerned with this matter will not focus on texts and official rhetoric but on the way in which values operate on the level of ordinary life.

During one of my visits to Singapore, Vivienne Wee, a bright, young anthropologist of Chinese ethnicity, wanted to show me one of the increasingly rare areas of traditional Malay architecture. As we walked around the area, I agreed that the houses were indeed more attractive than the huge blocks of public housing favored by the authorities. Then Wee saw a flag sticking out from one of the houses. She exclaimed, "Ah, Chinese spirit temple! We have to go in!" The temple turned out to be an ordinary apartment. The owner happened to be in, a young electrician, who on one or two evenings a week functioned as a medium, putting clients in touch with the spirit world. He spoke no English, and Wee had to translate.

What he wanted to tell us about first left no doubt that this was an individual with an intact sense of the supernatural. He complained that he was harassed by a Malay demon, who lived in a tree behind the house. He felt that he had to explain that Chinese spirits could live in houses but not on any natural habitats, such as trees or rocks. On the other hand, Malay spirits could only live in natural habitats because, like human Malays, they were "sons of the soil."

He then took us to the living room, which contained a bookcase holding several shelves with statuettes of Chinese gods and spirits. On the top shelf was the Chinese goddess of mercy, occupying the most prestigious location in the little pantheon. The medium explained that he used all these characters to contact the spirit world, to bring deceased relatives on line (so to speak), and to answer prayers. He then described various denizens of his magical bookcase: "This one has been very useful. We have moved him up, right below the goddess. But this one is no good at all. We have put him on the lowest shelf. If he doesn't shape up soon, we'll throw him out completely." What impressed me was that this purveyor of supernatural services spoke of the spirits very much like a manager rating employees—with a peculiar mix of a mythological worldview and hard-nosed pragmatism. Perhaps similar combinations can be found in other peasant cultures, but this episode helped me understand the suggestion that the Confucian ethic rests on a foundation of a distinctive Chinese folk religion.

The behavior of children is particularly important because values first learned in childhood exercise a lifelong influence. (If modern psychology has taught us anything, it is this.) I had an instructive experience in this regard in Korea.

There was a break in the supposedly erudite conference I was attending in Seoul. I cannot remember what it was (as I cannot remember many such events that seemed so important at the time). I joined a small group that took a bus to a place at some distance from the city. This was a reconstructed traditional Korean village. After inspecting this theme park we were taken to a small amphitheater, were a folk-dancing performance was to take place. No folk dancers were in evidence. We sat down on the bleachers to wait for them. Shortly after our arrival, a bus full of schoolchildren drove up. They were all boys, aged somewhere between six and eight. The accompanying teachers made the boys sit down on the bleachers as well. The dancers still did not show up. It was summer, and it was uncomfortably hot. There was no shade. The boys wore uniforms made of some thick material. I could see that they were sweating. The teachers did what one does on such occasions. They played little games with the boys, told stories, led them in singing. The dancers were still not coming. We all sat waiting for them, for something like forty-five minutes, after which we and the teachers gave up and we all left for our respective busses.

What I found impressive was the behavior of the boys. During the entire period of waiting in the hot sunshine, there was not a single incident of disorderly behavior, let alone rebellion. The boys must have been very uncomfortable, but they sat quietly and did whatever they were told. I decided that I could not imagine a group of American or European children behaving like this. Were we seeing the Korean economic miracle at its biographically primordial roots?

Weber coined the phrase "this-worldly asceticism," an ethic of discipline and delayed gratification that is probably indispensable in the first stages of modern economic takeoff. I told Brigitte about the Korean schoolboys when I got home from this trip. She was not sure about my quasi-Weberian interpretation, observing that a hundred years ago German children would have behaved in the same way. At the time this seemed to me to cast doubt on my interpretation. Later on I thought that actually her observation supported my interpretation: German economic development in the late nineteenth century was roughly where the South Korean economy was a hundred years later. Much later I sharpened this thought: The "Protestant ethic" comes with an expiration date. Put differently: Only a wealthy society can afford misbehaving children (and, presumably, can afford me!).

What is important here is that in East Asia, elements of traditional culture have adapted to the enormous changes of development and modernization. Long after my Korea excursion, the Israeli sociologist Shmuel Eisenstadt coined the concept of "multiple modernities." There is not a single path to modernity. Modernization is not necessarily synonymous with Westernization. I increasingly came to look at Japan as the most important case in point—the first non-Western country to modernize successfully, while maintaining many elements of its traditional culture. I read a lot, especially about the period of rapid development in the last decades of the nineteenth century. My older son, Thomas, specialized in Japan as a political scientist. I learned a lot from him, and I visited him with some frequency during the three years he lived in Japan.

I have been particularly fascinated by the speed with which the modernization of Japan took place. In 1857 Commodore Perry of the US Navy steamed into Tokyo Bay and forced Japan to open itself to international trade. The shock of this naked act of imperialism was enormous to a nation that had successfully shut itself off from the outside world for about two hundred years. But the Japanese were not ignorant of how China had become a victim of similar acts of Western imperialism. In 1868 there was a coup d'etat against the feudal shogun regime, misleadingly called the Meiji Restoration. Supposedly the insurrection was to restore the power of the emperor, who had been a mere figurehead under the old regime. But the real power now resided not with the Meiji ermperor but with an oligarchy from the old warrior caste. The slogan of the new regime was "Revere the emperor! Expel the barbarians!" In other words: Avoid the fate of China! Maybe they did revere the emperor, but they did not expel the barbarians. Rather, they learned from them, turned the knowledge against them, and prevented them from colonizing Japan.

Soon after the events of 1868, the new rulers did something that must be unique in history. They assembled a large delegation that undertook a lengthy journey through all the advanced societies of America and Europe to see what they could learn that would be useful to Japan. When the delegation returned, the regime systematically reconstructed all the major institutions of the society—from a modern navy to a modern market economy. The feudal system was abolished, resulting in a very effective land reform and, ingeniously, allowing groups of feudal aristocrats to become capitalists by investing the funds they received in compensation for their lost lands. Yet all this occurred under a symbolic canopy of traditional values, changed yet preserved at the same time. Thus the feudal ethic of loyalty and discipline of the samurai caste became "democratized," taught to all classes of society, and transformed into a modern business culture. Bushido, the old warrior code, morphed into quality control and lifetime employment!

The trajectory in time of this transformation is breathtaking. The delegation to the West left a few years after the 1868 coup. In 1895, when the institutional revamping was in full swing, the imperial edict on education made primary schooling for all boys compulsory (it was later extended to girls and to secondary schools). Yet this modern system of education, a highly meritocratic one, instituted grueling examinations that bore a striking resemblance to the examinations of classical Confucianism. The process may be seen as culminating in 1905, when Japan defeated Russia, one of the great European powers, on land and on the sea. Changes that in the West had taken centuries had been compressed into a few decades.

The modernizing transformations in other East Asian countries since the 1950s happened even faster. Of course these processes were not without costs. Yet no one who visits East Asia today can think that these societies are mired in Third World poverty, or that they have become simple replicas of Europe or America. If present developments in the People's Republic of China continue, there will emerge a great power that will be undeniably both modern and non-Western. Someone once quipped that, if all the millions of Chinese jumped up and down at the same time, the planet would be thrown off its course. Perhaps they already have.

MAYBE GOOD NEWS?

In the midst of all this globalism I undertook my one and only foray into domestic social policy. Like so much else during those years, it began with conversations among Richard Neuhaus, Brigitte, and myself in the living room of our Brooklyn brownstone. Brigitte, who had increasingly concerned herself with questions of family policy, was the one who suggested to Neuhaus and me that some radical reformulations of social policy were much needed. We talked with other people about this, with the result that the American Enterprise Institute (AEI), the conservative think tank in Washington, asked Neuhaus and me to write a paper outlining what such a reformulation might look like.

We obliged and produced this paper in a very short time (neither of us, perhaps regrettably, suffered from writer's block). AEI published the paper as a booklet in 1977—*To Empower People: Mediating Structures and Public Policy*. This text was republished by AEI in book form, with added essays, on the occasion of its twentieth anniversary. The fate of this little text, barely fifty pages in length, has been rather amazing. As far as I know, the AEI book is still in print. Perhaps the ultimate sign of success is that the term *mediating structures*, which we concocted, is now used without mention of its origin—it has become a common noun like *fridge* or *coke*.

This is all the more remarkable since the argument we made was not terribly original. We did invent the term, but what it referred to was anything but new. It referred to the intermediate institutions that stand between individual life and the megastructures of a modern society, notably the state, the economy, and other vast bureaucracies. There is a long tradition in social theory arguing for the importance of these institutions: They protect the individual from feeling alienated in society, and they bestow legitimacy on the megastructures by linking them to the living values of personal life. The classical French sociologist Emile Durkheim paid intense attention to these institutions. But there are also analogous arguments in theories of the Right (Edmund Burke's praise of the "small platoons") and the Left (Georges Sorel and the ideology of "syndicalism"). Very importantly, one finds such ideas in Catholic social thought with its concept of "subsidiarity," which suggests that policy should always prefer those typically small institutions that are close to the actual lives of ordinary people. Last but not least, there is a specifically American tradition of "communitarianism" to which our approach could appeal.

Be this as it may, our argument was succinctly put. Without mediating structures, individuals will experience the social order as alien or even hostile, and the large institutions of society, especially the state, will lack legitimacy because of this remoteness from the values by which people live. We discussed four such institutions—family, neighborhood, church, and voluntary association (by *church* we meant any religious institution, not just Christian ones). We proposed that the policies of the welfare state often undermine these institutions. We then made two overall recommendations. The first, echoing the maxim of the Hippocratic oath—"Above all, do not harm!"—urged policymakers to take great care not to weaken or destroy mediating structures. The second recommendation was the more debatable one—that, as far as possible, social policy should utilize mediating structures in realizing specific purposes.

The book was a big success almost immediately. Despite its publication by a right-of-center think tank, it was applauded across the political spectrum. It was also misunderstood across that spectrum, which no doubt explains its success. On the right, the concept of mediating structures was understood as including all institutions except the state; that is, it was understood as synonymous with the broadest possible understanding of "civil society." Thus General Motors would also be called a mediating structure, which would be absurd; it is not just the political sphere that brings forth megastructures. On the other hand, small political units (say, a local government that stays close to its constituents) can serve a mediating function. On the left, mediating structures were understood as grassroots organizations that are agents of social change. Of course this may be the case with some of them. Others, however, can simply be local branches of megastructures seeking to mobilize people, who become, if you will, objects of colonization by this or that large institution. Also, this understanding is much too narrow. There can be mediating structures without any activist purposes—for example, the African American churches before the civil rights era, which provided havens of meaning and dignity to an oppressed people.

In the intervening years, especially on the occasion of anniversary celebrations, claims have been made (not by Neuhaus or me) that *To Empower People* has had a great influence on social policy in the United States, such as on various reforms of welfare or on the developments that led to the faith-based initiative. I am skeptical of such claims. What I rather think is that the little booklet came at just the right moment, when serious questions were raised about the efficacy of the American welfare state and about the unintended consequences of the large bureaucratic institutions that administered its programs. The concept of mediating structures legitimated these concerns and became a handy term for reformers of just about any ideological coloration.

Over the years Neuhaus and I have discussed what we wrote in *To Empower People.* We agree that we still stand by its argument. But we would be more careful to clarify what the term *mediating structures* means and, importantly, what it does not mean. Against the two misunderstandings, we should have made clearer that mediating is as mediating does. There is a parallel here with the diverse understandings of another concept, which became popular a little later—the concept of "civil society." The Mafia, for instance, could be subsumed under either concept—it does mediate between personal values and the larger society for the Mafiosi, and it definitely is not an arm of the state (except perhaps in New Jersey). But the values it upholds are certainly not civil, and the mediation it performs is socially undesirable.

The analogy with good and bad cholesterol is suggestive. Doctors used to think that all cholesterol is bad; then good cholesterol was discovered. We tended to think that all mediating structures are good, but there are also bad ones. What one must ask then is not just whether a particular institution mediates but what are the values that are being mediated.

Also, I think that we greatly underestimated the corrupting effect that frequently occurred when grassroots organizations became agents of government programs. A few years earlier Great Society programs were mandated to include "maximum feasible participation" by community groups. The corrupting (and of course unintended) consequences of this were sharply exposed in Patrick Moynihan's book *Maximum Feasible Misunderstanding*. When Max Weber discussed the unintended consequences of social action, he did not call his position "Murphy's law." He might have.

AEI sponsored a research project built around the argument of the book. The project was generously funded. Neuhaus and I assembled a team to explore how mediating structures could be deployed in specific policy areas—health, education, housing, and crime prevention. Some of the papers produced by the team were interesting. But I think it is fair to say that the project as a whole did not lead to any startling insights.

CRIA, where our little periodical *Worldview* was located, also housed an office of the project. Some of the team meetings were held in the posh quarters of the Lehrman Institute, which was also on the Upper East Side. Right up until my move from New York to Boston in 1979, Neuhaus and I had a Manhattan division of our floating coffee-house conversation, sort of an extension of my Brooklyn living room, with an expanding and varied group of interlocutors. P. J. Moriarty's remained our favorite feeding station.

The most interesting team was the one dealing with crime prevention. It was led by Robert Woodson, an African American activist whom I met at the Urban League. He had become increasingly skeptical of the liberal approach to the racial problem. One of his favorite exclamations was, "The helping hand strikes again!" Our concept of mediating structures immediately struck a chord with him. He was then in the process of founding the institution he still directs in Washington, DC, the National Center for Neighborhood Enterprise—its name succinctly describes its approach. In the same vein he looked into local, largely informal community initiatives to prevent juvenile crime.

The most memorable occasion I recall from the time of the AEI project was a conference organized by Woodson to discuss the possibility of steering juvenile gangs toward legitimate economic enterprises. The conference took place at the Mayflower Hotel in Washington. Brigitte and I were the only outside consultants. Except for Woodson's small staff and us, the attendees were all gang members from various inner-city neighborhoods on the East Coast. As they filed in, dressed up in leather and metal clasps right out of central casting, the Mayflower waiters were visibly tightening up. I am quite sure that hotel security was put on alert. Woodson was very much in charge of the discussion, presiding with great verve. As was to be expected, the discussion was brash and lively. Overall the gang members reacted positively to Woodson's proposals, though I don't know to what extent they followed through.

My most vivid recollection is of a group from a Latino gang from the Bronx. The gang leader was there, a self-confident young man, accompanied by his strikingly attractive girlfriend. It was a motorcycle gang. Woodson pitched this idea to him: His members obviously knew a lot about motorcycles. Supposedly there was a shortage of repair facilities for motorcycles (I have no idea how Woodson knew this). Why not have this gang start a network, perhaps a national one, of motorcycle repair shops? Various technicalities were discussed. I asked the gang leader whether he was sure that his members would want to work in these shops. He smiled in a rather sinister way: "If I tell them, they will!" The girlfriend chuckled.

6

POLITICALLY INCORRECT EXCURSIONS

In 1979 Brigitte received an offer to become sociology chairman at Wellesley College. It seemed like a more interesting job than her professorship at Long Island University. (It turned out to be interesting in a rather unpleasant way: Wellesley was then, as it is now, a fortress of doctrinaire feminism, which Brigitte found uncongenial and which motivated her to go elsewhere after a few years.) I was not greatly attached to Rutgers, and I had no professional hesitations about relocating to the Boston area. I quickly found a job on the faculty of Boston College, where I stayed for two years before moving to Boston University for a more attractive appointment as a university professor—an interdisciplinary post, supposedly in sociology, religion, and theology.

Both of us did have personal hesitations about leaving New York and its cosmopolitan dynamism for the more sedate environment of Boston academia. Shortly after moving I read a newspaper article about people who had made the same move. It contained one memorable observation: In Boston your waiter reads Dostoyevsky, because of course he is a student; in New York your waiter is a character out of Dostoyevsky.

At the time we could not anticipate the length of our stay: At this time of writing it has been thirty years since our move to Boston. We have found it a generally pleasant place to live—leaving aside the weather in January and February, in anticipation of which I had purchased a forbiddingly heavy overcoat, which made me look like a Russian general and which I wore only once or twice.

But it is fair to say that we did not become fully naturalized Yankees. Indeed, whenever I am asked where I am from, I recall an old Jewish joke: This ultra-Orthodox rabbi from the Lower East Side goes to visit his son, who has started a business in a small town in Mississippi. The old man descends from the bus exhibiting a complete Orthodox persona—beard, side locks, black hat, kaftan with fringes. A few kids are gaping at him. He says to them, "What's the matter with you? Have you never seen a Yankee before?"

First impressions are often instructive. Early on Brigitte observed, "This is not a city. It is a federation of campuses." True enough. The fact is double-edged. On the one hand, it is satisfying to know that there is no field without an expert within a fifteen-minute drive. Not long after our arrival, at a party in Cambridge, I met Harvard's professor of Mongolian literature. On the other hand, there is a left-leaning political culture that can be oppressive (and not only at Wellesley). Another joke, this time Yankee rather than Jewish: The very last headline in the *Boston Globe*—"World Ends Tomorrow. Women and Minorities Hit Hardest."

Logically enough, my first encounter with this culture occurred at Harvard. (Sociological finding: Contrary to Marxist theory, the wealthier a locale is, the more left-leaning it will be.) One of the things I had looked forward to in moving to the Boston area was its large number of theological institutions. I hoped that this would provide more theological interlocutors than were available in New York. I sent out some feelers and was appointed as a supposedly prestigious William James Lecturer at the Harvard Divinity School for the academic year 1979–1980. This simply involved teaching one course in the sociology of religion. My first disappointment came when no one on the faculty there took any notice of my arrival, with the exception of Harvey Cox, who was always amicable despite our large theological and political differences. I soon realized that both the mainline Protestant and the

Roman Catholic institutions in the area were dominated by the local political fundamentalists, with whom useful conversation was impossible. Not so dominated were two outriders—the Evangelical Gordon-Conwell Seminary and the Greek Orthodox Seminary of the Holy Cross—but there were of course other problems of communication. This situation, by the way, has improved slightly since then, as the "sixties generation" is tottering from tenured faculty positions to Medicare entitlement. But the sharpest disappointment came soon after I started my course at the Harvard Divinity School.

After a few sessions of the course I was presented with a long, somewhat incoherent letter signed by most if not all the female students. The letter was fairly polite in tone. It addressed me as "*Lieber Herr Doktor*" and began by saying how much the undersigned had learned from my work. But then it protested sharply against my conduct of the course, which, it was claimed, "linguistically excluded [the women in the course] from both the form and content of your class as presently constructed." Actually, there was no protest against any of the content that was taught; the protest was against the content that was *not* taught—that is, the standard topics of feminist ideology. But what evidently irked the letter writers most was that I used "gender-exclusive language"—that is, the generic masculine. The letter stated that it was intended to invite not battle but dialogue.

I (in retrospect foolishly) accepted the invitation to dialogue. I had not yet learned the lesson that dialogue with fundamentalists is futile. A time outside the regular class schedule was agreed upon, and most of the students showed up for the occasion. Given the usual tenor of such events, it was relatively civilized. After all, this *was* Harvard; not long afterward a lecture of mine at the London School of Economics was noisily disrupted and terminated by a screaming mob. (What enraged this lot was my saying that sociology was radical in its debunking perspective but conservative in its practical implications.) Nevertheless, here there was no dialogue of any sort but rather an endless repetition of the same denunciations. There was no follow-up to the confrontation, but I finished the course mechanically without any real rapport with the students.

It is impossible to have lived through the last few decades in American or European academia without encountering this type of feminist militancy (though, as mentioned above, it has mostly diminished in decibel). There are aspects of feminism with which, I think, any decent person would agree—notably the determination to proscribe all forms of legal or social discrimination against women. I recall a conversation in the early sixties with a male sociologist who said, without embarrassment, that he would adamantly oppose the appointment of any more women in his department. Such a conversation would be impossible today, and that is real progress. I also have no problems with the feminist affirmation of a woman's sexuality in any form she finds plausible. Another matter, though, is the continuing definition of women as victims—and that in the Western societies which have accorded to women a degree of privilege unequalled in human history and indeed unequalled in any other contemporary society.

As to the linguistic issue, which so agitated my Harvard students, it struck me as absurd from the first moment I came across it. The very substitution of *gender* for *sex* already implies an empirically untenable proposition, namely that there are no significant differences between men and women (except for the presumably minor difference in the shape of the genitalia). *Sex* is a biological term, *gender* a grammatical one—and grammar is completely arbitrary and therefore freely changeable. As to the generic masculine, I doubt whether, prior to the advent of recent feminism, any child over the age of five believed that the generic use of *man*—as in "the rights of man"—excluded women. The empirical reality is the opposite from the one assumed in the feminist rhetoric: the old syntax was simply standard English and in no way excluded women, but the new syntax, self-defined as "inclusive," deliberately excludes and marginalizes all dissenters from feminist ideology.

There is an analogy that I have found useful in thinking about this issue (I did not use it in my Harvard "dialogue," because it would have enraged these students even more). Modern Italian, like most European languages other than English, makes a linguistic distinction between informal and formal communication. The informal address, used in intimate communication, is *tu* (as in German *du*). The formal address is *lei* (as in German *Sie*). Modern English, possibly to its impoverishment, cannot make this distinction with its status-neutral *you*. Grammatically, Italian *lei* is third-person plural. It is as though in formal conversation in English, one asked an individual, "Do they want more coffee?" Sometime in the 1930s Mussolini made a speech about this. He said that *lei* was effeminate. Since the Fascist revolution intended to restore Roman ideals of virility, the good Fascist did not say *lei* but *voi* (which is second-person plural, actually like English *you*, though what Mussolini had in mind was the Latin *vos*). Now, in terms of the empirical reality of modern Italian diction, this made no sense at all. Before Mussolini's speech it would have not occurred to anyone that *lei* was effeminate. But after his speech no one could use these terms innocently. Whoever said *voi* gave the linguistic equivalent of the Fascist salute (the outstretched arm, another Roman thing). And whoever said *lei* made, however mutedly, an anti-Fascist gesture.

Come to think of it, Mussolini was inconsistent. Both men and women Fascists were instructed to say *voi*, but presumably only men were to aspire to Roman virility. To be consistent, Mussolini would have had to devise different languages for men and for women. But that would have meant imposing Japanese syntax on the existing Italian language, which, apart from its inherent difficulty, would have negated Mussolini's Roman project.

"I THANK THE HONORABLE REPRESENTATIVE OF THE UNITED STATES FOR HIS STATEMENT."

If I had "been struggled" at a mass meeting in a postrevolutionary America, as some of my Maoist students may have wished, there would at least have been three accusations against me. I was clearly guilty of linguistic oppression of all female comrades. Two other counts would probably have been added: serving as a propagandist for American imperialism and giving comfort and aid to the merchants of death (also known as the tobacco industry). On second thought, the last count might have been omitted: all the comrades (male or female) whom I met during those years smoked like chimneys.

As a result of hanging around with the neoconservative crowd, I knew several people in the newly elected Reagan administration. One of them was Elliott Abrams, who was first assistant secretary of state for international organization affairs and soon afterward for human rights (this was before he moved over to the Latin America bureau, where he became entangled in the Iran-Contra debacle). Early in 1981 I received a phone call from him, which he opened rather solemnly: "Peter, I want you to do something for your country." For one scary moment I saw myself engaged in some sinister clandestine exercise (Did I have an intuition of what Abrams would be up to a little later?), but the mission turned out to be less dramatic: I was to represent the United States in a newly formed offshoot of the United Nations Commission on Human Rights called the Working Group on the Right to Development. It sounded interesting, right up my alley. What was also promising was that two other individuals from the *Commentary* crowd were being appointed to relevant positions—Jeanne Kirkpatrick as ambassador to the United Nations and Michael Novak as American representative to the Commission on Human Rights. Relieved that I was not to be parachuted into a Warsaw Pact country, I accepted the assignment.

I spent a day being briefed in Washington, DC. I saw Abrams for only a brief meeting. I remember only one moment from that occasion. I was with some other people visiting the State Department, one of whom asked if he could smoke. Abrams replied: "In this administration you can smoke *anywhere*!" Those were the days.

I spent a long time being given the background of this newly proposed right to development and how this related to various American interests. It had been invented some years previously by a group of Senegalese law professors. I was not told how this came about. In any case, this putative contribution to international law gathered dust in some government office in Dakar, until it was discovered and enthusiastically endorsed by a French law professor, who wrote a book about it. This individual was close to the newly elected Mitterand government, which became interested in this matter (presumably as part of an intention to look good in the eyes of the Third World). Not surprisingly, the French law professor was appointed as his country's representative to the working group—my counterpart in that historic exercise.

The main American interest in this affair was, if possible, to forestall yet another effort to use a United Nations platform to attack the United States as the major proponent of imperialism, capitalist exploitation, racism, apartheid, and similar accusations typical of Third World demonology. I was then given a sizable list of formulations that I must never accept. On the flight back to Boston I realized that I had been given no positive instructions whatever.

The working group was to meet in Geneva, and I was on my way there within a couple weeks of the Washington briefing. I was met at the airport by a lawyer attached to the American mission, a pleasant individual whom I called my babysitter. He was at first suspicious of me, assuming that as an appointee of the Reagan administration I must be some sort of right-wing fanatic; he mellowed very soon, as I did not seem to correspond with his original assumption. He apologized for bringing this up when I must be jet-lagged, but the French were very eager to meet with me and would like to have dinner this evening. I agreed, got a couple hours of sleep in the afternoon, then went to the dinner.

There were four people there—in addition to my babysitter and me, there were the law professor who was my French counterpart and his babysitter, a diplomat of Algerian-Jewish background (who later gave us to understand that he regarded the entire affair as being utterly senseless). It was an excellent dinner, lasting for several hours. At about 10:00 in the evening, when I was barely awake, I found myself saying with great assurance that the United States had this position, would not accept that position, and other statements in this vein. I returned to my hotel with a greatly impaired sense of reality and phoned Brigitte to restore that sense.

The next day I said to my babysitter that I really had no idea what I should say when the working group convened, other than some polite remarks—I had no instructions. He said that was easy—I should write my instructions myself—that is, I should write what I thought I should say. I did this, essentially writing a very brief essay on my understanding of the nature of development and on why formulating a right to development made little sense. Two days later the reply came back from Washington. It repeated verbatim the statement I had sent there, just with the syntax changed: where I had written "the American representative suggests saying the following," the text now read "the American representative *will say* the following." I asked my babysitter whether this is how it usually worked. He replied, "No, only in matters about which Washington does not care."

As I recall, the full working group assembled, for the first time, two days after my arrival. It was a thoroughly depressing group. The chairman, logically enough, was the Senegalese ambassador, an enormous black man who was driven in a shining Mercedes and who only spoke French. He was invariably courteous. The only two countries that, one hoped, might support us were France and the Netherlands. That hope did not materialize, since both had their own axes to grind and were eager to please the Third World representatives. That list included

Algeria, Cuba, Ethiopia (then ruled by a Marxist dictatorship), and Syria—a noble crew in a gathering about human rights. There were representatives from Panama and Peru—I cannot remember their ever saying anything. Two countries that later turned out most promising for our side were India and Yugoslavia. And of course there was the Soviet Union, with Poland as a sidekick.

It is hard to imagine a less inspiring bunch. The Soviet representative was a sour, seemingly depressed person of middle age. We always sat next to each other, USA and USSR in alphabetical order. Of course we always disagreed, but at least he was minimally polite. The Cuban was my particular nemesis, a young ideologue who attacked me shrilly and personally in rapid Spanish (which, unfortunately, I understood without putting on my earphones). When I began to dream about him, I realized that I had probably participated in these meetings long enough.

I was a member of the working group for about two and a half years, going to Geneva twice a year for about a week at a time. The work (if one can call it that) proceeded at a snail's pace. Most statements were made "*ad referendum*," which, as I learned, meant that they were preliminary and would have to be referred back to the home government. There were endless debates over minor clauses in various proposed formulations of the alleged right to development, mostly wrapped in this or that ideological rhetoric.

There was an additional delay, which at first I did not understand: Every time after someone spoke, the chairman, in impeccable French, would say, "I thank the honorable representative of So-and-So for his statement," and then *repeat* what was just said in somewhat shortened form. I came to understand that this seemingly pointless exercise had two useful functions. It gave everyone some time to consider a response. But also (as I understood when the chairman did it to me), he very slightly changed what had been said, smoothing the rougher edges and pushing the statement, even if by a little mistranslation, in the direction of a possible consensus. The man knew his business.

He was very friendly to me, once inviting me to lunch at his apartment, which turned out to be embarrassing: Only he and I were there, along with his manservant—a white Englishman, who, I think, was drunk, as he kept stumbling and dropped a dish. I did my best to pretend that I did not see the antics of the unfortunate fellow, but the ambassador was mortified, and it was a thoroughly trying occasion.

My trips to Geneva became a routine, at times boring but also mildly interesting on occasion. I think I went to Washington one more time, but, as had correctly been pointed out to me, nobody there was really interested in the right to development. Jeanne Kirkpatrick wanted to be briefed. I had dinner with her and some of her staff in New York. (I did not like her. She impressed me as arrogant and opinionated.)

The French gradually lost interest as well, but I was asked to come to Paris at one point, when it seemed that we might get through a compromise. The State Department's low degree of interest was manifest on this occasion: I had asked for my babysitter to come along, because legal issues were likely to come up, but permission was refused; when I asked the legal counsel of the American embassy in Paris to come to the meeting, he said that he had another meeting that he had to attend. The French (in addition to the law professor, a couple of lower-echelon foreign ministry officials) treated me in a politely patronizing manner and took me to lunch in a rather sleazy bistro.

Apart from reiterating disagreement with the more egregious reiterations of Third World and Soviet ideology, the American position was focused on one point: human rights pertained to individuals, not to collectivities. If the putative right to development was to belong to collectivities, notably to states, then it could not be a human right. This disagreement came up again and again.

Somewhat to my surprise, my most useful contacts were with the Indian and Yugoslav representatives. The Indian was not an official of the foreign ministry but a civil servant from the state of Kerala—one of the most successfully developing states. He was also a very pious

Hindu. We struck up something like a friendship, based on a number of searching conversations. He knew enough about development to know that Third World rhetoric was nonsensical. Gradually we cooked up a compromise: Yes, the right of development could be called a human right, if its bearers were individuals, but it could have a collective dimension by way of the right of association and the right of self-determination. I presented this formulation to the State Department, which okayed it (absentmindedly, I surmise). The French and Dutch were willing to go along. The Indian got New Delhi to agree, and the Yugoslav (a Slovenian apparatchik, who advertised his socialist credentials by always addressing the Russian and the Cuban as "comrade") got an okay from Belgrade. The Indian thought that he could get the nonaligned caucus (the so-called G-77) to agree as well. He was wrong. The Cuban succeeded in mobilizing the opposition, and our draft was voted down.

At that point I wrote to the State Department that my usefulness in this matter had come to an end. I had tried to play the role of "good cop"; if the United States was to be represented in the working group at all, it should be by a "bad cop" who would offer no compromises at all. (Verbally I suggested a secretary from the Geneva embassy, who would say nothing beyond voting no and would ostentatiously read the *Wall Street Journal*.)

I don't know whether I had a successor in the working group. I received a very gracious letter of thanks from Elliott Abrams. The working group adopted a formulation of the right of development, which contained all the provisions that were unacceptable to the United States and which was duly passed by the General Assembly. Of course it signified nothing.

Apart from having some fun, I learned a number of things from this episode. About American foreign policy, I realized how isolated the United States is in this type of forum, but I also noted that, whenever I spoke, everyone, including the Russian and the Cuban, listened very carefully. I was also very favorably impressed by all the American foreign service officers I met both in Geneva and in Washington. About the United Nations, I had no romantic illusions, but, if anything, I gained a slightly more favorable view of it. Of course most of what is said there is empty rhetoric, with no relationship to empirical realities, including talk about that mythical entity "the international community." But there is at least one useful function—the big powers don't need the United Nations to deal with each other—but small countries, like Senegal, do need this forum, in which they can have their voice heard and have some influence on the course of events.

But the main reason for including the episode in this book is that it was a concrete case in which insights gained as a social scientist—in this case, on the meaning of development—could be applied to a political process. I found this fact gratifying, even though the locale of the application frustrated its usefulness.

There was one slightly bizarre incident toward the end of my career as a "running dog of American imperialism." In late 1983 I received an invitation to attend a meeting of a group of businessmen concerned with Central America and the Caribbean. Except for a visit as a tourist to Guatemala years before, I knew little about Central America. But I had become interested in the Caribbean for two reasons. A former student of mine, Barry Levine, had become editor of a new journal, *Caribbean Review*, which I read both for its lively style and for its information about a fascinating region. And I had been intrigued by the election in 1980 of Edward Seaga as prime minister of Jamaica. He had trounced Michael Manley, who had loudly embraced Fidel Castro and announced that he would lead Jamaica toward socialism. Seaga (who was elected almost simultaneously with Ronald Reagan) launched the country on an unambiguously capitalist development plan. He actually referred to East Asia as his model. Obviously, that was relevant to me. Jamaican culture is about as different as one can get from the "post-Confucian" cultures of East Asia. Thus Jamaica could become a test case for the role of culture in development.

I accepted the invitation to what turned out to be rather strange event. The meeting took place on a ranch in western Texas belonging to a very wealthy businessman, a veritably stereotypical Texan (big hat and cowboy boots included). I flew by commercial airline into Dallas, where a private plane picked up me and another participant. We touched down on a landing strip in the middle of nowhere, on a ranch that, we were proudly told, was roughly the size of the state of Delaware. Its owner did not actually live on this property but used it for various meetings. There was a caretaker couple, a retired Marine and his wife, and a young man who on this occasion ferried people from and to the landing strip in a pickup truck. The accommodations were simple but comfortable.

I was one of three or four invited intellectuals, all deemed to be friendly to the Reagan administration. Then there were four or five businessmen, friends of the owner. They flew in on *their* private planes. As I recall, we were on the ranch for two working days, though I could not see much work being done. The meetings were informal. The discussion was exclusively about Central America and US interests there, especially with regard to the Sandinista regime in Nicaragua. No one except me seemed interested in the Caribbean. I had difficulty figuring out why I had been invited or, for that matter, what the meeting was all about.

I found out some years later. I don't know whether any discussions took place without my presence (the ranch was spacious). But I later learned that all the businessmen present were sympathetic to the US efforts to undermine the Sandinista regime. Since I was never made privy to whatever secret involvement the other participants had with these efforts, I can only imagine that I was invited to give some sort of academic cover to the meeting. At the time I was rather puzzled. Asked what I might be interested in doing for the group, I mentioned that I would like to take a closer look at Jamaica. I was promptly commissioned to visit Jamaica and write a report to the group about the situation there. The exercise was generously funded.

I spent the following weeks reading assiduously about Jamaica and the Caribbean and, with the help of Levine, preparing my trip there. That turned out to be a successful exercise of "sociological tourism." I spent a week in Kingston, interviewing a remarkably broad spectrum of people—some in the Seaga government and some in the opposition party, intellectuals of different ideological positions, and two officials from the American embassy. It was an intensive week. Since I found Kingston to be a dangerous and generally unattractive place, there were no distractions. When I left, I had an unusually rich store of information about the country. I wrote a lengthy report titled "The Case of Jamaica" for my "clients," who appeared totally uninterested and immediately gave permission for the text to be published, which I did in *Caribbean Review*. And that was the end of my brief career as a Jamaica expert.

Apart from acquiring an unexpected and only temporarily relevant acquaintance with Jamaica, and apart from being tickled retrospectively about possibly having been on the fringes of a clandestine operation, what did I learn from this episode?

I had some refreshing insights into Texan culture. On the ranch I was impressed by the democratic character of our host. He prepared breakfast for everyone, saying that the caretaker couple were elderly and should not be bothered that early in the morning. The pickup-driving young man always ate with us, participated (not very intelligently) in the conversation at table, and at one point contradicted something said by his boss (who did not seem to mind).

The latter was obsessed by the issue of illegal immigration. He favored stringent border controls, including some sort of physical barrier. He took us up on his plane, flying along the Rio Grande, so we could see ourselves how vulnerable the border was. He later told us that hundreds of illegals came across his property every week, so that he had set up a soup kitchen for them, apparently with no thought of turning them in to the authorities. When he was asked whether this was not in contradiction with his policy recommendations, he replied, "That has nothing to do with it. People who are on my property are my guests, and I will not let them leave hungry."

More important, this was my first attempt at getting an overview, as a social scientist, of an entire country. Admittedly it was not a very large one. But the exercise not only validated my methodological prejudice in favor of "sociological tourism" but was a useful rehearsal for my much more demanding engagement with South Africa about a year later.

"NONSMOKERS MUST ALSO DIE."

Overlapping in time with my brief career as a diplomat was a stint as a consultant to a consortium of European and North American tobacco companies—two roles which, had they only known about them, would have certified in the minds of my Harvard students my status as a politically incorrect individual (more so, I imagine, than my failure to use gender-neutral language).

I witnessed a little incident on what was then the Eastern Airlines shuttle between New York and Washington, DC. A middle-aged Korean passenger was told that the smoking section was full and that he had to sit in a nonsmoking seat. He was visibly angered and ostentatiously lit a cigarette. Naturally a flight attendant came over and told him to put out the cigarette. But what impressed me was the tone in which she did. It was not the kind of tone that she would have used if, say, he had neglected to secure his seat belt. Rather, it was a tone of moral outrage and barely contained fury—as if, say, he had defecated on the floor. I asked myself where this fervor came from. I concluded that it came from the fear that smoking was a lethal threat and that, conversely, the antismoking movement was a modern continuation of the age-old quest for immortality: "Stop smoking, and you will never die."

This was when I could write anything I wanted in *Worldview*. So, as I mentioned previously, in 1977, I published a short piece entitled "Gilgamesh on the Washington Shuttle," referring to the hero of the ancient Mesopotamian epic who, devastated by the death of a friend, embarks on a journey in search of the plant that can bestow immortality. (By the way, when he finally finds the plant, a snake comes and eats it. Whereupon Gilgamesh sits down and weeps.)

A few weeks later I received a phone call from an official of the Philip Morris company who had read the piece. He invited me to a one-day meeting to discuss nonmedical aspects of smoking, as the tobacco industry had realized that more than medical evidence was involved in the campaign against smoking. It was an interesting event with about ten participants. An economist spoke about the place of tobacco in the world economy, a lawyer about legal restrictions on smoking, an anthropologist about smoking as a cultural symbol. I had little to say, except to state my recently acquired hypothesis.

At the end of the meeting each participant was asked what sort of research he thought the industry should undertake. I said that this was really not something I was interested in, but, on the principle of knowing one's enemies, the industry should have a study done on the antismoking movement: Who are these people? What are their interests? How are they funded? Not long after the meeting I was asked whether I would conduct such a study. I said no, as I was fully occupied with other projects, but that I would find someone for them. I did.

Aaron Wildavsky, the prominent Berkeley political scientist, had done work on risk avoidance, and that was the angle that interested him. He assembled a small team, which undertook a study of the antismoking movement in the United States and the United Kingdom. But I was asked to be a consultant, specifically to attend and report on three international antismoking conferences organized by the World Health Organization, respectively in Stockholm, Winnipeg, and Tokyo. It was an instructive experience.

The Stockholm conference met in 1979. It was still billed as a scientific conference, though it was clearly an antismoking rally. (Later on the latter definition of these meetings was openly admitted, on the assumption that the science was all in and that there was nothing more to discuss other than strategies of implementation—forebodings of Al Gore and global warming!) This was also the first such conference with strong representation from Third World countries, whose representatives were flown in with funds from the Swedish government. It was a very large meeting, with about a dozen undercover observers from the industry. We met for breakfast and dinner every day, first deciding who should go where and then exchanging impressions.

An amusing incident occurred on the first day. There was a reception in the ornate Stockholm city hall. I noticed a delegation of three representatives from the Cuban ministry of health. They spoke only Spanish and stood together rather forlornly. I felt sorry for them and went over to join them. They were grateful. After some chitchat I asked the leader of the group whether the Cuban government was really serious about the antismoking cause. I had a mental image of Fidel Castro puffing on his cigar. Absolutely, he replied, and took out of his pocket a half-smoked packet of cigarettes, obviously his. He proudly showed me the warning on the packet. I cannot reconstruct the precise Spanish text, but it was suffused with subjunctives—something like, "It is possible that smoking is probably bad for health." He then looked at my nametag, which of course did not state my affiliation but did say "USA." He said, "Of course, if it were not for the American embargo, we could export other things." The logic of this was not immediately clear, but I let it go.

My report to the consortium was, in retrospect, the most interesting of the lot. I still have it in a file. After telling my clients, the "merchants of death," what happened at the conference from my observations (of course they had the reports from the other industry observers), I made two major points. First, I wrote that the antismoking campaign was driven by an alliance of two very different entities—the movement proper, consisting of the usual mix of passionate believers and moral entrepreneurs (who had probably worked for other causes before), and bureaucrats from both governmental and nongovernmental organizations. They had quite different interests. The movement people wanted, as far as possible, to *eliminate* smoking; the bureaucrats wanted to *regulate* it (which would mean a huge new job opportunity for them). I suggested that, for obvious reasons, the bureaucrats were more likely to make compromises with the industry.

Generally, I observed that the opposition always used the phrase "tobacco interests," which of course was empirically valid, but that one should also understand what the "antismoking interests" were. In other words, it was not a matter of disinterested idealists battling the vested interests—there were hard material interests on both sides. In any case, the strength of the campaign came from just this alliance of ideals and interests.

This conclusion, of course, comes straight out of the sociology of knowledge. Comparison: The Protestant Reformation, born out of the definitely "disinterested" struggle of a lonely monk with his oversensitive conscience, would not have gotten far if it had not been linked with the long-standing interest of German princes to steal monastery-owned real estate. Incidentally, the unpublished report of the Wildavsky study came out a little later with a similar description of the antismoking campaign, except that it used the rather awkward terms *sect* and *caste* to refer to the two components of the campaign.

I made a further observation. At least in Western democracies the antismoking campaign ran into a serious difficulty: If I smoke and kill myself as a result, this is my business and no one else's—the function of government is to protect people from each other, not to protect them from themselves. Therefore, the campaign had to find an "innocent bystander" (I did not use this phrase in the report but used it later in talking about it). Two possibilities were emerging: The argument based on so-called social costs—I die early because of my smoking, but society has to pay the costs of my medical care, the provisions for my surviving family, and the loss of my productive contribution. And the argument based on what was then called "passive smoking"—the negative effect on the health of others in whose company I smoke. I argued that the first argument was too abstract to get very far. (A few years later an economist actually came out with a calculation that society would *gain* from my early death from smoking—saving on the medical costs and the pension costs resulting from longevity.) I suggested that the latter argument was likely to win the day, as indeed it did.

In my career as an accidental sociologist, my observations on the antismoking interests and on the argument about "passive smoking" constituted my most successful predictions. I think I can be quite proud about this. It is too bad that I could not have predicted more important societal developments.

A Scandinavian participant at the Stockholm conference defined the goal of the antismoking movement as follows—to make smoking an activity in private undertaken by consenting adults. In 1979 this statement seemed a little crazy. It turned out to be prophetic. It describes the situation today, thirty years later, at least in developed societies.

In my report on the Winnipeg meeting in 1983 I could describe the increasing bureaucratization of the antismoking campaign, especially by governmental bodies regulating smoking behavior. Research was increasingly focused on the alleged effects of "passive smoking." I witnessed a telling incident illustrating the "sectarian" character of the movement. Two Danish scientists reported on a study of theirs, which showed no ill effects from "passive smoking." The audience turned on them with sustained fury, not only questioning their data but insinuating that they must be in the pay of the tobacco industry. They were no better off when they protested that they were staunch opponents of smoking and that their study was not conclusive.

It reminded me of a meeting I had attended, years before, of a group interested in "unidentified flying objects." On the agenda was a report of an alleged UFO landing somewhere in America. The report was enthusiastically received, but when one person at the meeting questioned the reliability of the report (it was made by the local sheriff, who, it was mentioned in passing, liked to drink), the rest of the audience furiously pounced on him. Sectarians are especially allergic to cognitive dissonance. In any case, it was becoming quite clear in the early 1980s that, as I put it, antismoking had "become a formidable social and political reality."

The last conference I attended, in Tokyo in 1987, had a certain ironic quality. Many if not most of the Japanese participants smoked as soon as they left the meeting rooms. In my report I described the conference as "a chastity rally in a house of ill repute." Even so, while the commitment to the cause of the Japanese participants was somewhat questionable, the overall mood of the conference was triumphalist. Movement activists and bureaucrats had fully amalgamated. Research into "passive smoking" was richly funded and had of course multiplied. There was a big push for restrictions on smoking in public places and in the workplace and for discrimination against smokers in insurance and employment. There were overt calls for "segregating and stigmatizing" smokers. It was (accurately) predicted that smokers would offer little resistance, because the campaign had made them feel guilty about their habit. In other words, the antismoking campaign was becoming both triumphal and nasty.

The next conference was to be held a few years hence in Perth, Australia. It was strongly suggested that observers from the tobacco industry should be barred from attending. I don't know if this happened, but I was not asked by the consortium to go to Perth. In any case, by then much of the industry, especially in the United States, had given up the fight. They adopted a strategy of compromise and adaptation. What happened since the 1980s saw, in effect, the full success of the antismoking campaign, at least in the Western world. Restrictive legislation became globalized, even in developing societies (though enforcement there was problematic). The peculiar character of American tort law made possible lawsuits against tobacco firms resulting in astronomic payments, not only to individuals, but also to states (supposedly compensating them for costs incurred from the medical treatment of "smoke-related" illnesses). The aggregate amount of these lawsuits must constitute the largest extortion in human history.

Smoking is not an important personal concern of mine. I gave up smoking after I had heart surgery, and the antismoking issue is not something that I frequently think about. But I have described my involvement with the issue at some length here because I came to understand it as a result of insights derived directly from my role as a social scientist. The antismoking movement, which I followed from its beginnings, is the most successful social movement in my experience. I learned a lot from observing it—specifically, about the combination of ideology and material interests in the anatomy of a successful social movement; about the use and misuse of science in politics (the scientific data on the effect of smoking on smokers are overwhelmingly clear, but on the effect on "passive smokers" much less so); about the importance of fear in mobilizing public support; and, in America, about the power of litigation in extracting huge sums from any entity with "deep pockets," no matter the merits of the alleged torts.

I have described the two episodes—my experiences at the United Nations and with the tobacco industry—in some detail. Although these were hardly high points in my career as a social scientist, I did this for two reasons. One, as indicated above, I learned a lot from both cases, and that was at least in part due to the intellectual tools of a distinctive kind of sociology I had fashioned over the years. But there is another reason: My approach to each of these cases was radically debunking—of the United Nations, of the rhetoric of the so-called Third World, of the pretensions of a supposedly idealistic movement. Yet throughout these exercises of what Nietzsche had called "the art of mistrust," I upheld a number of political and moral convictions. In other words, my practice of debunking did not come out of a cynical worldview; neither did it lead to one. And this is a conclusion that I believe to be generalizable. In the case of my Geneva excursions, I did not for a moment give up my conviction as to the superiority of the values of democracy and individual rights represented, however inconsistently, by the United States. In the case of the antismoking campaign, my skepticism about it did not derive only from doubts about the validity of its assumptions, but also from a moral revulsion against sectarian fanaticism and against the totalitarian implications of what so often passes for humane concern.

Interestingly, what the two cases have in common (and what is perhaps an important component of so-called political correctness) is an aversion to risk. Socialist utopias are supposed to protect against the risks of a market economy. The utopias implicit in this and other versions of the cult of health seek to avoid the risks that are an intrinsic feature of the human condition. This is why I have chosen as a heading for this section the title of an essay by the Austrian writer Friedrich Torberg—"Nonsmokers Must Also Die."

There is yet another, more political point to be made. I have continued to believe what so enraged the students who disrupted my lecture at the London School of Economics—that sociology is radical in its debunking analyses but conservative in its practical implications. In the 1980s I moved in right-of-center circles and was, almost by definition, politically incorrect as seen from the Left. But neither was I correct in terms of the other side. Of course I was willing to defend the United States against the diatribes of my Cuban nemesis in Geneva, and I strongly recommended market-based development policies as against the socialist alternatives. But I was not uncritical of all American policies in the Third World, from my early opposition to the war in Vietnam to my difficulties with the Wilsonian democratism of George W. Bush. Domestically, I distanced myself from the neoconservatives as they embraced (whether out of conviction or for tactical reasons) the positions of the Christian Right on abortion and homosexuality. And long before I became critical of George W. Bush for his foreign policy, I was appalled by his record on capital punishment while he was governor of Texas. I think that at least some of my political buddies from the early 1980s smelled out my incorrectness from their point of view, which may account for my being invited to that ranch meeting in Texas as a sort of useful idiot. As to the tobacco industry, I refused to demonize it as the antismoking movement did and I had no moral problem with giving it sociological advice, but I did not doubt that it too used data as selectively as the other side. The basic political issue here, in my mind, was the right of individuals to choose how to live and the protection of this right against the totalitarian inclinations of even the most democratic regimes.

To go back to the title of my earliest book, sociology does indeed lead to a "precarious vision" of the social order. For that very reason it fosters a sense of the fragility of all institutions, and of the twin dangers of tyranny or chaos when institutions are hastily dismantled. To move all the way to my most recent book, *In Praise of Doubt*, a morally sensitive social scientist will, I think, instinctively move toward middle positions (middle between radical change and stubborn preservation) on most issues.

7

FROM MBULWA TO GÜTERSLOH

In 1981 I moved, so to speak, down the road, from Boston College to Boston University to take on a position as university professor. The two institutions are only some ten minutes apart by car, going in one direction or the other on Commonwealth Avenue, but they differ greatly in atmosphere. Boston College (BC) is still a Jesuit institution, though its Catholicism is rather muted (much, I understand, to the chagrin of the Vatican). However, it still retains (or at any rate did when I worked there) the sociological aura of its beginnings, when it was the gateway into the middle class for the children of Irish and Italian immigrants. By contrast, Boston University (BU) has a decidedly more cosmopolitan atmosphere and a much more visible Jewish presence. It already had a sizable building of the Hillel Foundation when I started there; it has now been replaced by an even more impressive edifice.

The urban ambience of the campus appealed to me from the beginning; indeed it reminded me a bit of the New School. No attempt here to scatter faux-Gothic buildings across an imitation English village, as is typical of so much academic architecture in America. Lecturing in a building overlooking Commonwealth Avenue, one could easily have the impression that the streetcars were actually going through the classroom.

One physical benefit of my move was that I now lived right next to my place of work. When we came to Boston, we bought a house that was only a short drive to BC. Now I had a five-minute walk to my office at

BU. Brigitte observed that I must be the first person in academia who first acquired a house and then found a job to go with it.

In most American institutions the title of university professor just signifies an honorific status bestowed on an individual. At BU it also meant affiliation with a separate academic division. The University Professors Program, generally referred to by the abbreviation UNI, was a free-standing unit, separate from any school or department, reporting directly to the president. John Silber, the legendary president who had transformed BU from a backwater into a reputable research university, created it in the 1970s. UNI was abolished not long after Silber's retirement.

In 1981 it was going strong. Silber's idea was to create an interdisciplinary "center of excellence," whose influence would radiate throughout the university. It was an interesting idea, and in many ways a commendable one, very much in line with Silber's ambitious plans for BU. Not surprisingly, it did not quite work out as intended.

Some UNI faculty were indeed remarkable scholars. Others could not be so described by the most generous stretch of intellectual judgment. In a number of cases (including mine, I am sure) Silber used UNI as a mechanism to get in people with problematic relations with their own field. Various attempts were made to routinize interaction among the affiliated professors, along the lines of the Oxbridge "high table." This only partially succeeded, since people were busy and had little time for conversation with others working in fields far removed from their own interests.

As to radiating influence, pretty much the opposite happened. There was widespread resentment in the wider faculty against UNI's alleged elite status, its arbitrary recruitment procedures not subject to regular departmental procedures, and, last but not least, the reduced teaching loads and the reputedly high salaries of UNI faculty.

The program did indeed attract some gifted graduate students, often eccentrics who could not easily fit into conventional doctoral programs, though this had the downside of these individuals subsequently having a difficult time on the job market—degrees were always in two fields, which led putative employers to wonder which field a candidate was really qualified in. UNI did have an effective undergraduate program, but it competed with an honors program in arts and sciences, thus creating additional resentment.

Be this as it may, I found UNI to be a very pleasant base for my teaching. UNI faculty had to be affiliated with at least one other division of the university; I was affiliated with three (I don't know whether this was Silber's idea)—the departments of sociology and religion and the School of Theology. Each of these had to approve the affiliation, but since my salary did not come out of their budgets and probably because they were afraid of Silber, approval was readily given.

This setup had an enormous advantage. University departments are famous for holding innumerable plenary and committee meetings. It was clear that I could not possibly attend meetings in all three entities with which I was affiliated, and so I attended none. The UNI faculty met very rarely.

Over the years I supervised the doctoral work of a considerable number of interesting students. To mention some: Charles Glenn, who has become an internationally known expert on church-state relations in education; Craig Gay, who has become known as an up-and-coming Evangelical thinker on social issues; Cecilia Mariz, doing interesting work on religion in Brazil; Gillian Godsell, the wife of the man who got me involved in South Africa (see below) and who is active in teaching and research on black entrepreneurship in that country; Uwe Siemon-Netto, a German journalist concerned with Lutheran political ethics; and Caesar Mavratsas, who became the first professor of sociology at the University of Cyprus. My two most recent "doctor-children" are Tulasi Srinivas, a daughter of S. N. Srinivas, a founding father of Indian anthropology, who herself works on Hinduism and modernity; and Inna Naletova, who is immersed in studying the religious situation in post-Soviet Russia.

On top of all this, UNI allowed me to teach pretty much what I wanted (almost like an old-fashioned German professor). I will only mention one pioneering seminar, which I cotaught with Claire Wolfteich, a Roman Catholic on the faculty of BU's School of Theology. It was a one-year affair with a deliberately vague title, "Church and Theology in the Contemporary World." It allowed students to work on a serious research project, for which they had access to funds from a sizable grant we obtained from a foundation. We had some interesting projects: one by an Air Force chaplain, an Evangelical woman who was confronted by the demand to facilitate worship by a group of self-defined witches; another by a middle-aged minister from Nigeria, who wrote a paper castigating Western churches for abandoning such practices of early Christianity as miraculous healing, prophecy, exorcism, and raising the dead (he claimed to have witnessed an incident of the last). Wolfteich and I struggled with the question of how we should grade this effort.

John Silber was president for most of my time on the faculty of BU. He hovered over the campus as a palpable presence. In the public eye, not least in the reporting of the *Boston Globe*, he *was* BU. Within the faculty there was a large group that detested him and a probably smaller group of fierce loyalists. I did not fall into either category. But I appreciated what he had done for the institution and for the generous way in which he supported me. And, though I did not meet him too often, I got along with him and indeed liked him. Of course, here as elsewhere, most professors went about their business without paying too much attention to the wider affairs of the university.

In person Silber came across as sharply intelligent, opinionated, bellicose, and equipped with a rather malicious wit. He made quick decisions, sometimes very bad ones, much more often good ones. In many ways he was an embodiment of a cranky Texan. Some on the faculty perceived him as a right-winger, which was certainly a misperception. He was a lifelong Democrat, very much in the pre-1960s tradition of Democratic Party liberalism. But he was an American patriot, staunchly anti-communist, opposed to abortion on philosophical grounds, and contemptuous of fashionable political correctness.

He also had a propensity for malapropisms. My favorite one came in an interview with a journalist, who asked him whether it was true that he was homophobic. Silber vehemently denied the charge, mentioning that several important individuals in his administration were gay and insisting that he had nothing against homosexuals. He added, "But I don't like them pushing their agenda down my throat." His irascible temperament harmed his political ambitions, as when, during his campaign for governor of Massachusetts, he fatally spoiled his chances by lashing out against a friendly journalist who asked him a personal question.

I have used the past tense in describing Silber. At this time of writing he is very much alive, still residing in his house just off campus. But there has been a far-reaching effort to eliminate what has been labeled "the Silber legacy"—a faithful enactment of Max Weber's theory of the routinization of charisma. After the visionaries come the bureaucrats. Although a small street alongside the main administration building has been renamed Silber Way, the Silber era is indeed in the past tense. Sociologically, this may be inevitable. It is also very sad.

I will mention two incidents with Silber that I witnessed. One illustrates his cocksure crankiness, the other his profound faith in the value of a liberal education. Silber hosted a lunch for Helen Suzman, a heroine of the struggle against apartheid in South Africa and one of the most impressive individuals I have ever met. I had come to know her in South Africa, as a result of which I sat at the table with her and Silber. Throughout the meal Silber was holding forth with his views about Suzman's country. She was obviously taken aback, but, gracious as ever, she did not interrupt him. The other incident occurred at, of all occasions, a meeting with parents of incoming freshmen. Silber spoke about his vision of a university education. Then he said: "I hope that your children will have a great future after they graduate. But I would like to think that, if something terrible happened and they died soon after they graduated, you would feel that their four years at BU had been worthwhile." The parents were visibly shocked by that sentence, but I had the impression that most were moved rather than offended.

WITNESSING A COUNTRY'S TRANSFORMATION

Two significant changes in my career as a social scientist occurred in 1985. I started my own research center at Boston University. And I stumbled into a project that led me to try to understand the transformation of an entire country. I will deal with the first development in the next chapter. The second began with an unexpected phone call from Johannesburg.

The call came from Bobby Godsell, who was then in charge of labor relations at Anglo American, the huge South African mining corporation. I did not know Godsell (he has since become a good friend). He had read some of my writings. He informed me that Harry Oppenheimer, the mining tycoon and a strong opponent of apartheid, wanted to set up an international commission to study the future of South Africa. Godsell was coming to America and wanted to meet me to see whether I would agree to chair such a commission. I asked, "Why me? I have never been to South Africa and I know nothing about it." Godsell replied, "That's why we want you as chairman." I understood of course what he meant—they wanted someone with no axe to grind—but I observed that this was the first time in my career that I was being asked to do something on the grounds of proven ignorance.

Godsell and I met. We hit it off right away. I agreed to do what he asked. For the next three years I visited South Africa with regularity, and I have become intellectually and indeed emotionally involved with the country ever since. I got caught up in its dramatic transformation. Something very big and very good happened there, and I have been rooting for the process to succeed.

The first visit was quite extended. Of course I was doing a lot of reading. But Godsell had me meet a number of informative people from different sectors of the society. The main task at hand was to constitute the working team (we early on gave up the term *commission* as too pretentious). Most of them were South Africans, and I met them personally. A few were Americans, and I met them when I returned home. The team ended up with twenty individuals from a wide range of professional backgrounds (by no means only in the social sciences). Of the South African members eight were white, four nonwhite.

The project was named South Africa Beyond Apartheid (SABA). Oppenheimer's foundation as well as a group of South African and American corporations very generously funded it. Over the years the research team formed close ties (several of its members attained important positions in the postapartheid period), and I made lasting friendships—in addition to Godsell and his wife Gillian (who came to Boston University and did a doctorate with me), with Ann Bernstein (who then worked for the Urban Foundation, a business organization working against apartheid, and who started an influential think tank of her own after the transition to democracy) and with Lawrie Schlemmer (a sociologist then on the faculty of the University of Natal, now an independent consultant). Overall I was enormously intrigued by my first contacts with the country. For a while, as Brigitte observed, I first turned at breakfast to whatever news the *New York Times* carried about South Africa. In those years there was such news very frequently.

Oppenheimer's idea for the project was somewhat vague. I soon discovered that there was a large number of already published books speculating about the future of South Africa. I saw little point adding yet another. Godsell and I redefined the agenda to produce, not the thinking of the team about the future, but the thinking of all the major political actors about what the country should and would likely look like

after the demise of apartheid. The team as such would make neither recommendations nor predictions. Rather, it would carefully record those
made by the various actors. In terms of the sociology of knowledge, we
would map the normative and cognitive definitions of reality made by
the actors. Those ranged across the spectrum, from the extreme
(Afrikaner) right wing to the extreme (black) resistance groups in the
townships.

I asked Godsell why he thought that all these people would talk to
us. He smiled and said, "If Harry Oppenheimer invites you, everyone in
South Africa shows up." He turned out to be right. In the course of the
project I met Oppenheimer several times. He was an impressive individual, immensely successful, possibly one of the richest individuals in
the world, yet unassuming in demeanor. He was passionately opposed to
apartheid on moral grounds and had been so long before most of the
business community had concluded that apartheid was bad for the
economy.

We assigned members of the team based on the likelihood that representatives of a particular actor would speak to them. This did not necessarily mean that the team member sympathized politically with the
actor. Thus Bernstein researched the business community, with which
she broadly sympathized, while Schlemmer interviewed members of the
government, of which he was sharply, and publicly, critical. But he was
an Afrikaans speaker, and Afrikaners have a strong feeling of community
even with members of the *volk* whose political views they reject. The
members of the team were strongly urged to keep their views to themselves while interviewing. But it must be remembered that the project
took place during a time of intense political conflict, with passions flying
high. People wanted to know how everyone stood on the conflict.

Therefore, at the outset, we hammered out four normative assumptions with which every member of the team agreed, though the assumptions
were not to be paraded in the interviews: "Apartheid is morally repre-
hensible and should be abolished. It should be replaced by a democracy

and not a tyranny. In the process of transition the productive capacity of the economy should not be destroyed. The costs of transition, especially in human terms, should be kept to the minimum." This obviously left room for a lot of disagreement, as between those who sympathized with armed struggle as part of the resistance and those we called "incrementalists." Each group had its icon, respectively Nelson Mandela and Helen Suzman. It is worth noting that the two were friends from the time that Suzman visited Mandela in prison until her recent death.

A project undertaken by such a diverse team of researchers is obviously in danger of incoherence. It was my task to provide the group with a coherent conceptual framework applicable to each actor being studied. The scheme I produced was essentially based on the sociology of knowledge, though it carefully avoided the technical language of *The Social Construction of Reality*—with one exception: I defined our agenda as producing an accurate account of the *cognitive maps* operative in South African politics (I invented this term ad hoc). But the agenda went beyond the sociology of knowledge in seeking to provide an account of the social character and the strategy of each political order.

In addition we tried to do what Godsell called "reality testing": without criticizing the normative presupposition of a strategy, we asked whether it had a reasonable chance of success. For example, we did not question the moral grounds of armed struggle, but we asked whether it was likely to lead to the demise of the apartheid regime (we thought that it was not).

The method proved to be highly successful. The book published in 1988 with the findings of the project, *A Future South Africa: Visions, Strategies and Realities*, was a bestseller in South Africa. Everyone wanted to read it to see if they were correctly described (each chapter was sent back to the interviewees before it was put into its final form) and to obtain a better understanding of what the other parties thought. After publication of the book, we received quite a few letters of protest. *But not a single one protested what we had said about the party of the letter writer.* The protests were all about what had been said about other parties, along the lines of "You were deceived about the real intentions of these bastards!" I found this methodological validation very encouraging, and I have used similar analytic schemes since then.

After the research team was organized, we all met at a place in the eastern Transvaal called Mbulwa. It was some sort of hunting lodge owned by Oppenheimer, but it was also used for less bloodthirsty gatherings. It was in the middle of nowhere—the kind of place that gives my highly urbanized psyche the creeps. As our bus went farther and farther into what appeared a sinister wilderness, I felt panic coming on. I did what I usually do in panicky situations—I made a joke. I asked: "Did you know that *Mbulwa* means hay fever in the Swazi language?" Only two people with whom I sat heard me. One smiled. The other said: "That's a strange name to call a place." I decided at once that the latter's contribution to the project would not be good. I was right. Once the program began, I overcame my feelings about wilderness locations (what man-eating animals were making those noises outside my bedroom?), and I made a valiant attempt at translating Schutzian phenomenological sociology into the vernacular. It seems that I was successful.

I had the most instructive exchange with one member of the team, Helen Zille, a very bright young journalist. Her assignment was the Afrikaner right wing (that is, the groups to the right of the Nationalist government). They knew who she was, a fervent opponent of apartheid, but she was an Afrikaner herself and the aforementioned *volk* belongingness ensured that these people would talk to her—as they did. Zille at that time described herself as a Marxist (since then she has moved very far politically—she became mayor of Cape Town and is now leader of the Democratic Alliance, the official opposition party in parliament). In my presentation I, of course, strongly emphasized the need for objectivity. Zille strongly protested this: "We should be part of the struggle against apartheid, and objectivity is neither possible nor desirable." I argued with her for a while, then gave up and simply told her to do the best she could.

In the event she wrote one of the best papers for the project. If one did not know her, one could think that she was part of the group she was describing. In other words, *she did brilliantly what she said could not be done*. I have on a number of occasions mentioned this incident when speaking about objectivity. But Zille was wrong on one point. Her report ends with this sentence: "The Right is no paper tiger." As events developed in the years after 1988, the Afrikaner extremist groups, the ones graphically called the "bitter-enders," turned out to be, precisely, a paper tiger.

During the SABA project I was asked a few times whether, apart from the fact that I knew very little except very general facts about South Africa, I had any surprises after I got there. There was of course the sheer beauty of some parts of the country. But beyond that I could come up with two, only seemingly contradictory facts.

One was the dehumanizing quality of apartheid for black people, not just in the most glaring atrocities committed by the regime but in ordinary, everyday life. One black member of the research team told of a recent incident. He had caught a young black man who had attempted a burglary in his house. Just then appeared three "comrades" (the name used by underground resistance youths in the townships), who had also come upon the hapless burglar and were about to impose "revolutionary justice," which in such cases often meant summary execution. A curfew was on, and the streets were being patrolled by security forces in armored cars—they tended to shoot before asking questions. Our colleague told how he cowered behind a bush in his backyard so as not to be seen from the street, trying to convince the "comrades" not to kill the burglar (successfully, it turned out).

The other surprise was that I developed a certain empathy with the Afrikaners—that small white culture stuck on the southern end of a black continent, speaking their archaic form of Dutch and struggling with their contorted Calvinist conscience. I was especially taken by the beauty of the wine country of the Western Cape, with its center in the university town of Stellenbosch (one of the most charming campuses in my experience). None of this, of course, is to deny the abhorrent regime, which Afrikaners had set up in 1948 and which the majority of them supported in the following decades.

I recall a conversation I had with a Stellenbosch professor who had been a vocal critic of apartheid all along. I asked him if he knew the then state president (whose policies he abhorred). "Oh yes," he replied, "we have known each other from before we had shoes." It turned out that their families had adjoining farms and that boys rarely if ever wore shoes before they started school.

During the three years of SABA there were quite a few memorable incidents—some disturbing, some moving, some funny. I just want to recount one that was positively surreal. Godsell thought that I should meet Mangosuthu Buthelezi, chief minister of KwaZulu. This was one of the so-called "homelands" set up by the apartheid government, in this instance to be the allegedly "independent" state for the Zulu ethnic group. Buthelezi had accepted the government-approved position (for which the main resistance groups considered him a collaborator), but he had rejected the phony "independent" status and had made his Inkatha party an important element in the "incrementalist" camp.

There were no commercial flights to Ulundi, the capital of KwaZulu, so Godsell, a visiting American lawyer, and I flew there in a company plane. We landed on a deserted airstrip and stood there for some thirty minutes, observed by a few heavily armed men from a watchtower. Eventually a shiny Mercedes arrived to take us to the government buildings, which rose like a strange, modernist mirage out of a lonely veld landscape. We went through a rigorous security check and were ushered to a waiting room. The chief was running late, we were told. With us in the room were two other people, a South African army officer in uniform and another white man (we learned later that he was a very right-wing American journalist).

Nothing happened for a while. Then suddenly a door opened and a group of about ten people, some wearing yarmulkes, hurried through, on the way to see Buthelezi. This was some sort of fact-finding mission by American Jews—I had heard about them but had not imagined that I would run into them in Zululand. I knew two or three of them. They were in our room for just a few moments, but several of them called out:

"Look, there is Peter Berger."

"Hello, Peter."

"What are you doing here?"

This sociable scene was quickly over, the group was out, and it was quiet again.

That was surreal enough. But then the South African officer came over and said, "I'm sorry, but I couldn't help overhearing. Are you the Peter Berger who wrote *Invitation to Sociology*?" When I pleaded guilty, he went on, "Oh, that is a wonderful book. I read it in university. There is one sentence you wrote that I never forgot: 'marriage is a thousand bleary-eyed breakfasts.'" I denied ever having written this; he insisted, and I again denied it. (I later verified that he was right, though he had taken the line out of context. Who knows what Afrikaans domestic tragedy lay behind this memory of his?)

After this mad exchange there was another waiting period. When we were finally ushered into the presence of the chief of the Zulus, I was so disoriented that I couldn't think of anything to ask him. It did not matter. He talked the entire time.

In 1987 Godsell and I coauthored an article in *Commentary*, trying to dispel some American conceptions about South Africa. I think that the picture we drew of the situation was quite accurate. But we made two predictions, both of which were wrong. In cautioning against the expectations for quick change held by many in the antiapartheid movement, we wrote that "strategies for change need to be framed in terms of years, perhaps even decades." In the event, the whole system started to unravel just a couple of years down the road. Then we criticized the idea, often voiced by outside observers, that it was now "too late for negotiations." On the contrary, we wrote, it was too early for negotiations. We

added that negotiations would only begin when both sides had concluded that they could not win, and that had not yet happened. Of
course, just about then took place the first contacts between intermedi-
aries of the government and the exiled African National Congress
(ANC). We had not understood how a set of different processes would
rapidly gel to convince the ruling elite that the status quo was untenable.

First, there was a significant split in the constituency of the Nationalist party (the Afrikaans business elite joined its English-speaking counterpart in opposing apartheid as economically disastrous). Then the
Dutch Reformed Church (which had been a strong supporter of government policy) declared that apartheid was a sin. Added to this was the
increasing unrest in the country, as well as the economic and psychological effects of being branded internationally as a pariah state (though this
factor was probably less important). And as far as the ANC was concerned, we could not have anticipated the (equally unpredicted) collapse
of the Soviet empire, which began in 1989—the Soviet Union had been
the most important foreign supporter of the ANC. I had the fantasy of
someone at the exile headquarters of the ANC in Lusaka who had to call
a certain number in Moscow for instructions every Monday—and his
surprise one day when an Orthodox priest answered the phone.

It was a rare gratifying experience for me to be able to contribute to
a morally worthwhile political process. SABA was also a great learning
experience. It was exciting to begin to understand the basic processes of
transformation in an entire country and especially the fragility of what
at first seemed to be an invincible structure of oppression. I was also
gratified in seeing once more, in an important research exercise, how the
particular approach to sociological analysis that I had helped develop
could be useful for understanding a very complex social and political situation. And then there is the recollection of the view from Table Mountain over Cape Town and its stunning environs.

"HOW DOES ONE GET FROM DELHI TO GÜTERSLOH?"

I will briefly leave aside the chronological sequence I have followed through most of this book in order to look at a project that I directed a few years after the SABA book came out. It was a study of eleven countries with normative and political conflicts, commissioned by the Bertelsmann Foundation (an arm of the huge Bertelsmann global publishing company) and designated as a report to the Club of Rome (the rather absurd organization that some years before had issued a report predicting an imminent world catastrophe because of overpopulation). I do so for two reasons: In many ways this project was an internationalization of SABA with the same underlying concern—how there can be a resolution of seemingly irresolvable conflicts in a society. It used the same team methodology as SABA—one coffee house morphing into the next coffee house, as it were. But also the Bertelsmann project brought together a number of people who constituted a core of the international network of scholars of the new research center at Boston University—an alliance of coffee-house habitués.

In each country the research sought to describe the nature of the normative conflict and its political ramifications and then went on to ask which institutions were in a position to mediate between the parties to the conflict and to help bring about a peaceful resolution. Thus, for example, there were studies of the so-called culture war in the United States between progressives and conservatives, of the challenge by Muslims to the secularist ideology of the French republic, and of the attempts by movements such as feminism and environmentalism to change the ideological consensus in West Germany (to name only the topics of the first three chapters of the book). In each of these cases, despite sharp normative disagreements, the institutions of political democracy and civil society succeeded in containing these within a framework of peaceful contestation.

The project, while it involved other individuals, consolidated the relations among a group of scholars with whom I continued to collaborate in a variety of activities. They were the following (in the order their chapters appeared in the book): James Davison Hunter—who did his doctorate in sociology with me at Rutgers, went on to the faculty of the University of Virginia, and first used the phrase *culture war* to describe the normative conflict in contemporary America; Danièle Hervieu-Léger—probably the best sociologist of religion in France, who later became president of the prestigious Ecole des Hautes Etudes en Sciences Sociales in Paris; Janos Kovacs—a Hungarian economist, affiliated with the Institute on Human Sciences in Vienna; Arturo Fontaine—director of the Instituto de Estudios Publicos in Santiago, which played an interesting role in the peaceful transition to democracy after the Pinochet regime in Chile; Ann Bernstein—previously mentioned as a member of the SABA team, who now had founded and become the director of the Centre for Development and Enterprise in Johannesburg; Robert Hefner—an anthropologist at Boston University, who early on became associate director of the new research center founded in 1985 and in 2009 succeeded me as director—who is an expert on Indonesia and has branched out to deal with the encounter of Islam with modernity in different countries; and Hsin-Huang Michael Hsiao—a sociologist at the Academia Sinica in Taiwan, who has worked on social change in several countries in the region and who was coeditor with me in 1988 of the much-discussed book *In Search of an East Asian Development Model* (which itself was the result of a conference organized by CRIA in New York—coffee houses piled upon coffee houses!).

It would be an exaggeration to say that here was the kernel of a school of thought. These people shared a common focus of interest in the relation of culture and social change but not a common approach to this topic. In any case, I had long given up the ambition of starting an intellectual school, ever since the collapse of this utopian notion during my all-too-brief chairmanship at the New School. Still, it pleased me that these people stayed in touch with and worked with each other even on occasions where I did not convene them in a formal way. And perhaps, like Cicero's augurs, they wink at each other when they meet.

There were meetings of the group in Berlin, London, and New York (lack of funds has not been a problem of the Bertelsmann Foundation). The final meeting was in Gütersloh, the headquarters of the corporation as well as of its foundation. Gütersloh is a nondescript small town in a hard-to-reach location in northern Germany. It was the seat for many years of a minor Protestant publishing house, which morphed into the Bertelsmann empire after World War II. Perhaps the most revealing question was asked by the author of the India study: "How does one get from Delhi to Gütersloh?" In the event he made it, with some difficulty, though I was tempted, when he asked the question, to repeat the punch line of an old New York joke about a tourist in Times Square asking a police officer how to get to an obscure address in Queens: "You can't get there from here." Perhaps a mantra of globalization skeptics?

I don't know how or why the Bertelsmann Foundation defined this operation as a report to the Club of Rome, most famous for pronouncing wrong prophecies. In any case, we were supposed to "report" to this organization at a meeting (I think its annual get-together) in Ponce, Puerto Rico. Two Bertelsmann representatives were there, with myself and a few others from the research team. The impression I got from the meeting was of a gathering of mostly elderly and retired big shots, or rather ex–big shots, from Europe and Latin America. They evidently thought of themselves as very important people. Presiding over this gathering was the crown prince of Spain, a pleasant enough young man, who was accompanied everywhere by his military aide in full uniform (perhaps carrying in his briefcase the keys to Spain's secret nuclear arsenal?). We said what we had to say at one session of the meeting, but we were excluded from most of the proceedings, which were limited to members of the Club of Rome. We felt a bit like strolling musicians performing briefly at an aristocratic family event. We ended up renting a car and driving around the island.

The book *The Limits of Social Cohesion* was published in 1993. I have no idea who read it, and I did not see any reviews. It did not contain any startling conclusions, though some of the country studies were very interesting; for example, Kovacs's account of the reemergence of the old normative conflict between Budapest and bucolic populism in post-communist Hungary; or Fontaine's description of how academic institutions could bring together opposition intellectuals with more moderate elements in the military regime; or the account by Serif Mardin (a political scientist, regrettably only a temporary member of the coffee-house clientele) of the continuing conflict between Westernizers and Muslim traditionalists in Turkey. Bernstein, of course, was able to tell the fascinating story of the role of big business in the transition to democracy in South Africa. Perhaps the most interesting finding of the study was that very different institutions are able to mediate normative conflicts—NGOs, religious institutions, corporations, and even agencies of the state (Hervieu-Léger described the successful intervention of the government to resolve a conflict between native Melanesians and Europeans in New Caledonia, a French territory in the South Pacific).

In my own thinking this reinforced an insight that came out sharply in the SABA findings—that both micro- and macroinstitutions can perform mediating functions in society. And that, of course, is relevant to the antistate bias implicit in the "mediating structures" approach by Richard Neuhaus and myself in *To Empower People* (Neuhaus, by the way, did a paper on the role of the churches for the SABA project—coffee-house membership tends to have an "indelible character," to borrow a term from the Catholic definition of priesthood).

The Bertelsmann project had a small but pleasant sequel. At my suggestion, Thomas Luckmann (by then a distinguished professor in Konstanz and, indeed, the central figure of a kind of "school" in sociology) was invited to be a critic at meetings of the project. He and I were then invited to produce a booklet in a series Bertelsmann published on what it called "cultural orientation." We produced this booklet in 1995,

Modernity, Pluralism and the Crisis of Meaning. It was very nice to work on a text together. I think it is fair to say that we did not say much here that we had not said elsewhere. Our focus was the loss of an overarching and taken-for-granted order of meaning in modern societies—for reasons that both of us had dealt with many times before.

For my own thinking, the little booklet was the first place in which the dichotomy between relativism and fundamentalism was explained as constituting two sides of the same coin—to wit, modern pluralism. Luckmann had for many years done empirical studies, mostly in Germany, of moral judgments uttered in ordinary conversation. One of his findings was the dominant place occupied by tolerance in the relevant value system—tolerance being the one surviving moral absolute in the worldview of relativism. In any case, we did not join in the widespread chorus of lamentations over the meaninglessness of modern life. We emphasized that there were "communities of meaning" (our term) that sustained individuals even if there was a dearth of meanings in the society as a whole. Luckmann made effective use of a concept coined by his wife Benita (herself a political scientist)—that of the "little life-worlds" that provide meaning (and indeed "cultural orientation") to ordinary people.

THREE BOOKS AT THE WRONG TIME

In the course of the 1980s I came out with three books. The first was coauthored with Hansfried Kellner (my brother-in-law) and the second with Brigitte—a sort of family firm at work. I wrote the third by myself. None of these books could be called successful. That fact is significant in terms of my career as a sociologist.

The book with Kellner, *Sociology Reinterpreted: An Essay on Method and Vocation*, was published in 1981. It came about as the result of a conversation the two of us had with Brigitte. We were going on about the unfortunate dichotomy that was coming to dominate the field— between those for whom only quantitative methods were deemed to be properly scientific and those who disdained all claims to scientific objectivity in favor of ideological advocacy. Brigitte said, "Why don't the two of you write a book on methodology?" Well, we did. It turned out to cover a somewhat broader ground, as we felt impelled to deal also with the ethical issue of the proper vocation of the social scientist in society.

The substance of the book was not intended to be particularly original. It was a forceful restatement of an understanding of sociology through a mixture of Max Weber and Alfred Schutz. We began describing sociology as a "way of seeing." The core chapter was entitled "The Act of Interpretation." Here Kellner's contribution was essential— he was and is competent, much more than I, in the kind of methodology developed in Schutz's phenomenology. But we did not want the book to be a dreary exercise of philosophical pedantry. I think we succeeded in making a number of concepts alive and even entertaining.

The main example in the chapter was a somewhat raunchy vignette: A young woman, a graduate student of sociology from the Midwest, is attending an academic conference at a hotel in California. In the midst of a conversation with another woman attendee, the latter, out of the blue, invites her to an orgy in one of the rooms upstairs, with the charming explanation that they could use another woman. The point of the exercise is that, from that moment on, our young woman must engage in a series of interpretations, beginning with the obvious questions: "Have I heard right?" "Is this a joke?" "Could this be an attempt at lesbian seduction?" Then, step-by-step, we follow her as she tries to incorporate the incident into the "stock of knowledge" available to her, first as a person socialized in a specific American milieu, then as a social scientist.

The key Schutzian categories employed here are "typification" and "relevance structure." As soon as the graduate student starts to interpret the incident, an array of possible typifications comes into play, all constituting attempts to make sense of it. For example, as a midwesterner she has at hand a typification of "a California lifestyle": Does this type give meaning to what is happening? As the act of interpretation continues, different relevance structures come into play—there could be a sexual one (she may be aroused) or one of simple curiosity (are Californians really like that?). But later, if she remembers that after all she is a sociologist, the distinctive relevance structure of the discipline will become conscious (how does the performance of an orgy in a convention hotel fit into what we know about the culture of the professional class?). If she then decides to undertake a systematic research project on the sexual mores of social scientists attending conventions, there will be a much more rigorous relevance structure, involving bodies of theory and data. All this is taking place within an overall situation with which the young woman is basically familiar.

We interweave this example with another one, where she is invited not to an orgy but to a ceremony of human sacrifice—a totally unfamiliar situation, where relevance structures have to be constructed from scratch. Needless to say, we had fun with all this.

Of course our main purpose here was to elaborate on the specific character of the sociological relevance structure. We used that concept to defend the ideal and the practical possibility of objectivity. We also argued that sociological analysis is compatible with the idea of human freedom and, in its political implication, is conducive to it. Sociological understanding makes one averse to any form of fanaticism. Sociology should not become an ideological instrument. The sociologist must necessarily find a balance between being an objective observer and a morally engaged member of society. We called this balance the sociologist's "dual citizenship."

The book was barely noticed. There were just a couple of mildly critical reviews in sociological journals. No one seemed particularly annoyed by the book. Hardly anyone seemed particularly interested.

The War over the Family: Capturing the Middle Ground, by Brigitte and me, appeared in 1983. It was much more her book than mine, since it dealt with the area of family sociology in which she had specialized for years. The book was a combination of sociological analysis with advocacy of a political position we called that of "the middle ground." Much of the book was a description and analysis of the feminist assault on the conventional family, beginning with Betty Friedan's 1963 book, *The Feminine Mystique*, and erupting into full-scale "culture war" in the wake of the 1973 Supreme Court decision in *Roe v. Wade*. In the 1960s there was as yet no organized resistance to the assault, though of course many socially conservative people were repelled. That changed in the 1970s, as social conservatives (many of them on religious grounds) began to organize and exert political muscle. Many of them had pinned high hopes on Jimmy Carter, who presented himself as an Evangelical. They were severely disappointed in him after he became president. A pivotal event was one presided over by Carter, which was originally billed as a White House Conference on the Family and then under feminist pressure renamed White House Conference on Fami*lies*. These developments led to a polarized politics, which is still very much in evidence today. On one side the pro-family and antiabortion ("pro-life") movements merged, while on the other side the pro-abortion ("pro-choice") movement allied itself with other socially progressive causes. Probably more by accident than by deliberate decisions, the social conservatives became an important constituency of the Republican Party, while the social progressives assumed a dominant role in the Democratic Party. Abortion became a doctrinaire litmus test on both sides.

The book also contained a fairly detailed statement of Brigitte's central hypothesis: Contrary to the commonly held view that the nuclear family (parents and children forming a unit separate from larger kinship groupings) was a result of modernity, Brigitte argued that this form of the family was *a cause* of modernity. The hypothesis, buttressed by a sizable body of historical evidence, was original and quite startling. The modern nuclear family came into its present shape with the rise of the bourgeoisie. Thus the term *traditional family* is rather misleading—the "tradition" is, at the most, a little over two hundred years old.

This insight, not so incidentally, puts into question the conservative view that the contemporary family is based on the Bible. The totally different biblical view of the family can be quickly grasped by one look at the tenth commandment, where a wife is listed among other items of property such as cattle (that, of course, is in the Hebrew Bible; things don't get much better in the New Testament).

In any case, the bourgeois family brought about a revolution, in the relations both between spouses and between them and their children—increasingly an egalitarian revolution.

We argued that the bourgeois family, now under attack, is the best setting in which children can be socialized to become responsible adults—a precondition for a successful democracy. This argument was neither philosophical nor theological but was based on Brigitte's reading of the empirical evidence. We then undertook what we called a reasonable defense of the bourgeois family. This was indeed a "middle ground." It annoyed both sides.

We annoyed the progressive side by defending an institution they had defined as repressive and because we took a nuanced position on abortion, which rejected the rigid "pro-choice" position. We annoyed the conservatives for that reason as well (with no embrace of the equally rigid "pro-life" position) but also because our version of history put in question their view of the bourgeois family being "traditional" (let alone grounded in natural law). As if to make sure that everyone remained equally annoyed, I contributed an excursus in which I compared two contemporary versions of linguistic bowdlerism—the old proscription of "dirty talk" (I called it "Goshspeak") and the new one of "gender-exclusive" language (which I called "Femspeak"). We did not touch on the question of gay marriage, since it was not yet an issue.

Annoyed or not, few people paid much attention to the book. There was a favorable review by Robert Coles in the *New York Times Book*

Review and a dismissive mention in a review of several books in a socio-logical journal. But the fate of this book adumbrated what happened later. Brigitte continued to work on this issue throughout the 1980s and 1990s. She published some articles, but her major book, *The Family in the Modern Age*, did not come out until 2002 (it was finally published by Irving Louis Horowitz's Transaction Publishers, after several other publishers had turned it down). It contained a much fuller statement of the central hypothesis on the vital relation of the bourgeois family to three core institutions of modernity—the capitalist economy, the demo-cratic state, and civil society.

Of course it was again opposed to progressive ideology because of its undogmatic position on abortion; it was also at odds with the Left because it strongly advocated a privileged legal status for the bourgeois family and now explicitly opposed gay marriage, again on purely pru-dential grounds and not because of any animus against homosexual rela-tionships. We have no such animus but are inclined to believe that chil-dren are best off when raised by their biological parents—a hypothesis that may yet be falsified by new data. In the meantime it seems impru-dent to hastily weaken an institution that has been around for a very long time (i.e., marriage limited to heterosexual couples). The legitimate grievances of same-sex couples can be accommodated by other means, such as contracts or civil unions.

But the opposition to conservative ideology was, if anything, even sharper—not only because the book took an "incorrect" position on abortion but because of a tolerant view of divorce and premarital cohab-itation—precisely on the grounds that these probably supported the bourgeois family, the former by getting people out of destructive mar-riages and then possibly into more benign ones, the latter by socializing people into the often demanding adjustment of living in an emotionally charged monogamous relationship. The book received one favorable review in a right-of-center publication.

The third book, of which I was the only author, was *The Capitalist*

Revolution, published in 1986. It was the fullest statement of my conclusion that capitalism was the only viable model of development. The
book was organized in fifty propositions, arguing that capitalism was
best suited to lift large numbers of people into decent levels of material
prosperity, to create societies with reasonable equality of opportunity,
and to lead to political regimes that provided safeguards for human
rights and liberties. The book, however, was not a manifesto. Its propositions were in the form of hypotheses. I suppose its tenor is best caught
by the title of one of Irving Kristol's books, *Two Cheers for Capitalism*. In
1991, when it was clear that the major socialist alternative to capitalism
had collapsed, I wrote a new introduction to a paperback edition, obviously claiming that my argument was being reinforced. It did not do
much to help the book.

When the book first came out, it did indeed receive a good deal of
attention. It was widely reviewed. The reviews were mostly predictable—quite favorable in right-of-center publications, critical in liberal ones (such as the *New York Times Book Review* and the *New
Republic*). Yet the book had little influence and soon went out of print.
Years later I found out that it had become an important point of reference in one ideological subculture, the libertarian one, though there I
was mildly criticized for having given only *two* cheers for capitalism.
Some people are hard to please.

There is a somewhat depressing conclusion to the fate of these
books. By the late 1980s Brigitte's and my alienation from the polarized
cultural and political scene had become fairly clear to others as well as to
ourselves. As the generation of the 1960s came into positions of influence, we increasingly noticed their imprint on mainstream culture and
academia. In sociology the mantra of "class, race, gender" had come to
dominate work in most areas of the discipline; a diffuse left-liberalism
had in many places hardened into a repressive orthodoxy.

For a while we had felt comfortable in the milieu of the neoconservatives (and, not so incidentally, had received funding for our work by foun-

dations that subsidized that milieu). In 1986 Brigitte and I published an article in *Commentary*, "Our Conservatism and Theirs," in which we spelled out our differences with the old social and cultural conservatives (the article was triggered by Brigitte's attendance at a conference of the Philadelphia Society, in which neocons were attacked in a particularly venomous way). The irony here is that, beginning about then, the neocons themselves were entering into an alliance with just those conservatives, first in the area of sexual politics, later by endorsing the adventurous foreign policy of George W. Bush. Abortion, of course, became the rigid litmus test in the various right-of-center coteries. Our middle position on this and most other relevant issues was unpalatable all around.

I remember a conversation we had with Norman Podhoretz (we had become friendly, and still are, with him and his wife, Midge Decter). When we brought up the middle ground, he said emphatically that the middle ground is an illusion. He was wrong, of course. There are plentiful data to show that most Americans are, precisely, in the middle of most of the issues that divide our polarized ideological scene. His view, however, is a self-fulfilling prophecy. It pertained to the course of the neoconservative movement. And it also describes the sectarian atmosphere that marks the committed activists on both sides (two minorities in the population, but very vocal and well organized, and therefore enormously influential).

My own political alienation from this whole scene reached a certain end point in 1997, when *First Things*, the journal edited by my old friend Richard Neuhaus, ran an issue devoted to the question of whether the American political system was still legitimate. Some of the articles were more strident than others, but the overall thrust was that the American system was no longer legitimate because it had established a right to abortion. The most strident piece was the editorial by Neuhaus, which compared abortion in America with the Holocaust and spoke of the Christian right of resistance against tyranny in the line of Dietrich Bonhoeffer's joining the conspiracy to overthrow the Nazi regime.

I had been a member of the journal's editorial board from its inception. I had become disturbed by its increasingly dogmatic tone following Neuhaus's conversion to a very conservative Catholicism. But I felt that this issue was moving into right-wing-militia territory, and I resigned from the editorial board. Other people connected with the journal were also disturbed. Midge Decter wrote a letter to the editor, criticizing Neuhaus's editorial, but she did not resign. The only other individual who did was Gertrude Himmelfarb (Irving Kristol's wife). I should add that Neuhaus and I preserved our friendship until his recent death, but the old camaraderie could not be restored.

When people are shooting at each other, it is not a career-enhancing move to be in the middle. Brigitte paid a higher price than I did for not joining the militant battalions on either side. Her field of family sociology was virtually obliterated under the aegis of "gender studies." I was luckier in that I straddled several fields—the sociology of religion was less embroiled in the culture war than the sociology of development. What is more, I was (and am) theologically quite liberal but politically moderately conservative. This makes some people seasick. On the other hand, some people who like my theology are willing to forgive my politics, and vice versa.

I remember my asking a sociologist some years ago what her specialty was; she replied that it was "victimology." The term was new to me, though I understand that it has become more common now. I do not intend to make an autobiographical contribution to this noble field. Neither Brigitte nor I was seriously persecuted; she made a reasonably good career, I a very successful one. But, in a book that seeks to give an account of my trajectory as a social scientist, it seems necessary to pay attention to the cultural and political context of this trajectory.

In the last few pages, and indeed in other parts of this book, I have mentioned several political positions advocated by Brigitte and myself. Our having done this in no way contradicts the view of objectivity that both of us have held for many years. Objectivity pertains to the attempt by a social scientist to understand the world. It does *not* describe his total existence. Using Weber's term, science, if it is to be science, must be "value-free." But a "value-free" *scientist* would be something of a moral monster.

The idea of "dual citizenship" is a useful one in this connection. The social scientist wears two hats. He is a member of a community of scholars committed to specific canons of analysis. He is also a member of a political community, subject to the same moral considerations as anyone else. The two hats are quite different. For the sake of honest advertising, it should always be made clear under which hat a particular statement is being made.

Perhaps I have overused the coffee house as a metaphor for a methodological habitus. It may simply be a reflection of a romantic image derived from my Viennese origins. It certainly does not intend to convey an aversion to disciplined intellectual effort. It does intend to convey a particular attitude toward such an effort and to the social setting in which it occurs. The attitude is one of open-mindedness, of not taking oneself too seriously, of appreciating style and wit as enhancing understanding. Most important, it is a metaphor for a very important insight—that there are few pleasures in life to equal that of sustained conversation with intelligent, articulate people in a congenial environment. I will add a politically incorrect observation: It helps if the conversation is fueled by coffee and is enveloped in pungent tobacco smoke.

8

CONDUCTOR RATHER THAN SOLOIST

For quite a few years it had been clear to me that I needed collaborators from different fields if I were to pursue most of the topics that interested me, especially as I had come to believe that a cross-national comparative perspective is close to indispensable for social-scientific work today. As a result I had fantasized about a situation in which a group of people from different disciplines and with different area specialties would work together for a sustained period of time. The fantasy came true in 1985, when John Silber authorized me to start a new research center at Boston University devoted to exploring the cultural bases for economic activity in general and for a capitalist economy in particular. In my own mind, obviously, this was a "neo-Weberian" agenda, though we did not use this quasi-sectarian term. We called the baby Institute for the Study of Economic Culture (ISEC). Later on, for uninteresting reasons having to do with the interests of donors, we changed the name twice—first to Institute on Religion and World Affairs (IRWA), then to Institute on Culture, Religion and World Affairs (CURA). For convenience's sake, I'll stick to CURA throughout. The agenda of the center did not change. I became its director, and for the next twenty-four years this position determined my work as a social scientist.

We began very modestly. At first I simply operated out of my office at the University Professors Program, with part-time access to a secretary, and after a while BU gave us a small office of our own. Then I received a small grant, which allowed me to employ a part-time associate to help with fundraising and conceptualizing the research agenda. I was lucky with the individual I found for this function, Laura L. Nash, who had been trained as a classicist and had somehow come to develop a program on business ethics at the Harvard Business School. She stayed with CURA for several years, moving from the original administrative role to research projects of her own. To my surprise, we were very successful in raising funds. I had never done this before, and at first I felt awkward about it. Then I grasped a simple fact: foundations needed me as much as I needed them—they had to make grants to stay in business, and there were only that many viable ideas around.

Two kinds of foundations funded us. First, there were foundations with a pro-capitalist orientation—they felt, correctly, that CURA shared that bias and that its findings could be politically useful (though we always made clear that we were a research center, not a propaganda agency). And second, there were foundations with no particular ideological orientation who were simply interested in objective research on matters of public importance. At one point, within a few weeks, one foundation dropped us because, as they candidly told us, we did not sufficiently share their right-wing agenda; another foundation, a little more subtly, turned down our application as being *too* right-wing. I felt reassured by this double rejection. One foundation that faithfully stuck by us through most of the following years was the Lynde and Harry Bradley Foundation, which did have a political interest but which also understood the importance of nonideological, "value-free" research.

In the first five years of CURA's existence we started some large-scale projects, but a big change occurred in 1990. It came with one of those stories that one could head "Only in America!" and Europeans find hard to understand. Southern Methodist University was trying to recruit me. I felt no urge to leave BU and I had no great desire to live in Dallas, so I had reacted quite negatively, but they persisted in a very nice way. So I went down for a visit. I had a long interview with the dean. He offered me a bigger salary, but I said that I really made enough money. He offered a reduced teaching load, but I said that I liked to teach. He became quite exasperated: "What *would* you want?"

I told him about the research center I was trying to develop. He showed great interest.

The very next day he arranged lunch at the Petroleum Club with some five tycoons from the oil industry. We were sitting in a dining room on the top floor of a skyscraper, looking out over all the other skyscrapers of downtown Dallas. For a moment I thought (perhaps blasphemously) of the devil taking Jesus to a mountaintop and showing him the kingdoms of this world. I described what I had in mind. One of the men scribbled something on the back of an envelope, then asked me: "Would a ten-million-dollar endowment be enough to get you off the ground?" I said that, yes, I thought so. He nodded and said: "Well, we could talk about that."

Needless to say, I returned to Boston in a rather pensive mood. I told only two people about my Dallas adventure, Brigitte and my best friend on the faculty, Howard Kee (a distinguished New Testament scholar). Without telling me, Kee told Silber. Two days later Silber called me: "Berger, I understand that you are talking with SMU." I admitted that I had been. Silber went on: "I regard Texas as recruiting ground for BU, not the other way around. Come see me."

When I did, he said that BU did not have the kind of rich alumni who might give me $10 million, but he offered me four lines for research faculty, support staff, and much bigger quarters. Of course I accepted, relieved that I did not have to live in Dallas. CURA moved to its very attractive space, just off campus. We celebrated the new location at a reception, for which I hired a Mexican mariachi band. Thus we inaugurated this new phase in CURA's history with trumpets blaring out "Guadalajara!"

CURA has been impressively productive. The first books coming out of CURA-sponsored research were published in 1990. The list of such books topped one hundred by mid-2009 (we never bothered to list articles). That number is a little misleading, since the list includes some foreign translations and some booklets, but it includes over fifty full-length books originally published in English. Not all these books, naturally, were of top quality. Many were and some have become points of reference for their particular topics. I think we can be satisfied with this result. (Zulu proverb: "If I don't beat my drum, who will?") Since 1985 the format of my own work has changed significantly. I have written some books of my own, some on topics not on CURA's agenda, but mostly I have stimulated and raised funds for the work of other people. In other words, much of the time I have performed as conductor rather than soloist. On some occasions (which I will describe presently) I did play first violin—that is, I directed a research team myself.

CAPITALISTS WITH OR WITHOUT CHOPSTICKS

It would be tedious to go through all these CURA projects one by one. I will limit myself to the major ones, which focused on two overall issues—the general cultural concomitants of economic behavior and the religious ones in particular. To denote the first issue, we used (and, I think, coined) the term *economic culture* intentionally as an analogy with the common term *political culture*. We decided to tackle this issue by first looking at what was becoming an astounding phenomenon— the great economic success stories of East Asia. In the mid-1980s, when we began this research, mainland China was still in the throes of the Maoist economic disaster. The success stories were first, of course, to Japan, then the so-called "Four Little Dragons"—South Korea, Taiwan, Hong Kong, and Singapore—and, perhaps most intriguing, the over-seas Chinese, arguably the economically most successful group of people in the world. Our first project explored the economic culture of this remarkable population. What cultural factors might help to explain this success?

The project was directed by Gordon Redding, a British management expert, at the time dean of the business school of the University of Hong Kong (he subsequently moved to INSEAD—Institut Européen d'Administration des Affaires—the business school near Paris). Redding was aware, of course, of the "post-Confucian hypothesis," but he was not concerned with such broad historical questions. Rather, he wanted to find out the worldview and the value system that could be detected as underlying the everyday economic behavior of this group. Redding and his associates interviewed CEOs of Chinese companies in Hong Kong, Taiwan, and Singapore.

I attended one set of interviews in Hong Kong. These were fascinating occasions. Redding invited five top businessmen at a time to dinner in a private room at the Hong Kong Hilton. No serious questions were raised during the excellent meal, but there was a lot of drinking (under the circumstances an important methodological tool). When coffee was served, Redding (a superb interviewer) opened the discussion with a few questions. He did not have to lead the discussion for long. Very soon his guests started to interview each other; he could lean back, intervene occasionally, and just make sure that the tape machine was running. I doubt whether this format could be duplicated in other places. After all, these people were Chinese—they were self-confident, they appreciated good food, they could drink a lot without getting drunk, and they liked to talk. In this particular context, Redding's methodology (if one could call it that) worked wonders.

Redding's book on this first project, *The Spirit of Chinese Capitalism*, was published in 1990. Its findings were compelling. He described a worldview marked by a pervasive sense of insecurity, against which the individual had to pit himself with ingenuity and ruthlessness. He also described a value system centered on the family for one overriding reason—family members were the only people one could trust. For this reason, the ideal Chinese business was the family firm. Almost by defini-tion, it had to be relatively small—if it got too big, one would run out of relatives one could trust. There were some large Chinese firms, but they tended to be enterprises where the central office could be kept small—for example, shipping companies. The contrast with Japanese economic cul-ture is striking. The Japanese are very good at building large organiza-tions. By contrast, the most successful Chinese business is small, family based, informally organized, and thus very flexible.

CURA has continued an East Asia focus ever since. Redding has continued research on the business cultures of East and Southeast Asia following an agenda he calls "comparative capitalisms." In 1990, Robert Weller, a BU anthropologist and Sinologist, became a CURA faculty associate. He has been conducting a number of research projects in the region, including in mainland China after that became possible in the wake of economic reforms.

One result of this East Asia focus was the book that I coedited with Hsin-Huang Michael Hsiao, *In Search of an East Asian Development Model* (1988), which I discussed in chapter 5. It contained excellent con-tributions by Gustav Papanek (a BU economist), Lucian Pye (an MIT political scientist), and Iwao Munakata (a sociologist at Sophia Univer-sity in Tokyo).

CURA also sponsored a small study of new individualist trends in the Japanese economy by Kuniko Miyanaga (an anthropologist con-nected with a research center in Tokyo).

In 2008 CURA started a program of summer seminars on religion in the contemporary world in collaboration with Fudan University (Shanghai) and Renmin University (Beijing). To prepare for this pro-gram, some colleagues and I had a meeting in Beijing with the State Administration of Religious Affairs (SARA), the agency of the Chinese government seeking to control all religious activities in the country (including, incidentally, permissible reincarnations by Buddhist sages). We got a green light to proceed with the seminar program.

Over the years CURA undertook a number of projects to explore different economic cultures, some in history, some contemporary. Claudio Veliz (a Chilean historian who joined the BU faculty) wrote a study of the divergent economic cultures of North and Latin America. Our first published book, by Shelley Green and Paul Pryde (both freelance consultants at the time), dealt with black economic enterprise in the United States. Hansfried Kellner and Laura L. Nash participated in studies of therapeutically oriented personnel policies in America and Germany. Janos Kovacs directed a study of the transition to capitalism in several ex-communist countries in Europe. Brigitte edited a book on the "culture of entrepreneurship" (the only CURA book that, for whatever reason, was translated into Arabic). I could go on. But this may suffice to make clear that we did not limit our research to cultures where people eat with chopsticks.[1]

The focus on economic cultures naturally suggested collaboration with economists. We tried. On the whole we failed. Economists turned out to be the one group of social scientists with whom it was generally impossible to work. Kovacs was a notable exception (his being from Central Europe may have something to do with this). Curiously, we found plausible collaborators among two coteries of economists who are usually perceived as coming from opposite ideological camps: adherents of the so-called Austrian School, because their iconic figure, Friedrich Hayek, had a keen interest in history; and development economists, because culture is hard to avoid if one bums around exotic countries far from home. Peter Boettke (George Mason University) came from the former group, Gustav Papanek from the latter—we had fruitful interactions with both. Most other economists we encountered were as impervious as fundamentalist mullahs to any language other than the one allegedly revealed to them, and to them alone.

Soon after CURA got going, we convened a conference to discuss the concept of economic culture with what we thought was a particularly hard-nosed bunch, mostly economists associated with the so-called public choice school. (I think that some of them later preferred the label "rational actor.") The conference was a complete fiasco. Every time one of us said anything, one of them would translate what had just been said into their language. At one point a speaker tried to explain that immigration policy was often dictated by motives other than rational economic interests, indeed was often economically irrational. They firmly denied this, maintaining that all motives in this area were based on economic rationality.

Exasperated, the speaker asked, "Don't you accept that some people act for reasons of conscience?"

"Oh yes," said one of the economists. "Conscience—we call it internal price controls."

I was chairing this session, supposedly in an impartial way. But I lost my cool then. I told the following story: I used to have a colleague, an accomplished church historian. But his main claim to fame, in his own mind, was as one of the founders and leading members of the American Society for Spoken Latin. In that capacity he had translated the comic strip *Pogo* into Latin. I concluded: "What one must ask is this—*What is gained by translating* Pogo *into Latin?*"

The economists failed to see the point. I should have known that one must not tell jokes to mullahs. Sometime after this event I recounted it to Bernard Lewis, the distinguished Islam scholar. He nodded and said, "I am thinking of writing an essay on economics. So far I have only the opening lines: 'In the history of human thought science has often come out of superstition. Astronomy came out of astrology. Chemistry came out of alchemy. What will come out of economics?'"

At one time we thought of producing a collective volume about the concept of economic culture. We never did, mainly because all of us were busy with less ambitious projects. But over the years I was able to reach a number of worthwhile conclusions about the relation of culture and economic activity. Most important: The relation is not a one-directional one between an independent and a dependent variable—

that is, neither cultural nor economic determinism can explain all cases. Sometimes culture drives the relation, as when people are inspired by powerful religious or political ideas. At other times economic rationality is in the driver's seat, typically, I suspect, in less emotionally charged situations. Theories that assume either determination are prone to distort reality.

Take an "economistic" interpretation of a jihadist suicide bomber: there he is, engaged in a rational cost-benefit analysis—on the one hand, being blown up; on the other hand, looking forward to seventy virgins. Or take a "culturalist" interpretation of the East Asian economic miracles—chopsticks, and whatever goes with them, will do the trick every time.

I found it more useful to speak of a "comparative cultural advantage." Take the demographically disproportionate role of ethnic Chinese in the economies of Southeast Asia—a very small minority of the population controls a large segment of the economy—despite concerted efforts in several countries to discriminate in favor of ethnic Malay "sons of the soil." Of course not all Chinese are successful; of course some Malays are successful. But the concept of "comparative cultural advantage" can be put very simply: It helps to be Chinese.

Another important conclusion: The advantage was not always there, and it may not last. The economic functionality of cultural factors may be "latent" for a long time and then suddenly start operating as circumstances change. The change may be spontaneous and unplanned, or it may be deliberately designed. Traditional Chinese culture, especially as articulated by Confucianism, did not favor economic enterprise. To be sure, there was a merchant class, but it was subordinate to the mandarins, who despised grubby moneymaking in favor of such exquisite accomplishments as reciting classical texts or painting dragons on silk screens. But the so-called post-Confucian virtues suddenly burst into economic functionality when Chinese migrants had to survive on the streets of Jakarta or Manila—in the absence of mandarins (or, for that matter, of third cousins wanting a piece of the action). That development of course was not planned by anyone. But the same cultural mobilization occurred with the economic reforms in mainland China—here a changed situation resulting from a political plan.

A similar argument of latency can be made concerning the transformation of a feudal ethos into a modern economic culture, deliberately designed by the Meiji regime in Japan. This example can serve to explain that the economic advantage of cultural traits may not last—may, in other words, come with an "expiration date." The transformation of Bushido into a postfeudal ethic was highly functional as Japan developed as an industrial economy. Today Japan is well into a postindustrial, knowledge-based economy. Arguably, the old ethic of Japanese business—highly disciplined work habits and loyalty to the firm, both rewarded by lifetime employment—may no longer be functional. More hedonistic and individualistic values may now be called for.

Yet another important insight: Economically functional values need not be distributed equally throughout a population. Quite often the driving force in an economy can be an entrepreneurial "vanguard," which will indeed be animated by values of competitive ambition, life discipline, and risk taking. The rest of the population may then go on with a much more relaxed, hedonistic lifestyle. To put this in a more personal way, a vanguard of frenetic workaholics may be needed to maintain a society that can afford me.

A potentially poisonous situation may arise, of course, when the vanguard is of a different ethnicity from the majority population. Envy can be an explosive political force. The Jews in Europe and the Chinese outside their homeland are prototypical cases of this. Their histories are tragic examples of the point that people may act against their own economic rationality. The European rulers who welcomed Jews into their domains understood that it is foolish to kill the goose that lays the golden eggs. The resentful peasants who engaged in pogroms did not.

I remember a conversation I had with some black people in South

Africa. They expressed strong resentment about the continuing privilege of the white minority despite the demise of the apartheid regime. I said that I could understand their feelings, but I suggested a mental experiment: Forget the race of these people for a moment. Just look at their economic functions, which the country needs and which blacks especially need. Then look at them as an economic asset to be exploited, not for their sake but for yours. My argument failed to convince.

A topic that does not neatly fit under the category of economic culture, but that occupied me quite a lot in the wake of the SABA project, was the relation of capitalism and democracy and, more specifically, the role of business in transitions to democracy. Business had clearly played an important role in such a transition in South Africa. Could one generalize from this case? Ann Bernstein, Bobby Godsell, and I had a number of conversations about this in the early 1990s. Out of these conversations came a project exploring the topic in a number of countries. Bernstein was the key person in this undertaking, and she was the major editor of the book resulting from the project, *Business and Democracy*, published in 1998. I don't think that it was much noticed outside South Africa, but it was useful there during a period when the postapartheid government embarked on a pro-capitalist economic policy very much at odds with its Marxist past.

A number of CURA stalwarts contributed to the project—Gustav Papanek, Gordon Redding, Robert Hefner, and Laura L. Nash, as well as Myron Weiner, an MIT political scientist who had been friendly with us for several years.

One incident from this project sticks in my memory. We had a meeting in Hong Kong, where Redding had arranged interviews with a number of leading businessmen. Bernstein, who was still on a high after the triumph of democracy in South Africa, was increasingly disturbed by the remarkable lack of interest in democracy on the part of most of the businessmen. Their overriding concern about the imminent takeover of Hong Kong by the communist government of China was whether the city's vibrant economy would be allowed to continue. They could not care less about the lack of democracy in the People's Republic. Bernstein's sharpest shock came during a conversation with a young executive of a new, very successful airline. Asked about democracy, he said that he could put his view in a syllogism: "Democracy means that there will be a welfare state. We know that the welfare state is bad for economic development. Therefore, we must be against democracy."

The conclusions of the book were not startling but were quite in line with my own a few years earlier in *The Capitalist Revolution*: Business does not necessarily require democracy to flourish, but neither does it necessarily lead to democracy. However, it releases social pressures that, in the long run, have a democratizing effect. Business creates a social space outside the state, which eventually can become politically significant. Business contributes to economic growth and modernization, both developments that favor democracy. We adopted a phrase coined by Redding—the "thickening of civil society."

He used it in a paper for the project, which analyzed the noneconomic consequences of the opening of the new Shanghai stock exchange—all consequences that were outside the control of the stock exchange and unplanned by it. For example, the stock exchange needed trained accountants and reliable financial news. It could not fill these needs itself, but neither could the state. There appeared schools to train accountants and independent agencies to accredit the schools—all ingredients of a nascent civil society. Similarly, there arose economic news media, independent both of the stock exchange and of the state. Of course these were nonpolitical, at least initially, and their appearance certainly did not herald the advent of freedom of the press. But, again, here was an opening of social space that had democratic potential.

The most controversial portion of the book was a discussion of the conditions of conducting successful business enterprises under a nondemocratic regime. The conditions first strike one as cynical, but upon reflection they constitute a realistic assessment. Of course they very much represent the South African experience of Bernstein and Godsell. Here they are:

The state is in effective control of the country and has the ability to provide a stable social environment over an extended period of time. The state pursues intelligent economic and social policies—that is, it favors economic growth and has a concern for the welfare of its population. The state refrains from outright terror. And (perhaps closest to cynicism) corruption should be kept within "reasonable limits."

As far as this last condition is concerned, I had an instructive conversation with Papanek. We agreed that, in certain situations, corruption might be a useful factor in doing business under predictable circumstances. We also agreed that there were limits to such usefulness. I asked him why economists could not distinguish "good" from "bad" corruption. He replied that he could do that and then enunciated what he called the "Papanek principle of corruption," which stated that "the corruption may not exceed the corruption itself."

He gave an example: It is acceptable corruption if the head of government appoints his wife's uncle to a position in which he has nothing whatsoever to do (indeed he may have an office without a telephone that he ritually visits once a month to collect his salary check). But, as a result of the position, he draws a huge salary, lives in a government-supplied villa, and drives a government-supplied Mercedes. However, the corruption becomes unacceptable if the position entails real power over a sector of the economy—such as the power to wreck the state-controlled electricity company.

The book concluded with a call to business to enter into the public discourse, wherever possible, and to stop apologizing for itself (an unfortunate habit of business in many countries). This has been an important theme in Bernstein's work ever since.

This study reinforced another insight of my own, which I had held for a long time (on philosophical as much as sociological reasons)—that it is better to appeal to self-interest than to morality. Of course there is a place for moral argument, and there are people who will be persuaded by it. But, human nature being what it is, people more easily deceive themselves about the morality than about the self-interest of their actions. Therefore, an intelligent Machiavellian will try to achieve the morally desirable outcome by working with people's selfish motives rather than with their putative values. It is a question of the safer bet.

The South African experience was a good example of this. Of course there were people like Harry Oppenheimer, whose conscience made them oppose apartheid (and would have done so even if this had been against their own interests). And of course moral appeals had an effect, as when the Afrikaner elite had to cope with the eventual condemnation of apartheid by the Dutch Reformed Church. But business as a whole, including its Afrikaans sector, only swung into the antiapartheid camp after it had become convinced that the status quo was going to destroy the economy.

Similarly, hard-nosed Chinese businessmen will not become pro-democracy from hearing ringing speeches about freedom and human rights but through an argument that, in the long run, a democratic regime is more likely to provide the stable environment that business needs. One must, as far as possible, work with the logic of institutions. Business is an institution whose logic is profit seeking. To want business to act as a moral agency is like wanting an elephant to tap dance. Hegel used the telling phrase "the cunning of reason." Let me paraphrase: To achieve moral results in the real world is to practice the cunning of conscience.

"MAX WEBER IS ALIVE AND WELL AND LIVING IN GUATEMALA."

In most of the world, if one speaks about culture, one speaks about religion. Quite apart from my own bias as a Godder, it was only natural that from the beginning CURA's research focused heavily on religion. It was also plausible that our first project on a religious topic addressed the most amazing phenomenon on the global religious scene—the explosive growth of Pentecostalism. The topic has remained on CURA's agenda.

As I mentioned much earlier in this book, I first encountered and was impressed by Pentecostals when I did research as a graduate student on the streets of East Harlem. On and off, in the years since then, I had come across the phenomenon and become aware of its rapid expansion in many parts of the world. Thus it was not an accident that I decided on this topic for one of the first CURA projects. I did not quite realize the scope of the phenomenon. I continue to be fascinated by it.

The term *Pentecostal* of course refers to the event described in the Book of Acts, when the disciples of Jesus, soon after his disappearance from this life, gathered in Jerusalem for the Jewish feast of Pentecost (Shavuot). According to the New Testament account, the Holy Spirit descended upon the gathering, and the defining characteristic of Pentecostalism first appeared—glossolalia, the "speaking in tongues"—which to an outside observer seems to be gibberish but which believers understand to be foreign languages or the speech of angels or both. Glossolalia has been a recurring phenomenon in religious history, but Pentecostalism properly speaking appeared quite recently as a movement within Evangelical Protestantism. It asserted that to be a true Christian one had to undergo the "baptism of the spirit," which then bestows the "gifts of the spirit" (New Testament charismata). In addition to glossolalia, these gifts consist of miraculous healing, exorcisms, prophecy, and (at least occasionally) the raising of the dead. Pentecostals claim, very correctly, that in these things they replicate the practices of the early church—a claim that is, or should be, embarrassing to sedate mainline churches, which have long left these practices behind.

Pentecostalism, by its very nature, is spontaneous, often unorganized, without a settled hierarchy. Thus its boundaries are hard to specify. There are Pentecostal denominations, but there are also numerous local groups with no wider ties. The term *Pentecostalization* has been used to refer to the spillover of this type of charismatic Christianity into mainline churches, including even the Catholic Church.

There were several charismatic eruptions in the early years of the twentieth century, but a pivotal event marking the advent of modern Pentecostalism was the so-called Azusa Street Revival. In 1906 William Seymour, a one-eyed black Baptist preacher, came out of Texas and started services in an abandoned stable on Azusa Street in Los Angeles. He must have been an impressive individual. Within a few weeks he had brought together a sizable congregation, an interracial one to boot (not a common occurrence in California at that time). Very soon the characteristic Pentecostal practices appeared. The event attracted media attention. Contemporary newspaper stories reported in a tone of amusement the strange happenings on Azusa Street. Seymour and his flock were unfazed. They started a magazine and sent out missionaries, first to other parts of the United States, then abroad.

There were remarkable Pentecostal eruptions in Britain, Sweden, and India. Pentecostalism became a significant element within American Protestantism. But the truly massive explosion of the movement occurred after World War II—in parts of Asia, throughout sub-Saharan Africa, and most dramatically in Latin America.

Putting Pentecostals into a broader category of charismatic Christianity, a recent multicountry study by the Pew Research Center puts the total number at about 400 million. This may be a bit of an exaggeration. But, in any case, Pentecostalism since Azusa must be the fastest-growing religious movement in history. CURA cannot be accused of having picked a trivial subject.

We started the research in Latin America, beginning in Chile. The principal researcher was the British sociologist David Martin (London School of Economics). His first book on the subject came out in 1990, *Tongues of Fire: The Explosion of Protestantism in Latin America*. Since then, together with his wife, Bernice Martin (another sociologist, University College London), he has studied Pentecostals throughout the world, has written two more books and many articles, and has become a sort of dean of Pentecostal studies. The question most commonly asked is, how can one account for the great attractiveness of Pentecostalism? Martin has been providing a very full answer.

Here is a religion that provides a robustly supernatural faith—a miraculous God is never far away. It also provides a very strong community, giving social support to people who have been torn away from traditional ties. The highly emotional form of worship provides psychological catharsis, relief from the pressures and frustrations of marginalized social existence. Religious salvation is linked to physical healing—as encapsulated in the most common Pentecostal bumper sticker in Latin America— "*Cristo salva y sana*" ("Christ saves and heals"). Thus there is an all-round promise of what Martin called "betterment"—religious, physical, psychological, and social. The emphasis on conversion—being "born again" in the spirit—is very individualistic. Pentecostalism thus provides a distinctively modern combination of individualism and community. As such, it is highly adaptable and "transportable" across cultural and geographical borders.

Last but not least, it provides a morality that is functional for people taking their first steps into a modernizing economy—a disciplined lifestyle, delayed gratification, sobriety, an emphasis on the education of children, and an egalitarian relation between men and women—precisely the key ingredients of the "Protestant ethic" that Max Weber claimed to have found in seventeenth- and eighteenth-century Protestantism in Europe and North America. Hence my nickname for Martin's project: "Max Weber is alive and well and living in Guatemala." (That country, for reasons I am not quite clear about, has the highest percentage of Protestants—almost one-third of the population, mostly first-generation and Pentecostal.)

In Latin America, in particular, this is also strongly a women's movement, with an antimachismo ideology. The preachers are mainly men, but the missionaries and organizers are mostly women (such as the *visitadoras*, who go from house to house, helping where they can and inviting people to join the church).

Martin's description of the Pentecostal "package" and his explanation of why it is so attractive are widely agreed upon. But there has been an ongoing debate about his (let us say) "neo-Weberian" hypothesis. Some other scholars have questioned that Pentecostalism is a vehicle for social mobility, instead arguing that it is a version of the so-called "cargo cult"—a religious movement in the South Pacific, promising the coming of ships bearing all the fruits of modernity, from cars to washing machines; all these gifts are bestowed on people who did not have to make any effort at all, who need only faith (and presumably make donations to the prophets of the cult).

I have come down strongly on Martin's side in this debate, which tallies with my own observations and my reading of the evidence. But there is actually a very simple resolution to the debate: We are dealing here with an immense population, in many countries. It is very plausible that there are "Protestant-ethic" Pentecostals in some places and "cargo-cult" Pentecostals elsewhere. I would reiterate here what I wrote earlier about entrepreneurial "vanguards": the "Protestant-ethic" Pentecostals are such a vanguard and therefore of very great social importance. Thus it does not really matter if other Pentecostals just pray, put money in the collection plate, and wait for the magical cargo of modernity to arrive.

In a later book Martin described Pentecostalism as a "forbidden revolution." Intellectuals everywhere tend to be in favor of revolutionary transformations on behalf of the poor, but they do not like *this* revolution. In fact, much of the time they do not even perceive it happening. I had a vivid experience of this when I visited Chile at the beginning of Martin's research.

I had spent the day in La Cintana, a poor suburb of Santiago that was then about 80 percent Pentecostal. One noticed the difference as soon as one entered the town. The houses were neater, with many small stores and shops, and the children were better dressed. I was enormously impressed by some of the *visitadoras* I met. In the evening I attended a party at the research center that hosted the project. I was asked whether this was my first visit to Chile—it was—and then was asked how I had spent the day. When I said that I had been in La Cintana, people got very interested: "But that is where all the Protestants are!" And then: "Tell us about it!" I should note that the suburb was about a half-hour drive away from where the party was held. Clearly none of these people had ever been there. They asked me, a first-time visitor to their city, to tell them about it—as if I had just come back from Mongolia.

A little later that week I attended a lecture by a prominent progressive Catholic about the future of Chile. I asked him what he thought would be the place of Protestants in that future. He replied, "Oh, these are very uneducated people. They are of no importance." At that time the Protestant minority in Chile was estimated at 15 percent.

CURA's most recent foray into the Pentecostal world was a study in South Africa. The main hypothesis, which was generally supported by the findings, was that Pentecostalism there functioned much as it did in Latin America. Along with some colleagues I visited one of many Sunday services at a Pentecostal megachurch in a suburb of Johannesburg. It claims to have thirty thousand members, a credible claim in view of the number of people attending this particular service. There must have been about seven thousand people in the huge barnlike auditorium—about 85 percent black, 15 percent white—and, judging by the cars and busses parked outside, spanning a spectrum of class. The noise, of course, was earsplitting. Black or white, poor or rich—everyone was dancing, shouting, seemingly relaxed. The preacher was the senior pastor of the church, a white ex-bodybuilder—sort of a born-again Schwarzenegger.

The sermon was nothing if not charismatic—self-confident, powerful, and very loud indeed. It had two themes. One: God does not want you to be poor. And two: You can do something about this. These themes are generally seen to be part of the so-called prosperity gospel—faith will make you rich.

As my colleagues and I left the service, we asked each other whether this was a message we would quarrel with. We decided that we would not. What is more, empirically speaking, the promise is not empty: If people really lived in accordance with the ethic recommended by this church, they would indeed experience "betterment"; they would probably not become rich but would very likely escape the worst poverty. It is noteworthy that the church ran a small business school. Being Sunday, it was closed, but we got a brochure. Of course the school was not designed to train people to work for a multinational corporation. But it taught people the basic skills needed to run a small business.

The Catholic Church, and not only in Latin America, has understandably been disturbed by the growth of Pentecostalism. It has tried to compete—by having folk masses, healing services, even tolerating glossolalia. There is, however, one big impediment: The Catholic Church cannot give up its hierarchical structure; if it did, it would cease to be the Catholic Church.

Cecilia Mariz did a doctoral dissertation with me published under the title *Coping with Poverty: Pentecostals and Christian Base Communities in Brazil* (Philadelphia: Temple University Press, 1994). She compared three religious groups in Recife, one of the poorest cities in Brazil, in terms of their capacity to cope with extreme poverty: members of Catholic "base communities" (politically oriented groups inspired by liberation theology), adherents of Afro-Brazilian cults, and Pentecostals. She found that the last were best prepared to cope with poverty (not necessarily to escape from it—Recife offered few opportunities for that). Being Catholic herself, she did not like this finding. But she summed it up insightfully: The Catholic Church has proclaimed a "preferential option for the poor" (a formulation created by the Catholic bishops' conference in Medellin, in 1968—a high point of liberation theology in Latin America). But the syntax makes clear that the church itself is not poor—the option is *for* the poor. By contrast, the Pentecostal church *is* poor. Therefore, the poor opt for it.

If the (let us call it) "neo-Weberian" hypothesis about Pentecostalism is valid, Protestantism still has a comparative cultural advantage in the early stages of modern economic development. In other words, Protestantism still helps. This does not mean that *only* Protestants can make it. A number of CURA projects looked at what sociologists call functional equivalents of the Protestant ethic—that is, value systems that inculcate behavior patterns with the key characteristics of that ethic (Weber's "this-worldly asceticism") but with other or no religious concomitants. The moral habitus of the Chinese entrepreneurs studied by Gordon Redding clearly represent such a functional equivalent.

An institution that we thought of but never followed up with a research project is the military in developing societies. Often, in such societies, the military is the only institution that inculcates in its members, specifically its officer corps, values of rationality, discipline, and sobriety. It should not surprise then that the military turns out to be a key institution in these societies. Here of course there need not be any religious concomitant. But of special interest in this connection are two religious traditions that are commonly cited as lacking the relevant Protestant values—Catholicism and Islam.

Let it be stipulated that in their earlier history these traditions may have evinced this particular lack (as Weber himself argued). But this does not mean that they are fated to continue in the same way. CURA undertook a study of the role of Opus Dei in the recent history of Spain. Joan Estruch (a sociologist at the Autonomous University of Barcelona) conducted the study and wrote a book on the findings. It appeared in Spanish, Catalan, and English versions and attracted considerable attention. Opus Dei was, and still is, a theologically ultraconservative Catholic order containing both priests and laypeople. In Spain and elsewhere the order concentrated on infiltrating political, economic, and cultural elites. From its beginnings it was close to the Franco regime. In other words, it was hardly the kind of organization that progressive Catholics have in mind as an agent of change.

It turned out to be just that. At some time in the later years of the Franco regime, the leadership of Opus Dei decided that Spain should move in the direction of a market economy. It was in a good position to help along that move. There were several Opus Dei members in the cabinet, and the overall influence of the order was at a high point. The regime began a rapid modernization of the economy. Opus Dei, among other things, opened the first business school in Spain, with its graduates taking leading positions all over the economy.

This story is interesting for two reasons. Most relevant to the present argument, it demonstrates that Catholicism, even in a theologically orthodox version, can generate a surprisingly "Protestant" ethic. The story is also a prime example of another Weberian insight—the principle of unintended consequences. Opus Dei wanted to make Spain into an "integrally" Catholic society, which happened to have a capitalist economy. Spain got that economy, as Opus Dei intended. It also got democracy, secularization, and a profoundly Europeanized culture—all of which Opus Dei definitely did *not* intend. I summed up the result of Estruch's project as follows: Opus Dei intended Spain to be a suburb of Fatima. It helped make Spain into a suburb of Brussels. (Fatima is a pilgrimage center in Spain, the site of an alleged miraculous appearance of the Virgin Mary. Brussels, of course, is the capital of the European Union (EU). It seems that admission to the EU—the famous *acquis*—not only means submission to several thousand pages of European law but also to a package of pan-European culture, which among other items includes Eurosecularity—of which more in a while.)

Robert Hefner spent many years studying Islam in Indonesia, paying special attention to Nahdlatul Ulama, a huge Muslim organization with a decidedly moderate agenda.[2] It not only eschews any form of jihadist violence but has been advocating democracy, human rights, and the separation of the state from religion. In economic matters it has advocated capitalism and, among other activities, financed young Muslims to have internships in (mostly Chinese-owned) modern banks.

Through Hefner I had several meetings with Abdurrahman Wahid, the recently deceased leader of the aforementioned organization and a former president of Indonesia. We had some fascinating conversations about democracy, Islamic law, and religious freedom. I recall one conversation about economic matters. I asked Wahid how he could reconcile his view on banking with the Koranic prohibition of usury. He replied, "What the Prophet had in mind is excessive interest. There is nothing wrong with reasonable interest." Then he added, more significantly, "In any case, the Koran is not a textbook of modern economics."

Needless to say, there are other, much more orthodox Muslim voices in Indonesia. But this case demonstrates that an emphatically Muslim movement can advocate values that have a "Weberian" effect. And this movement is by no means marginal in Indonesia (which, not so incidentally, is the country with the largest Muslim population in the world and which now has a reasonably robust democracy).

A country at the other end of the Muslim world with somewhat similar religious and political characteristics is Turkey. At present it has an avowedly Islamic government, which affirms the secular republic and presides over a democratic and capitalist society. CURA undertook a small study of an organization of Muslim entrepreneurs in Turkey, but we did not follow this up in a larger way. In any case, both Indonesia and Turkey are key countries for any exploration of the relation of Islam to both capitalism and democracy.

Speaking of Catholicism, there is a rather entertaining episode I should mention. I had become friendly with Leon Klenicki, a rabbi of Argentinian origin who was then working for the Anti-Defamation League on Jewish-Catholic relations. A friend of his, a conservative Colombian bishop, had just become head of an important Catholic organization. He shared Klenicki's and my reservations about liberation theology's flirtation with Marxism, and he offered to help organize a conference to introduce Catholic intellectuals in Latin America to other views of economic development. Klenicki and I agreed to share the costs of such a conference, but he had to get the approval of his boss.

We went to see this man in his office in New York. I did not say much at first, but Klenicki went on about Latin American Catholicism, liberation theology, and socialist and capitalist models of development.

His boss listened attentively, then said, "This is very interesting. But why should *we* pay for this?"

Klenicki was at a loss for words for a moment, so I jumped in. "I can answer that. There are three possible directions for Latin America—traditional-authoritarian, socialist-totalitarian, capitalist-democratic. Only the last is good for the Jews."

He replied, "You have sold me."

The conference took place in Cartagena, the picturesque port on the Caribbean coast of Colombia. It was an interesting event, with a group of about twenty Catholic clergy and lay leaders. The key address was by Claudio Veliz, who did a brilliant job. It was clear that most of those present had never heard any argument that was not totally hostile to capitalism, be it on traditional or leftist grounds. I don't know whether the conference had any influence.

In the late 1980s, George Weigel (the biographer of Pope John Paul II), with the help of the papal nuncio in Washington, organized a little study tour to Rome to explore the Vatican's thinking on economic matters. The group included Richard Neuhaus (this was shortly before his conversion), Michael Novak, and me. I did not know at the time that Novak was very active in trying to persuade Curia officials to take a more favorable attitude toward capitalism. It's not clear how influential he was, although apparently he tried hard. In any case, not long afterward the encyclical *Centesimus Annus*, for the first time in the history of Catholic social thought, commented favorably on the market economy. (It made a distinction between the market economy as good and capitalism as bad. The distinction makes little sense and may be regarded as a sop to both traditionalists and progressives. But the encyclical was particularly important in view of the impending collapse of socialism in Europe.)

We spent five working days in Rome, interviewing Vatican officials, including four cardinals. Two things impressed me. One was the cosmopolitanism of the Curia. I had not been in the Vatican since I had chaired the conference on the "culture of unbelief" twenty years earlier. Then almost everyone I met from the Curia was an Italian. On this occasion only one of the people we met was Italian, and he was Italian-American. I was also impressed by the well-informed and open-minded quality of our interlocutors (of course we did not talk about doctrine).

One of them was then Cardinal Ratzinger—now Pope Benedict XV—who gave us an hour of his time. He showed a wide-ranging knowledge of world problems. One brief exchange was prescient. We asked him about the church and Marxism. He made a dismissive gesture: "Marxism is finished. It is no longer a challenge." We then asked where the next challenge would come from. "Islam," he said.

After our conversation I had an unexpected view of another side of the man. I was going somewhere with Weigel, and he asked me to wait downstairs while he looked up a friend. I waited in the courtyard of the building housing Ratzinger's outfit, the Congregation for the Doctrine of the Faith (it used to be known as the Inquisition; one could not help wondering what may still go on in the basement). After a few minutes a delegation arrived, a group of Bavarians in folkloristic costumes. They came to visit their former archbishop. He came down to meet them. The head of the delegation addressed him in a broad Bavarian dialect. Ratzinger replied in the same idiom. Then he joined the group in singing the "Bayernlied," the unofficial Bavarian anthem.

CURA did not overlook the larger Evangelical phenomenon, of which Pentecostalism is only a part, though arguably the most dynamic part. It is clearly the most dynamic part of American Evangelicalism. But it is important to understand that almost all of Protestantism in the Global South is Evangelical in character, theologically supernaturalist, and morally conservative—even in the Anglican churches, as the recent controversy about homosexuality has shown. Laura L. Nash undertook an instructive study of Evangelical CEOs of a number of American businesses.[3] At the time of this writing, CURA is leading a study of Evangelical intellectuals, directed by Timothy Shah (a political scientist, until recently at the Pew Forum on Religion and Public Life). The study opened with a well-attended conference titled "The Opening of the Evangelical Mind," heralding the entry of Evangelicals into the mainstream of American culture. The keynote speaker at the conference was Mark Noll, an outstanding historian of American Christianity and a well-known Evangelical intellectual (significantly, he moved fairly recently from Wheaton College, the Evangelical flagship institution, to Notre Dame). There are plans to extend the study beyond America.

I have become something of a persona grata in Evangelical circles, because, although I always say honestly that I do not belong to their community (I am *evangelisch*, in the Lutheran sense, but not Evangelical), I have spoken and written against the negative stereotype of Evangelicals still prevailing in academia and the media—as people who chew tobacco, sleep with their sisters, and join right-wing militias. This stereotype was never empirically valid; it is grossly remote from reality today.

CURA explored yet another corner of the Christian world in a three-year study of the relation to democracy of the Russian Orthodox Church. The study was directed by Christopher Marsh (Baylor University), a political scientist specializing in postcommunist societies (an extraordinarily versatile scholar, fluent in both Russian and Chinese, and, perhaps not so incidentally, an accomplished practitioner of martial arts). A number of publications came out of this study.[4] The study naturally focused on official institutions, those of the government and of the patriarchate. But it coincided with the research of my doctoral candidate, Inna Naletova, who studied movements of popular Orthodoxy, specifically pilgrimages and street fairs. Consequently I obtained a picture of two strangely unrelated developments going on simultaneously—an increasing closeness between the Putin government and the Orthodox Church, to the point where one felt taken back to the time before the Bolshevik Revolution, and a genuine revival of Orthodoxy among ordinary people, most of them not very interested in the political ramifications of postcommunist religion.

On that level one of my strongest impressions is of attending the liturgy in the cathedral of Saint Petersburg. The church was filled with people, almost all of them clearly worshippers rather than tourists. From things I had read, I expected a gathering of old women with babushkas. Instead the crowd consisted of young, old, and middle-aged people— judging by their clothes, both well-to-do and poor. The place was vibrant with piety.

We had an initial meeting in Moscow, followed by conferences in Washington, DC, and Vienna. One of our main interlocutors was Archpriest Chaplin, in charge of external relations of the Moscow patriarchate. He was a worldly-wise, self-confident man of middle age with a good command of English. His most startling comment was made, of all places, at the Woodrow Wilson Center in Washington—an unapologetic statement of an anti-Wilsonian ideology. This is, verbatim, what Chaplin said:

> From our point of view, the ideal form of government would be that of the Judges in the Old Testament, who were directly inspired by God. Unfortunately this is no longer possible. Short of that, the best government is a monarchy, with a monolithic unity of church and state. The worst situation is anarchy. We have decided that, to avoid anarchy, democracy is an acceptable form of government.

This ringing endorsement was then hedged in by various limitations on political and human rights, including the right of religious freedom (which was considerably limited by a law in 1997 that came perilously close to making Orthodoxy the religion of the state).

In 1996 I was asked to organize a lecture series on religion and world politics at the School of Advanced International Studies in Washington. The lectures were subsequently published in a book titled *The Desecularization of the World* (which was also the title of my keynote address). Although that title was poorly chosen (it suggests a sequence from secularization to desecularization, which is historically misleading), the book was very successful. It is still frequently cited. It was also my own sharpest retraction of my early work on secularization. Among the lecturers were a number of old CURA hands—George Weigel; David Martin; Tu Weiming, the Harvard scholar of Confucianism but also a very welcome newcomer to CURA; and Grace Davie (University of Exeter), one of the best sociologists of religion in Britain (more about her later).

In recent years, as I was trying to figure out the different relations between religion and modernity, I have found very useful a concept coined by the Israeli sociologist Shmuel Eisenstadt—that of "multiple modernities." I had much earlier concluded that modernization did not necessarily imply Westernization. In teaching, I tried to make clear the point that modernization is not a unilinear process leading to a Western-type society. I called the latter the electric toothbrush theory of modernization: Drop an electric toothbrush into the Amazonian rain forest, and after a generation the place will look like Cleveland. The case of Japanese modernization all by itself can serve to falsify this theory.

Gordon Redding's work on "capitalisms" makes a similar point on the level of the economy: Chinese capitalism is not like Japanese capitalism, American capitalism is different from Europe's, and there are even differences among different European versions. Eisenstadt's concept broadens the issue. There is no single type of modernity. Rather, there are different paths to modernity. To be sure, they all have some common traits—otherwise the very notion of modernity would make no sense. These traits are basically the ones we called "intrinsic packages" in *The Homeless Mind*[5]—the structures of rationality necessitated by technology and bureaucracy. But there are wide variations possible within these structures—indeed, a kaleidoscope of cultural possibilities.

These possibilities were already discussed in Egypt after the invasion by Napoleon's army, the first instance of France's "civilizing mission" in the Middle East: How could one accept the technology brought by the French and remain Muslim nevertheless? A similar question was hotly debated in China in the last decades of the nineteenth century, as Western imperialism penetrated the Middle Kingdom. And of course it was very much debated by the oligarchs in charge of Meiji Japan.

Today the question is not only intellectually interesting, but also of great political importance, as different parts of the world seek to define a version of modernity that will not destroy cultural patterns to which they are attached. Take the whole debate over so-called Asian values, first initiated by the Singapore regime, now taken up vigorously by the authorities of the People's Republic. Is there a distinctively Chinese form of modernity? If so, just what is it? It is clear that this is a rhetorical exercise that can be politically useful for authoritarian regimes seeking to proscribe any criticisms. But it would be a mistake to limit the problematic of "multiple modernities" to these ideological uses. There are legitimate concerns here that need have nothing to do with dictators branding democracy and human rights as culturally inappropriate. How can one be a faithful Muslim yet participate fully in the benefits of modernity? What is an authentically Catholic form of modernity? Is there an African modernity? And so on. I think that questions such as these will be increasingly discussed in the twenty-first century. Sociologists could make useful contributions to these discussions (if, that is, they can free themselves of the methodological and ideological hang-ups of the last few decades).

9

PLAYING FIRST VIOLIN

Du`D`uring the most recent decade there were three CURA projects that I directed myself, projects that were in the forefront of my own interests. They dealt with, respectively, the cultural aspects of globalization, the religious differences between Europe and America, and the dialectic between relativism and fundamentalism.

COMPUTERS AND HINDUISM

The globalization project was one fruit of the very hefty grant CURA received from the Pew Charitable Trusts, which designated CURA as one of ten "centers of excellence for the interdisciplinary study of religion." The project dealt generally with culture, not exclusively with religion, but Pew did not mind that. Given its funding (some other foundations contributed as well), the project did not have to skimp on expenditures. It went on for three years, and it covered ten countries. The final meeting of the research team took place at Bellagio, the luxurious center operated by the Rockefeller Foundation on Lake Como in northern Italy. Lake Como is one of the most beautiful places on Earth (I once described it as one of the arguments for the existence of God), but I did not like the center, which impressed me as pretentious and snobbish. The papers from the project were published in 2002 in a book entitled

Many Globalizations.[1] The book was very well received and continues to be cited.

I codirected the project with Samuel P. Huntington, the prominent Harvard political scientist. Toward the end of the project that relationship became rather tense, ostensibly because of some differences of opinion on the allocation of funds. I think that Huntington became uneasy about the project because its findings did not seem to support his thesis on the "clash of civilizations." However, Huntington's intellectual contribution was very important, and I benefited from it despite the fact that we never really hit it off on a personal level. He may also have resented that, with a couple exceptions, the team consisted mainly of (let us call them) CURA groupies—to wit (in order of appearance in the book) Hsin-Huang Michael Hsiao, Tulasi Srinivas, Hansfried Kellner, Janos Kovacs, Ann Bernstein, Arturo Fontaine, and James Davison Hunter.

The several country papers were full of rich data, which cannot possibly be summarized here. The title of the book nicely summarized its main conclusion—that there were many cultural globalizations, not just one steamroller imposing a monolithic global culture everywhere. We did not deny that there was indeed an emerging global culture to be found throughout the world—Western, indeed mainly American in origin, using the English language and populated by people who looked very much the same regardless of racial or ethnic origins. But we also proposed that this synthetic culture was not the only game in town and that it was received differently in different parts of the world, the reactions varying from supine acceptance to determined resistance. We also distinguished between elite and popular versions of this culture.

On the elite level, there is what Huntington aptly called the "Davos culture," after the Swiss village where the World Economic Forum meets annually. The population of this culture is best described as economic and political types, plus a sprinkling of so-called public intellectuals, who are either invited to Davos or (just as important) would like to be invited. There is another, though obviously less powerful, elite grouping, which I named (not too happily) the "faculty club culture"—an international intelligentsia, generally to the left of Davos ideologically. The lines may have become blurred—some businesspeople have greened, and some intellectuals have come to enjoy the emoluments of capitalism. To outsiders they offer choices. Thus Kovacs vividly described how people in ex-communist Europe all wanted to become part of the West but had to choose *which* West to emulate—Wall Street or Woodstock. In any case, both elites are carriers of unmistakably Western values and lifestyles—they are, if you will, agents of Western cultural imperialism.

On the popular level, there is, above all, popular culture, equally Western and mainly American in content. The world (especially its young) dances to American music, wears American clothes, aspires to the romantic lifestyles of Hollywood, and absorbs mispronounced American slang into its language. Finally, there are popular movements that are part of an emerging global culture. Some are political, such as feminism, environmentalism, or what Danièle Hervieu-Léger has called the "ecumenism of human rights." I kept insisting that Evangelical Protestantism must also be seen as an important popular movement, American in flavor despite its various forms of indigenization.

While all this is indeed going on, there are important countervailing cultural forces. Srinivas used the term *counter-emissions* to describe them. Some come from Latin America (salsa music), some from Africa ("Mandela shirts"). But the major ones come from Asia. Some may be deemed superficial, like the consumption of sushi or curry dishes (though one might argue that the substances one takes into oneself are not a superficial matter). Others are clearly more existentially significant, like martial arts or so-called spirituality. The British sociologist Colin Campbell has written about the "Easternization of the West" (the title of his 2007 book).[2] In other words, tribal people in India and Nepal may be converted to Pentecostalism, but Hinduism and Buddhism are returning the favor. Millions of Americans and Europeans meditate in the lotus position, try to communicate with the souls of trees, and believe in reincarnation.

I have proposed that one can distinguish between two types of cross-cultural consumption, regardless of whether it is Westernizing or Easternizing: profane and sacramental. Sometimes such consumption is simply a trivial preference—one need not absorb American culture by eating a hamburger or Japanese culture by eating sushi. To paraphrase Freud, sometimes a hamburger is just a hamburger. As James Watson showed in his wonderful study of McDonald restaurants in East Asian cities (*Golden Arches East*), they become simple eating places where they have been around for a long time. But when they first appear (as in mainland China a few years ago), they are seen as temples of American culture—each bite signifies a vicarious participation in Western modernity. Conversely, an American may practice yoga simply as healthy exercise. But, obviously, it can be much more than that—an internalization of certain Hindu or Buddhist notions of self and world.

A few months ago I had a conversation with a young American who wanted to teach a course on martial arts in an Evangelical university in the South. The dean had a long conversation with him to make sure that he would teach *Christian* martial arts. I first found this story funny, as if one were asked to do Christian basketball. On further reflection, I had to conclude that the dean had a point—martial arts can of course be simply a technique of self-defense, but it can also be something much more profound—a discipline to inculcate notions of a spiritual path at odds with the biblical view of man (at least as Evangelicals understand it).

Srinivas's India paper contains the most suggestive vignette, illustrating that globalization is not a homogenizing steamroller. In Hindu thought, all human acts of creativity are replications of the creative activity of the gods. In line with this idea, there has been a tradition of an annual festival during which artisans worship the tools of their trade. Srinivas focused her study on the computer industry in Bangalore—the flagship of India's recent economic upsurge and by the same token staffed by a modernizing elite. During the aforementioned festival the engineers and technicians put garlands on their computers, surround them with the paraphernalia of Hindu worship, and fold their hands reverentially before the tools of *their* trade. Multiple modernities indeed!

The most entertaining story in the book is in Bernstein's paper on South Africa, in which she discusses the efforts of the postapartheid regime to define a new identity for the "rainbow nation." A new flag and a new coat of arms were designed. The latter, which is full of African images, should have an inscription. That posed a problem. The old coat of arms had an inscription in Latin, which was clearly too Eurocentric. The new South Africa has eleven official languages—nine African languages, plus English and Afrikaans. In practice this means of course that the only national language is English. But one of the official languages could not be privileged by being put on the coat of arms.

The problem was solved by using an inscription in Khoisan, the extinct language of the aboriginal inhabitants of the country. Transliterated, it reads "*!KE E:XARRA//KE.*" The president, Thabo Mbeki, explained that this means "diverse people unite." Since no one knew how to pronounce this, the *Star* newspaper gave a pronunciation guide— "(CLICK)-EH-AIR-(CLICK)-gaara-(CLICK)—with the following helpful suggestions: "The first click is produced by flicking the tongue against the front of the palate. The second is produced by pressing the tip of the tongue against the front teeth. The third is made by sucking air through the side of the mouth." I don't think that the president demonstrated this exercise.

Unfortunately, this was not the end of the story. There are only two experts on the Khoisan language, both academics at different South African institutions. One designed and translated the aforementioned motto. The other one said that this translation was wrong, that the motto rather meant "diverse people urinate." Since there is no third expert to mediate this dispute, the matter had to remain unresolved. Perhaps both are right—urinating together may indeed symbolize unity in diversity—in the president's words "a commitment to value life, to respect all languages and cultures and to oppose racism, sexism, chauvinism, and genocide." Be this as it may, as Bernstein observed, "South Africans will be united in not being able to pronounce or understand their motto."

The globalization project also gave me the rare opportunity to see a social problem physically presented in front of my eyes. The Turkey paper was produced by two social scientists located in Ankara, where I had never been. Brigitte came along on this trip. We were planning a vacation in Istanbul, which we knew and were fond of. At a dinner with the researchers we asked what tourist attractions there were in Ankara. They could not come up with much, but they said that we should visit the mausoleum of Kemal Atatürk, the iconic founder of the Turkish republic. We did. The museum attached to the mausoleum is moderately interesting, but the startling sight was the panoramic view of the city from the hilltop on which the mausoleum is located. Ankara has exploded in recent decades, pushing outward from the center, which was Atatürk's capital. At the time of our visit only one big mosque was visible in the center; we were told that the Saudis had built it. But around the center there could be seen, all the way to the horizon, a ring of new neighborhoods. *Every one had a mosque.* Thus one could see, physically, the minarets of Islam besieging Atatürk's secular republic—a pretty accurate picture of the social and political reality of contemporary Turkey. Not just Turks but all of us have a stake in how this tension will be resolved.

TEXAS BUSINESSMEN AND A CLUELESS CONCIERGE IN LONDON

Another CURA project took up what for quite some time I had considered a key problem for the sociology of religion—the difference between America and Europe in terms of religion. This topic is of strategic importance for the question of religion and modernity: If secularization theory were correct in its assertion that modernity inherently secularizes, then America presents a major problem—a decidedly modern country that is also robustly religious.

I had written an article about this for the *National Interest*, then organized a CURA working group to explore the two questions in this matter: (1) Is the commonly alleged difference empirically valid? And if so, (2) How is the difference to be explained? The article served as a starting point for the project and became a chapter in the ensuing book, but naturally its argument was considerably modified as the project continued.

Essentially, the first question was answered in the affirmative, though hedged in with various reservations. When scrutinized more carefully, America is not quite as religious as it first seems, and Europe not quite as secular. Also, there are significant differences within Europe. Still, the difference between the two continents is real enough. As to the second question, no single factor explains the difference. Important developments in history hardly ever have a single cause. We came up with a fairly long list of causal factors. But when one takes all of them under consideration, the difference ceases to be a mystery; rather it becomes explainable.

My article opened with two episodes that, in my mind, succinctly summed up the difference. The first occurred when I was having breakfast in a hotel in Texas. At the next table sat two middle-aged men in suits reading newspapers. They looked like businessmen. One looked up and said, "Things are really heating up in the Middle East." The other man said, "Hmm." The first man added, "Just as the Bible said it would." The other nodded and again said, "Hmm." Then they went on reading. It struck me that two businessmen having breakfast in, say, Boston could have a similar exchange but would refer to a column in the *New York Times* instead of the Bible.

The other episode took place in London. I was alone on a Sunday morning and thought it would be nice to attend an Anglican service. I went to the concierge desk, which was manned by a young man whose name tag said "Warren" and who spoke with an unmistakable English working-class accent (evidently not an intern from Pakistan). I asked him if he could tell me where the nearest Anglican parish was, and for some reason I added "Church of England." He gave me a blank look and then asked, "Is this sort of like Catholic?" When I said, "Well, not quite," he shook his head and offered to look it up in his computer. In the event, the address he came up with turned out to be wrong.

In the article I did not mention the sequel. Later that week I went past Saint James's Church in Piccadilly (unaware that it was well known as an ultraprogressive outfit). I saw an announcement concerning an evening service. I decided to go, looking forward to the mellow beauty of evensong (preferably in the version of the Book of Common Prayer antedating the demolition job of a committee of liturgical reformers who translated what is one of the great monuments of the English language into a text reminiscent of a mail-order catalog). When I came in, there were some eight people, one of them wearing a clerical collar, sitting on the floor holding hands in front of the altar. The rest of the church was empty. The group seemed dejected. Their faces lit up when they saw me. The man with the clerical collar signaled me to join what was evidently some sort of encounter group. I fled as quickly as I could.

The CURA working group consisted almost entirely of European scholars of contemporary religion from a number of countries. The group met three times over a two-year period at the Protestant Academy in Berlin. It was chaired by the French sociologist Danièle Hervieu-

Léger. When she had to leave the project because she took over direction of the major center for graduate social-science education in France, Grace Davie and I took over the chairing of the group. The members of the group produced some excellent papers, but we were unable to find a publisher (perhaps in itself an interesting piece of data). In the end, the book was produced with three coauthors, myself with Davie and Effie Fokas, a young Greek sociologist. (There is a sort of apostolic succession here—she had recently obtained her doctorate with Davie, who had been a student of David Martin).

The book—*Religious America, Secular Europe?*[3]—was published in England in 2008. It was launched at an event at the London School of Economics with a discussion led by John Micklethwait, the editor of the *Economist*. At this time of writing it is a bit early to assess the book's reception, but it seems to be doing well. It is fair to say that, while all three of us contributed and signed off on the book together, Davie was the most important author. Her earlier book, *Europe: The Exceptional Case*, published in 2002, sharply formulated the main feat of our argument—to wit, standing the conventional view on its head. Conventionally it is America that is cited as the great exception. No doubt, America is exceptional (in some ways less attractively than in others) but *not* when it comes to religion. America is religious; so is most of the world; Europe is the great exception. It is the exception that must be explained.

We came up with a cocktail of explanatory factors. The most important is the relation of church and state. In this we were not exactly original—Alexis de Tocqueville had classically made this point. But I think we did a good job integrating this idea into a sociological frame of reference. It is not only that establishment of the state is not good for religion—every resentment against the state automatically turns into resentment against the church. It is also that, long after legal establishment has faded away or even been abolished, people look on the church as a public utility (Davie's term), there to be used if needed but not requiring any effort of one's own. That has been the case in most of

Europe—Catholic, Protestant, or Orthodox (though less so in Britain and the Netherlands).

By contrast, there was no successful establishment of religion in the English-speaking colonies in North America. There were attempts in Massachusetts and Virginia, but they foundered on the rock of an ineradicable religious pluralism. With the First Amendment to the Constitution of the United States, practical necessity was undergirded by normative principle—religious freedom became one of the pillars of the American political creed. The sociological consequence of this was simple but vastly important: Religious institutions, whether or not they liked it, became voluntary associations in competition with each other. One does not have to be an economist to say that competition makes for effort and innovation. A distinctive American form of religious institution emerged—the denomination—defined by the historian Richard Niebuhr as a church that accepts the presence of other churches in the society.

There are also important differences in the history of ideas. The Enlightenment took different forms in America than in most of Europe; it was in varying degrees hostile to religion in Europe, not so in America. Interestingly, the Enlightenment in Britain was more like the one in America in its friendliness to religion, but Davie suggested that it was pulled in the European direction because of the state-church situation. In any case, the two major versions of the Enlightenment produced two different forms of "high culture" and thus of the intelligentsia in charge of that culture. Anticlericalism morphing into a general animus against religion became an ingredient of European "high culture." It did not in America—more precisely, not until recently.

Differences in the educational system became important in this matter. Teachers in elementary and secondary school are not usually bona fide intellectuals—but they aspire to be. Using a sociological term, the intelligentsia serves as their "reference group." Schools are the major institutional vehicle by which the intelligentsia seeks to influence the general population, and until the advent of the mass media, they were pretty much the only vehicle. This became all the more important as schooling became compulsory in one country after another throughout the nineteenth century (the century, by the way, that is crucial for the secularization process). In most of Europe the educational system was a state monopoly, administered by a corps of teachers who served as missionaries of secularity.

No such thing in the United States: Throughout the period of European secularization, schools in America were locally run, and parents had a lot of influence on what went on in the schools. It should be emphasized that all this essentially refers to the nineteenth century. In the twentieth century, possibly beginning in the 1930s but becoming a major development after World War II, the American intelligentsia became, so to speak, "Europeanized" and thus more secular than the general population. The reasons for this cannot be pursued here (and were not pursued in our book), but this development is important for the so-called culture war in America.

The comparison between America and Europe yields other factors explaining the religious difference. In Europe there developed leftist political parties and labor unions, often led by intellectuals, with a bias against religion. Nothing like this in America. Conversely, religion in America had two social functions absent in Europe—assisting the assimilation into the society of the vast numbers of immigrants and serving as a marker of class (especially within the Protestant denominational system). Last but not least, a large Evangelical subculture developed in America, in itself a bulwark against secularization, while Evangelicalism played a much lesser role in Europe.

All this, needless to say, fits nicely under the categories of "multiple modernities." Both my Texas businessmen and my London concierge may be assumed to be modern men, but they are modern in very different ways. As we pointed out in the conclusions of the book, there are important implications for both domestic and international policies on the two sides of the Atlantic.

CONVICTIONS WITHOUT FANATICISM

A CURA project that turned out to be unusually fertile was "Between Relativism and Fundamentalism." Again, the topic was one that had pre-occupied me for a long time. How it came about is yet another one of those stories that one might head "Only in America!" It was financed entirely by one individual, David Kiersznowski, a businessman from Kansas. He had read some of my books, we had corresponded, and, when he had to come to New York for a business meeting, he made a side trip to Boston and we had a leisurely lunch. I told him about various CURA activities, but what really caught his imagination was the afore-mentioned one, which at that point was simply an idea in my head. Before he left, Kiersznowski wanted to write me a check large enough to cover the entire operation. I said that I could not simply go to the uni-versity with a check—I needed a letter stating what the check was for. Letter and check arrived a few days later. In the meantime, Kiersznowski has become a good friend for reasons that have nothing to do with his role as donor.

The idea of the project is simple but far-reaching. Modernity, because of the process of pluralization that I had grappled with before, relativizes all worldviews and value systems, including the religious ones. This relativization is intrinsic to modernity, just about impossible to avoid. It presents a deep challenge to all religious traditions and their truth claims. Another way of putting this is to say that religious certainty is now hard to come by.

There can be different reactions to this situation. Relativism is the reaction that abandons all claims to truth, which is viewed as unattain-able and possibly undesirable. Seemingly opposite is fundamentalism, the defiant reaffirmation of this or that set of truth claims to make cer-tainty attainable once more. The religious tradition thereby regains the status of taken-for-grantedness, maximally in the society as a whole, minimally within a sectarian subculture.

I argue that both reactions are to be rejected because both require a rejection of reason. And both subvert the cohesion of a society—relativism because it undermines the moral consensus without which social order becomes impossible, fundamentalism because it either balkanizes society or imposes unity by coercion. Thus there is an urgent need—philosophically, theologically, and indeed politically—to find a middle ground between the two extremes. In religious terms, this means to explain how one can have faith in the absence of certainty.

The project followed what by now has become the basic CURA formula—a working group met several times over a two-year period and produced papers, which could then be published as a book. The team consisted almost entirely of individuals with whom I had worked before, including three who had done their doctoral work with me. Grace Davie was a member of the team as well, this time not only as a sociologist of religion, but also as a lay canon in the Church of England. (Irrelevant but intriguing detail: She is attached to the Anglican bishop of Gibraltar, whose diocese covers all of continental Europe where most "parishes" are chapels in British embassies; she gets to visit them periodically.) Most of the team represented different Christian churches, but we wanted a Jewish and a Muslim voice. The Muslim participant had to withdraw for reasons of overwork (he is one of very few university professors of traditional "Islamic sciences" in Germany), but we had an excellent Jewish participant, David Gordis (former president of Hebrew College near Boston). Still, we regretted having downsized the project from Abrahamic to Judaeo-Christian. I chaired the group and served as editor of the volume of papers, which was published in 2009.[4]

The project engendered a second book, which had not been planned originally. As the project proceeded, I was increasingly preoccupied by a troubling question. It was clear to me, as to the others in the group, that one could indeed have faith in the absence of certainty. But I had to deal with the fact that I was completely certain about a number of *moral* convictions. Question: *Where does this certainty come from?* This went beyond the agenda of the CURA project, which dealt only with the religious aspect of relativization. I wanted to write a book, as author rather than editor, summing up my own approach to the relativism-fundamentalism dichotomy and dealing with the moral and political dimensions in addition to the religious one. This involved some philosophical matters on which I was not really competent. I wanted someone with philosophical expertise on board. So I invited an old friend to be coauthor, Anton C. Zijderveld, who holds degrees in both sociology and philosophy. Our book, *In Praise of Doubt: How to Have Convictions without Becoming a Fanatic*, was published in mid-2009 (New York: HarperOne). So far it has done very well. (The title contains an in-group joke, quite irrelevant to the argument of the book. Until his retirement Zijderveld was a professor at Erasmus University in Rotterdam. Erasmus's most famous work is *In Praise of Folly*. Many intellectual collaborations can quite accurately be described as folies à deux.)

The book restates in a more elaborated way the understanding of the dynamics of relativization of the CURA project. But in terms of the question of moral certainty, the book took a broader approach. For most people, it is fair to say, moral certainty is deduced from religious certainty—both proscriptions and prescriptions derive from the will of God. But that avenue is closed in the absence of religious certainty. There is then the venerable tradition of natural law—certain moral principles are universally inscribed in the hearts of human beings. Unfortunately, this seductive idea is empirically untenable. No matter what moral conviction one wants to cite, there have been many cultures in which this conviction cannot be found. There are more recent sociological and biological theories that ground morality in the imperatives of social order or in the survival values of evolution. These theories also fail empirically—both societies and species seem to survive in the absence of any number of moral convictions.

Take the case of slavery. I am certain in my conviction that slavery is morally abhorrent. No human being should be owned by another human being. Of course I know slavery was deemed morally acceptable for many centuries, and I know that my own conviction about this matter is relative to my location in history. But these insights do not in the least undermine my certainty. Why? Because, once the conviction has been established in my consciousness, it necessarily implies universality. In a conversation with a slave owner (such a conversation, alas, can still take place in some places even today), I cannot say, "I respect your point of view. Let us amicably agree to disagree."

We use a telling example from literature, Mark Twain's *Huckleberry Finn*. At one point of the story, as Huck is drifting on a raft in the Mississippi, an escaped slave climbs aboard. Huck, as a white child of the antebellum South, knows that he ought to return the slave to his rightful owner. Indeed, his conscience tells him to do just that. But, as they travel together, Huck finds that he cannot do this. He has not heard an abolitionist sermon, even less a voice from heaven. What happened was the appearance of a *perception*—the perception of the escaped slave as a human being.

There is, I think, an important insight here. Moral judgment is based not on a command but on a perception—not on the imperative *"Do this and don't do that!"* but rather on the exclamation *"Look at this!"* Of course this perception is historically and sociologically relative—it is not empirically ascertainable at all times and in all places. But once it appears, for whatever reason, it is morally compelling. I am sure that this proposition is in need of further elaboration (and I am open to the possibility that it might be interpreted as *a sort of* natural law theory). But this book could not provide such an elaboration.

We did go into some of the political implications. We proposed what we called a politics of moderation. It depends on a precarious balance (a "precarious vision," if you will) between doubt and certainty. Skepticism with regard to all programs of collective action is a primary political virtue. It is wonderfully expressed in a sentence addressed to Parliament by an exasperated Oliver Cromwell: "I beseech you, by the bowels of Christ, bethink that you may be mistaken." (The quaint reference to bowels, I understand, meant the essence of a person in seventeenth-century English.) Perhaps the sentence was known to a namesake of Cromwell's a couple of centuries later. Oliver Wendell Holmes Jr. served in the Union army during the American Civil War. Deeply affected by the atrocities committed by both sides, he returned from the war with the belief that all certainties were potentially murderous—a belief that influenced his later career as a judge on the Supreme Court. I don't know whether this included the certain conviction about the evil of slavery, but it definitely included some of the means that brought about its abolition.

In other words, the politics of moderation must be based on a balance between wide-ranging doubt and (inevitably few) moral certainties. I addressed this topic in an address in Berlin prior to the publication of the book. It was in the context of the much-discussed topic of "European values." In my view, these values are not dependent on Judaeo-Christian (or, if one prefers, Abrahamic) religious beliefs, as many conservatives claim. The values can be shared today by agnostics or atheists, or adherents of South and East Asian religions. Of course European civilization came out of a history shaped, among other things, by Christianity (along with Greek aesthetics, Roman law, Enlightenment thought). But it is not necessary to replicate the historical journey in order to hold "European values"—they are based on a distinctive perception of what it means to be human.

Hillel, the great Jewish sage, was once asked whether the meaning of the Torah could be stated while standing on one foot. He said yes and then stated what is probably the first formulation of the Golden Rule: "Do not do unto others what you hate being done to you." He added, "The rest is commentary." I suggested that the question of what is meant by European values can also be answered while standing on one foot. It is one sentence of the constitution of the Federal Republic: "The dignity of man is inviolate." The apodictic certainty of this sentence undoubt-

edly comes out of a specific historical experience—the horrific viola-
tions of human dignity perpetrated by the Third Reich, never to be
repeated by the postwar German democracy. But people who have not
gone through the history of Nazism can share the perception of
humanity that underlies the sentence. Clearly, however, there is room for
doubt on this or that measure by which the underlying moral judgment
is to be realized. "The rest is commentary."

TOWARD A LAUGHING SOCIOLOGY

During the period covered in this chapter I did produce three books
once again as a soloist. *Redeeming Laughter: The Comic Dimension in
Human Experience* (1997) tries to answer a question that has been occupying me for very many years—just what is it that makes us laugh? *Questions of Faith: A Skeptical Affirmation of Christianity* (2004) was an
attempt to sum up my own theological position, one of a decidedly het-
erodox Protestantism. A memoir of my childhood was published in
German only (*In the Dawn of Memory*, 2008).[5] All three might be
described as self-indulgences of an old man still suffering from "bibliorrhea." The first two were reasonably successful, especially for some
reason in German translations. The third flopped impressively, despite a
media circus produced by the Austrian publisher. The latter two books
do not plausibly fit into the agenda of the present book. But a portion
of *Redeeming Laughter* does, the chapter headed "The Social Construction of the Comic."

After discussing some philosophical and psychological interpretations of the comic, I begin the sociological discussion by using Alfred
Schutz's concept of "finite provinces of meaning"—realities into which
one may temporarily escape from the reality of everyday life (other
examples are aesthetic experience, religious experience, the worlds of
abstract thought). What we call a sense of humor may then be under-

stood as the capacity to perceive this other reality. There are distinct psychological and social functions of a sense of humor—relief from anxiety, a definition of community (those who share the joke, as it were), a political weapon by debunking this or that authority. I also discuss the institutions of the comic, such as that of medieval folly and of the modern clown (to which incidentally Anton C. Zijderveld devoted a wonderful book, *Reality in a Looking-Glass*).[6] These topics could be elaborated at great length. In the remaining pages of this section I would rather touch on something that, in retrospect, the book does not sufficiently deal with—the cognitive function of a sense of humor.

One may distinguish between a sociology *of* the comic and the comic *as* sociology. The former can seek to understand who laughs at what and the social locations and functions of the comic. That is a perfectly valid and indeed interesting line of inquiry. Even more interesting is how the comic perspective, often in a sudden flash, illuminates a social reality. Very often a joke does this in one or two sentences and more clearly than a scholarly treatise of many pages.

In his analysis of dreams Freud emphasized the *economy* of dreams—often a very complex reality is expressed by very compact symbols in a dream. The comic shares with dreams this economic quality. The joke—describable as a very short story with a punch line at the end—is actually the most economic form of the comic.

The comic as such is universal—there is no human culture without a sense of the comic. The joke, as just defined, is not. For example, African cultures are full of a sense of the comic—funny stories, situations, even institutional roles supposed to be funny. But two traditional Africans were (and still are) unlikely to meet in the village square and ask, "Have you heard this one?" The origins and history of the joke cannot, unfortunately, be pursued here.

This is the last chapter of the book. I may as well leave the reader laughing (or so I hope). Here then are some jokes to illustrate (should I say, *to prove?*) my contention that the comic has a cognitive function—

that is, can sharply illuminate a human reality and can indeed be a sort of sociology.

Countries

Israel: A scholarly treatise can explain in many pages how an Israeli identity was constructed in conscious detachment from Jewish identity in the European diaspora, but here's a more economical distillation of the treatise.

On a bus in Tel Aviv a mother is speaking to her little boy in Yiddish. This offends a Zionist fellow passenger: "You should be speaking Hebrew. Why do you speak in Yiddish to your little boy?"

"Because I don't want him to forget that he is a Jew."

Just about any country in *eastern Europe* (I heard it in Romania): Passionate nationalism persists despite, perhaps even because of, desperate circumstances.

Two worms, a papa worm and a little worm, live in a huge lake of horse manure. One day the two worms crawl to the edge of the lake and look out. The little worm asks, "Daddy, what is this beautiful green stuff over there?"

"That is grass."

"And beyond that, there are many beautiful colors."

"Those are flowers."

"And up there, what is this wonderful blue thing?

"That is the sky."

"Daddy, when there are such wonderful things in the world, why do we live in this lake of horse manure?"

"*Because it is our motherland!*"

Argentina: Argentinians think of Buenos Aires as the Paris of South America and their own culture as superior to that of any of their neighbors. (This of course is a joke that others tell *about* Argentinians).

What is a good deal? If you buy an Argentinian for what he is worth and sell him for what he thinks he is worth. (Uruguayans can't stop laughing at this one.)

Religious Traditions

Episcopalians: As we mention in our book *Religious America, Secular Europe?* there is a status scale of American Protestant denominations that provides indicators of class. In most places Episcopalians are at the head of the scale.

The children in an upper-class suburb in Connecticut are putting on a Christmas play. A little boy is supposed to play the innkeeper in Bethlehem who turns away the holy family. He is very nervous and cannot quite remember his lines. When Mary and Joseph show up, he says, "There is no room at the inn." He pauses anxiously, then adds, "But do come in for a drink."

Unitarians: They define themselves as a community of seekers and are proud that they have no binding doctrine.

How does the Unitarian version of the Lord's Prayer begin?

"To whom it may concern."

Southern Baptists: They are known for their strict code of behavior.

Why are Southern Baptists against premarital sex?

Because it might lead to dancing.

Situations

Refugees: A characteristic of refugees everywhere is a sorrowful nostalgia for the places from which they had to flee. This one is from the 1940s, when many refugees from Nazi-dominated Europe came to America.

Two poodles meet on Central Park West. One says, "In Vienna I was a Saint Bernhard."

Europe under Soviet domination: It was a very productive period for jokes. Most of them were mordant and profoundly pessimistic. This one was from Czechoslovakia.

Two Czechs are standing in front of the Lumumba monument in Prague. After a long silence one of them says, "You know, it was better under the Chinese."

Terrorism in the Middle East: This one was told about Pakistan.

The Good Samaritans have opened a branch in Karachi (presumably under a less Christian-sounding name). A man calls in and says, "I am desperate. Everything in my life has gone wrong. I want to kill myself."

The person taking the call pauses for a moment, then asks, "Can you drive a truck?"

Occupations

An *economist*: Someone who knows everything—and nothing else.

A *policy wonk* in Washington, DC: Someone who watches C-SPAN during sex.

And just so that I cannot be accused of exempting my own occupation:

What is a *sociologist*? A man who needs a one-million-dollar grant to find his way to the nearest house of ill repute.

Let me conclude with a maxim that always inspired my teaching: If they don't want to be educated, at least entertain them. (No aspersion on the reader is intended.)

A SORT OF EPILOGUE, NOT (or not yet) AN EPITAPH

I retired from my professorship in 1999 and as director of CURA in 2009. At CURA I now have the ambiguous title of senior research fellow, in which capacity I continue to be responsible for a number of specific projects and to occupy an office, in which I can sit and have great thoughts. These circumstances encourage a certain amount of taking stock about one's professional career and a lot of other things. A foundation has recently awarded me a "lifetime achievement award." On the one hand this is gratifying (especially as it was accompanied by a sizable check), but it also carries the disturbing suggestion that one's life is over. At my age one cannot simply dismiss this suggestion, although the available evidence strongly indicates that I am quite alive. I don't know when I will play the last sonata, but as of now I keep my violin robustly busy.

This book has been about my trajectory as a social scientist. As I take stock of my biography, I must ask myself how important this has been. If someone woke me at three in the morning and asked me who I am, I don't think that I would say, "I am a sociologist." I would say that my professional identity occupies third place in a hierarchy of identities. First, there is the formation of one's innermost self—from the dream world of childhood, through the emotional tumults of adolescence and youth, to the emergence of an approximation to maturity, especially manifested in marriage and parenthood. Secondly, in my case, there is a religious trajectory—a long journey of listening to the dark drums of God and trying to make sense of them. These two trajectories have been mentioned only in passing in the preceding pages. Thus the story told here is not the most important story of my life. Still, it is important—and, I think, rather interesting.

In recent years I have become somewhat detached from sociology as an organized profession. It has moved in directions that are uncongenial to me. Yet I have never given up the vision of the discipline I first encountered in the intellectual hothouse on Twelfth Street. At its center is the endless fascination with the vagaries of the human world and with the efforts to understand them. For whatever reason, this fascination seems to have deep roots in my character—or perhaps more accurately in what phenomenologists would call my mode of being in the world.

I cannot remember this incident—my parents told me about it. I must have been four or five years old. For my birthday or for Christmas I was given the present of a very sophisticated electric toy train. One could control its movements through multiple tracks and tunnels across a miniature landscape. I had no interest in the mechanical wonders of this toy. I did not even turn on the electricity. Instead I lay flat on the ground and talked with imaginary passengers on the train.

One might say that I have continued this conversation ever since. I never regretted it. It has been a lot of fun. It still is.

NOTES

1. Balzac on Twelfth Street

1. John Murray Cuddihy, *The Ordeal of Civility: Freud, Marx, Levi-Strauss, and the Jewish Struggle with Modernity* (Boston: Beacon Press, 1987).

2. Available in English as *The Phenomenology of the Social World*, trans. George Walsh and Frederick Lehnert (Evanston, IL: Northwestern University Press, 1967).

3. Available in two volumes: volume 1 trans. Richard M. Zaner and J. Tristam Engelhardt Jr. (Evanston, IL: Northwestern University Press, 1973); volume 2 trans. Richard M. Zaner and David J. Parent (Evanston, IL: Northwestern University Press, 1989).

3. From a Clique to a Failed Empire

1. Peter L. Berger and Anton C. Zijderveld, *In Praise of Doubt: How to Have Convictions without Becoming a Fanatic* (New York: HarperOne, 2009).

4. Globe-Trekking Sociology

1. Peter L. Berger, "In Praise of New York," *Commentary*, February 1977.

8. Conductor Rather Than Soloist

1. For complete references to the works by Miyanaga, Veliz, Green and Pryde, Kellner, Nash, Kovacs, Brigitte, myself, and others, see the publications page of the CURA website, http://www.bu.edu/cura/publications/book-list/.

2. See http://www.bu.edu/cura/publications/book-list/ for specific publications by Robert Hefner on this topic.

3. Laura L. Nash, *Believers in Business* (Nashville, TN: Thomas Nelson, 1994).

4. See publications 3, 5, 6, and 7 by Marsh and others at http://www.bu.edu/cura/publications/book-list/.

5. Peter L. Berger, Brigitte Berger, and Hansfried Kellner, *The Homeless Mind: Modernization and Consciousness* (New York: Vintage, 1974).

9. Playing First Violin

1. Peter L. Berger and Samuel P. Huntington, eds., *Many Globalizations: Cultural Diversity in the Contemporary World* (Oxford: Oxford University Press, 2002).

2. Colin Campbell, *The Easternization of the West: A Thematic Account of Cultural Change in the Modern Era*, Yale Cultural Sociology Series (Boulder, CO: Paradigm, 2007).

3. Peter L. Berger, Grace Davie, and Effie Fokas, *Religious America, Secular Europe? A Theme and Variations* (Farnham, UK: Ashgate, 2008).

4. Peter L. Berger, ed., *Between Relativism and Fundamentalism: Religious Resources for a Middle Position* (Grand Rapids, MI: William B. Eerdmans, 2009).

5. Peter L. Berger, *Redeeming Laughter: The Comic Dimension in Human Experience* (Berlin, Germany: Walter de Gruyter: 1997); *Questions of Faith: A Skeptical Affirmation of Christianity* (Malden, MA: Wiley-Blackwell, 2004); *Im Morgenlicht der Erinnerung: Eine Kindheit in turbulenter Zeit* [*In the Dawn of Memory: A Childhood in a Turbulent Time*] (Vienna, Austria: Molden Verlag, 2008).

6. Anton C. Zijderveld, *Reality in a Looking-Glass: Rationality through an Analysis of Tradtiional Folly* (London: Routledge & Kegan Paul Books, 1982).

MAJOR BOOKS BY PETER L. BERGER

Invitation to Sociology: A Humanistic Perspective. New York: Anchor Books, 1963.

The Social Construction of Reality (with Thomas Luckmann). New York: Anchor Books, 1966.

The Sacred Canopy: Elements of a Sociological Theory of Religion. New York: Anchor Books, 1967.

A Rumor of Angels: Modern Society and the Rediscovery of the Supernatural. New York: Anchor Books, 1969.

The Homeless Mind: Modernization and Consciousness (with Brigitte Berger and Hansfried Kellner). New York: Vintage, 1974.

Pyramids of Sacrifice: Political Ethics and Social Change. New York: Anchor Books, 1975.

The Heretical Imperative: Contemporary Possibilities of Religious Affirmation. New York: Doubleday, 1979.

Sociology Reinterpreted: An Essay on Method and Vocation (with Hansfried Kellner). New York: Anchor Books, 1981.

The War over the Family: Capturing the Middle Ground (with Brigitte Berger). New York: Doubleday, 1983.

The Capitalist Revolution: Fifty Propositions about Prosperity, Equality, and Liberty. New York: Basic Books, 1986.

A Far Glory: The Quest for Faith in an Age of Credulity. New York: Anchor Books, 1992.

Redeeming Laughter: The Comic Dimension in Human Experience. Berlin, Germany: Walter de Gruyter, 1997.

Questions of Faith: A Skeptical Affirmation of Christianity. Malden, MA: Wiley-Blackwell, 2004.

Religious America, Secular Europe? A Theme and Variations (with Grace Davie and Effie Fokas). Farnham, UK: Ashgate, 2008.

In Praise of Doubt: How to Have Convictions without Becoming a Fanatic (with Anton C. Zijderveld). New York: HarperOne, 2009.